SKYGATES
of the
MIND

IVAN KOS

Copyright; Ivan Kos, 2017.
ISBN 978-0-9920171-5-6
Edmonton, Alberta, Canada
All rights reserved.
Cover page; Branimir Kos

No part or the whole of this book may be reproduced by any means, be it electronic or manual, without express written permission from the publisher, except in the brief quotations embodied in critical articles and reviews.

Disclaimer

This book is presented for your information only, and is not intended for use in self-diagnosis or self-treatment of any condition or disease, be it mental or physical. Always seek advice from competent Health Professionals.

People who should not experiment with Conscious Dreaming are the ones who are unable to distinguish between waking reality and the construction of their imagination. Yogic Dreaming by itself will not cause you to lose touch with the difference between waking and dreaming. Exactly the opposite; lucid, conscious dreaming makes you even more aware, more conscious. If your sense of the difference between a dream and a waking state is in some way already compromised, please stay away from Lucid Dreaming, especially the higher levels of it.

DEDICATION:

To all the Spirit Voyagers.

INTRODUCTION

Dear reader; please understand English is not my primary language and I am not attempting to create a literary masterpiece here. All my books are non-fiction and instructional. As long as I convey the information across I feel I have accomplished what I set out to do.

I consider all spiritual and religious books of the world my heritage. There is something to be learned from all of them, especially if viewed with an inner eye. There is really nothing new under the sun. Modern man faces the same existential questions the ancient man did. But times have changed, people have changed. The mind of a modern man is radically different from the mind of a person 2,000 years ago. Yet the spiritual techniques have, for most part, stayed the same.

In my works I dedicated myself to modernizing the ancient spiritual methods by making them faster, more powerful and more effective. I also created some 'totally new' techniques, based on ancient knowledge. To the best of my ability I am attempting to provide a somewhat new point of view based on my experiences of the subconscious mind and SuperConscious. Of course; it is highly subjective, but never-the-less it provides a map that can be followed.

People will do anything, no matter how absurd, in order to avoid facing their own souls. They will practice Indian yoga and all its exercises, observe a strict regimen of diet, learn the literature of the whole world - all because they cannot get on with themselves and have not the slightest faith that anything useful could ever come out of their own souls.

There are only two kinds of people in this world, those who believe this universe is material and who keep looking for a primordial building block - the God particle; and those who KNOW the universe is of the mental nature.

There are also only two REAL directions in this world, outer and inner (six directions, up, down, left, right, forward and backward, do not count, they do not exist in the universe; it is so only in relation to you).

Believers in the material world, facing outer direction, should know what their fate is when their time expires. Just look far enough ahead.

"One does not become enlightened by imagining figures of light, but by making the darkness conscious."- Carl Gustav Jung.

The book: 'Biocentrism"- Dr. Robert Lanza (one of the most respected scientists in the world) - "The universe bursts into existence from life, not the other way around as we have been taught. For each life there is a universe, its own universe. We generate spheres of reality, individual bubbles of existence. Our planet consists of billions of spheres of reality, generated by each individual human and perhaps even by each animal." (That includes all lowly amoeba and all bacteria and viruses. After all, our human genome is in fact 90% bacterial.)

Biocentrism is the revolutionary view that life creates the universe instead of the other way around. In this new paradigm, life is not just an accidental by-product of the laws of physics. Biocentrism shatters so called 'scientific' ideas of life, time and space, and even death. Immortality doesn't mean a perpetual existence in time, but resides outside of time altogether. The concept of death as we know it "cannot exist in any real sense" as there are no true boundaries by which to define it. Essentially, the idea of dying is something we have long been taught to accept, but in reality it just exists in our minds.

At the same time, Biocentrism releases us from the dull worldview that life is merely the activity of an admixture of carbon and a few other elements; suggesting the exiting possibility that life is fundamentally immortal. It becomes clear why space and time, and even the properties of matter itself, depend on the observer. It also becomes clear why the forces and laws of the universe appear to be exquisitely fine-tuned for the existence of life.

Bottom line: What you see could not be present without your consciousness. Other words, the universe only exists because of all individual's consciousness of it; essentially life and biology are central to reality, which in turn creates the universe; the universe itself does not create life.

Science tells us with some precision that over 95% of the universe is composed of dark matter and dark energy, but must confess that it doesn't know what dark matter is, and knows even less about dark energy. Science is increasingly pointing towards an infinite universe, but has no ability to explain what that really means. Concepts such as time, space and even causality are being demonstrated as meaningless.

I hold the view that there is nothing material to the existence, it just seems so to those with a narrow view. As stated; this infinite universe is actually of a mental nature, energetic nature. Life is an adventure that transcends our ordinary linear way of thinking. Apparent solidity of mater results from our indirect sense perception, and workings of our minds.

Nothing has existence unless you, I, or some other living creature perceives it, and how it is perceived further influences that reality, and that includes time and space.

Even our dream world is not as simple as it is made out to be. Dream body can be more 'solid' and functional.

To illustrate what kind of predicament we are in, while happily frolicking around believing we are normal, I will tell you a short story. A hypnotist came to town. He invited about thirty people on the stage, out of the audience. He put ten people in a hypnotic trance. As the show went on, he kept final five. He gave them a suggestion they have a winning lottery ticket. Then he told them to open their eyes and take the imaginary tickets out of their pockets for there will be a ten million dollar draw. To one woman he said; your ticket is a bit wrinkled, and she promptly evened it up. As hypnotist kept calling the winning numbers, our five humans, their eyes wide open, were going nuts. As the final number was announced stage became a real pandemonium. They all won.

How is this possible? Well, they were hypnotized, right?! This is just a word; but what does it mean?

If a simple word can make you perceive and believe something totally nonexistent, could it be that most of the humanity is in the same predicament on many levels?

PREFACE

Intergenerational trauma and epigenetic research have discovered that trauma is passed between generations. The epigenetic inheritance theory holds that even environmental factors and your diet affects the genes of future generations.

It does not matter where you start; it matters where you end up.

I had my first conscious dream in 1973. It took over a year of research to find two references what that was; one in Tibetan Book of Bon and the other in Egyptian Book of Dead. Two sentences and that was it. Now you guys have literally hundreds of websites on the subject, dozens of books, thousands of articles, workshops, Dream machine, etc.

I feel I can contribute, at least a bit, to this knowledge and expand its horizons.

The term lucid dreaming represents a different orientation to the same experience; instead unconsciously dreams are experienced consciously. You know you are dreaming while in a dream world.

OBE (out of body) and a Lucid Dream are the same. Just like you can dream you are awake, or have more than one body, so you can dream you OBE-d your physical or your dream body. More important than OBE is knowledge how to exit the Dream World and see what is beyond.

Of course; many exercises can be performed during advanced Yogic Dreams. The beauty of it all is that Conscious Dreams and waking reality experiences both go to the same place; your memory.

Users and addicts of external DMT, LSD, THC, and many other drugs, substitute fantasies and verbal discussions for concrete work. The fictional idea some guru is going to liberate us by some magic touch is an illusion that serves to satisfy the needs of people to conceal the possibility of escaping from their situation by the force of their own efforts.

Instead of the beliefs we need action, action filled with a very strong positive emotion. When we are ready to give up being warriors of the sofa, to convert ourselves into committed practitioners, only then can something happen. What counts is the individual effort each person will make. Books, masters, gurus, schools, workshops, retreats are useful help only when we are ready to perform concrete acts in the vast task of knowledge.

One word of caution; at least 95% of so called gurus have failed or are outright con-artists.

Here is an example; insight into Ouspensky's mind and Gurdjijeff- Ouspensky "System" given by a friend. (also see my eBook; 'SuperConscious Meditation'; three chapters on the dark side of the coin.)

The Case of P. D. Ouspensky by Marie Seton Copyright © 1962 Quest, www. Gurdjieff-Bibliography.com

"He instructed me to cancel the lecture set for that evening because he wanted to go to dinner at this restaurant which had very good food and wine. I cancelled the lecture and informed as many of the people as possible. Ouspensky then asked me to go out to dinner with him. It was a most excellent dinner, but during it I felt the time had come when I must ask him for an explanation as to how he could consider that this dinner justified the sudden cancellation of a lecture. Where did such action fit into the System, and where also did his violent temper towards some people fit in?

The thought went through my mind several times: Is it I who do not understand? Is it I who have lost all sense of proportion? Is it I who am being temperamental in feeling I have a right to seek an explanation and not to take all this for granted as being in order?"

When the coffee came, I asked: "Can you, or will you,

explain how it is you could cancel a lecture at a few hours' notice for the sake of this dinner? I don't understand. And I am sorry to feel compelled to ask you; but do you lose your temper with people consciously, or because you have lost control of yourself? You do not lose your temper with me in this way."

"They are such fools," he said. "I've lost control of my temper."

"But surely, if we are to try to control our negative emotions, we cannot learn from you, if you can't control yours," I said.

Ouspensky answered bluntly: "I took over the leadership to save the System. But I took it over before I had gained enough control over myself. I was not ready. I have lost control over myself. It is a long time since I could control my state of mind."

"Will you not try to gain control over your temper for everybody thinks you are testing them when you fly at them," I said, for it never entered my head that Peter Ouspensky was not speaking the truth.

"They are fools!" he said contemptuously.

"But I really feel I have learned something from the System," I said.

"Then you are the only one who ever has!" said Ouspensky.

"I have really tried," I said, "tried for myself."

"The others are deluding themselves. They have never gained anything," Ouspensky said.

For some strange reason I was not aghast at such revelations. I was not even shocked. I was sorry because I did not feel for a moment that Ouspensky wanted to be in this predicament of disillusion and realization that he had tried to become a guru when he had not attained the resources in himself to keep control of himself.

"Why don't you give up the lectures and try to gain control of yourself again?" I asked.

"The System has become a profession with me," Ouspensky answered.

As the days went on, I thought of the predicament I was in with the young couple paying not only the rents and the bills for Mr. Ouspensky and Madam, but, that up to that moment, they had handed to me any amount of money that P. D. Ouspensky had told them to. And he had insisted that I take some of it for my own expenses.

Our Ego is part of the problem. When we are not capable of acting upon our mythology we convert into a dogma, into religion, useless rituals, into blind alleys. When this happens mythology loses its role as a liberator and becomes an instrument of oppression. A myth is something to live, and not something to believe.

Spirit Traveler is always struggling against personal weaknesses and limitations, and against the forces opposing this knowledge and power. The Spirit Voyager strives towards impeccability in every action doesn't matter how small. He or she gives the best in everything he or she does, which implies optimum use of individual's life-force. Even when everything looks hopeless, and all motivation disappears the Spirit Warrior will persist in acting impeccably, even if there is no reason at all to do so.

The world of ideas or desires has very little influence on the lives of the people unless there is energy, a personal life force that is behind it.

Energy determines what is possible and what is not. Everything we are, and do, requires energy. Average person's energy is totally consumed by the daily routine acts of their lives. Most of the behavior patterns are predetermined by people's past where nearly all of our energy is spent by everyday activities, leaving nothing for the exploration of the unknown. Undertakings on our part that reaches outside of a normal require extra available energy to accomplish it. This is the reason for the huge difficulty facing the ordinary person wishing to change; there is no energy available for such undertaking, so you just end up with wishful thinking. Spirit Travelers who venture into the unknown not only require a high level of energy, but also require high level of extra energy. It is paramount to know each act either increases or decreases the energy, so they become very careful about the nature of their actions, always stoutly striving for the optimum use of energy, to the point they stop thinking and perceiving themselves as physical bodies and Egos. Instead they think of themselves as the fields of energy.

The level of energy available to every individual depends on many factors, including the amount of energy with which they were conceived. The conception where both men and a woman orgasm is quite different if only a man did. This also depends on the energy charge of men and a woman prior to them conceiving a child. Energy level also depends on the manner in which the energy was utilized since birth. The form in which ordinary person uses energy is not a product of chance or a choice, rather it is determined by his or her past programming. But every person can redirect their life force, save energy and increase energy.

All human beings possess characteristics inherited from their ancestors, primarily their parents but also grandparents and their entire family tree. This is true not only of biological or physical characteristics, but of a psychological and energy levels as well. We inherited all biological, mental, emotional and energetic characteristics from our parents. Very important factor is how much energy did parents have to start up with, and how much of it was transferred over to the new being, created in the moment of conception. If a person is conceived with a great deal of passion in an orgasmic lovemaking, the large quantity of energy would become conveyed to the new being and he or she will be born with strong energetic patterns. If conception takes place through the low-level boring sexual intercourse, the energy at birth would be correspondingly low. This also greatly depends on a drug intake by parents, especially mother, and vaccinations of both mother and baby. These could be very detrimental. Huge factor is the birthing baby has. (See my eBook; 'Painless Effortless and Natural Birthing Method')

One technique to change the patterns through which we normally act is to perform unusual acts through which we create a disruption in habitual pattern of our energy use. For any action taking place, we should find a way to increase our energy, our life force. We generally do not know there are other ways besides eating to increase our energy. As a matter of fact too much food decreases the life-force.

Human beings can create extra energy through special exercises. If you wish to have more energy, you must first have some energy available to start up with. If we suspend our internal dialogue, at least to a degree, and a habitual response to the emotions, a certain amount of energy will becomes liberated which we can use to enter the unknown.

One of the biggest losses of energy is our habitual approach to sexual intercourse. White Tantric approach should definitely be studied. Examples of energy consuming habits and patterns include drugs, smoking and drinking, daydreaming, judging others, criticism and condemning, complaining, identification with violent fantasies, watching too much television, violent video games, etc. **Do not judge, do not criticize, do not condemn, do not complain!**

We should learn to distinguish between the emotions and feeling. Feelings is a natural reaction to what we perceive; our emotions are the product not of perception but the thought, of reasoning power. Feelings are not energy consuming while negative emotions definitely are one of the biggest losses. Surprisingly, so can positive emotions be. Emotions arise not from perception but from thought, they cannot be produced if you are without thoughts. Typical example of negative emotions are jealousy, wrath and self-pity, depression, etc. Most of everyday actions and emotions are repetitive and predetermined by personal history. Again; emotions cannot happen without thoughts, and what is more they cannot even be produced without particular thoughts. Let me clarify this; emotions without thoughts were possible before you learned to think.

When emotions are just beginning, we still have a choice; we can enter inner silence, a meditative state, double-arrow attention, and the emotion then cannot take a place. We can also at that moment change our thinking and our internal dialogue. Person can try thinking backwards, thinking in a foreign language, do simple mathematics, or remember nursery rhyme. Ego self-importance and ego building generally consumes over 90% of our life force giving nothing in return. Ego importance is a particular form in which we assemble and maintain reality.

If we are to become Spirit Travelers, it is paramount we learn to harvest the energy of the emotions.

But we are more than just physical body and its reactions. Our dream world can be entered consciously; our dream body can be made functional and the results are staggering. Dream world can be exited through the inner direction and the spirit world is now before us with all its opportunities. Humans are truly magical beings.

In the following pages I will try my best to address material and spiritual mind, scientific and religious mind, mind of a New Ager and a psychologist, mind of a believer and non-believer; in the hope they will seek knowledge and dispense with the beliefs.

CONTENTS

Chapter One: Yogic Dreaming	1
Chapter Two: Sleeping Mind	14
Chapter Three: False Awakenings	27
Chapter Four: Inner Visions of Dream Shamans	32
Chapter Five: Mutual and Group Dreaming	43
Chapter Six: Dream Body	54
Chapter Seven: Making a Dream Body Functional	67
Chapter Eight: OBE	75
Chapter Nine: Sleep Paralysis	88
Chapter Ten: Karma	99
Chapter Eleven: Demons of the Deep	109
Chapter Twelve: Dreamscape	157
Chapter Thirteen: SkyGates of the Mind	183
Chapter Fourteen: Clear Light	198
Chapter Fifteen: Spirit Voyagers	201
Chapter Sixteen: Recapitulation	210
Chapter Seventeen: Sun Yoga	217
Chapter Eighteen: DarkLight Meditation	230
Chapter Nineteen: Death - The Ultimate Dream	267
Chapter Twenty: Knowledge	274
Chapter Twenty-one: True Intent	291
Chapter Twenty-two: Crystal Body	295
Bibliography	297
About the Author	299

CHAPTER ONE

YOGIC DREAMING

Dream world, in so called average person, is a total chaos and total nonsense. It lacks organizing power. It lacks reason. In spite of this, dreaming personality, Ego, you, takes dreams to be real. Consciousness is at low level and Self-awareness is nonexistent. You are at the mercy of the subconscious. Even the slightest rise in consciousness results in lucid, conscious, dreams. For the duration of being in this slightly higher conscious state dreams have lost their power over you; you realize you are in a dream world. Instantly the dream world arranges itself into a bit higher order. You acquire a degree of intent, the will power. Regretfully, in the beginning, this freedom lasts only seconds. You just do not have enough energy, life-force, to power this somewhat higher awareness.

Wise person will realize what is happening and what needs to happen. Yogic Dreamer embarks upon a quest for total freedom. He/she begins learning relevant things, increasing intelligence, wisdom and reasoning power. Realizing that for the most part empathy was destroyed Spirit Voyager begins to reclaim his/her heart and feelings, bringing his emotions under conscious control. He aims to be Self-conscious 24 h per day, aims not to squander his life-force on irrelevant things.

We all dream about two hours each night, during the REM sleep, but for the most part we are clueless what is taking place. Let me make something perfectly clear; subconscious mind dreams 24 h a day. Why should all this matter? Well, dreams and waking experiences both end up in the memory banks; so they are of equal importance. Dreams produce corresponding chemistry. This chemistry produces an effect on your body and mind.

Average person's thinking process, emotional life and

level of awareness is very similar to unconscious dreaming. Such a person is 100% under control of subconscious mind, while all the time believing he/she makes their own decisions. All the decisions are made in the subconscious mind seconds before they surface to consciousness. We then believe we made them.

Not only we need to dream consciously; we need to live consciously. Presently this is much less than 1% of our potential.

Yogic dreaming is also known as Holy, Lucid, or Conscious Dreaming. It is a dream in which you are aware you are dreaming; you are not at the mercy of a dream situation and you have at least some freedom of action. In ordinary dreaming it is a dream that controls the dreamer, in lucid dreaming it is a dreamer who controls the dream.

Ordinary sleep is unconscious meditation; meditation is conscious sleep. Of course in Yogic Dreams we become conscious.

Your Lucid Dreams are limited only by your imagination. However, entering the lucid dreams is limited by your level of consciousness and amount of your life- force (ki, chi, mana, prana, vril, ruach, spiritus, nayatoneyah, barraka, pneuma, ka, hu, num, tachyon, orgone, ether, scalar waves, etc.), inadequate technique and a lack of real Intent.

Beside this, it is important to know how to prolong Conscious Dreams, and how to do reality check within dreams and upon awakening, to see if you are actually dreaming or awake. Most of the dreams, from the inside, look more real than waking reality, and sometime it is hard to tell them apart from so called waking reality. Reality check is needed. On your night table, at all times have a business card that says "I am dreaming". EVERY time you wake up or believe you have woken up, read the card, then look away and then read it again. If you are awake, it will read the same the second time. If you are dreaming the card will read differently. Another way is to levitate or fly. If you succeed, you can be 99.999999% certain you are still dreaming. At the deeper level of Soul Travelling this is indispensable.

Our dream world is our own, but there is also collective dream world, astral world.

When exploring 'southerly' direction (down, deep, dark) in a Lucid Dream, a dreamer can come across some very quick, powerful, nasty stuff; including archetypal. Not so innocent…

Remember; once the door to the subconscious opens, it is open both ways. Just like you can enter dream world, dream world can enter waking reality. You need to be ready.

Lucid dreaming has been scientifically proven for more than four decades (see the research by Stephen LaBerge).

Dreaming is most probably a right brain and cerebellum activity and most of the dreams are accompanied by rapid eye movement. The fact that waking reality eyes are directly linked to dream eyes was the fundamental discovery of Dr. LaBerge.

With learning and practicing lucid dreaming, we should keep in mind couple of things; the length of REM increases as the night proceeds, and the intervals between the REM shortens. This decreases time between the REM from 90 minutes at the beginning of sleep, to perhaps only 20 to 30 minutes. Eight hours later after five or six periods of dreaming sleep, you wake up for perhaps 10th time. This is how many times we wake up on average, even though we might not be fully conscious of it.

We can enter sleep consciously. The moment you are falling into the sleep is the moment to encounter the subconscious mind. You have fallen asleep many times but you have never seen it yet, never experienced that 'falling'. What is it; how it drops into dreams? You don't really know anything about it. You go to sleep every night and wake from sleep every morning, but that moment when sleep comes is unconscious.

Lay down, close your eyes, and then remember sleep is coming. Remaining conscious when it comes. This technique is very hard to do. It might take months and even years of dedicated practice before you succeed. Fortunately there is a faster way.

Upon the awakening learn not to move, do not think. Do not open your eyes, lie still with eyes closed and let the images come back to your mind. You will notice your body still vibrating at the different rate and you gently follow the images that present themselves. The full recollection of a dream will soon appear. When you're satisfies that you have remembered everything than you can get up and write the dream down. The tiniest fragment you can recall could be a trigger to remember the entire dream. Even lucid dreams should be written down because over time they will also fade and disappear from the memory.

The most important thing to remember during you dream is fearlessness. Dream images can baffle, instantaneously appearing out of nowhere, awfully fast, and immensely threatening. The Dreamer must realize or recognize the importance of raising his consciousness to much higher level to perceive those images without reacting to them instinctively. Sounds, noises, tastes, odors, the feel of objects, temperatures, kinesthetic sensations all seem real, however the physical pain is quite absent or at the very low intensity.

Lucid dreaming time is nearly equal to a cloak time of the waking state but not always. In a deep state even the time and space are subject to the dreamer's Intent and can change, even radically.

We can learn to control our dreams, directing and producing them in any way we desire, with the most miraculous results and insights.

Throughout the human history, by many cultures, and true psychics, shamans, mystics and gurus, it is asserted our waking world is NOTHING BUT A DREAM.

Shamans of old visited the realms of the Spirit to gain the healing power and insights for both themselves and their people.

The fact is that we are dreaming all the time whether we are awake or asleep; other words, the process by which the experiences arise is the same, no matter if we are awake or dreaming.

Lucid dreams can be used as a training ground to also WAKE UP in our "real and waking" world.

The world of dreams seems so real to a dreaming personality that 99% of the time we are coned into believing we are experiencing waking reality.

Then again, there are two sides to a coin. While "left side" is convincing you the dream is real and making you oblivious you are dreaming, "right side" is often inserting the cues within the dreamscape telling you BECOME AWARE, YOU ARE DREAMING. Developing the awareness of these cues is essential to further developing lucidity.

My first Lucid dream took place decades ago, while watching a cat that had only three legs, run across a street perfectly normally, which was impossible, and I realized "I must be dreaming." Lucidity lasted only a few seconds, but what a thrill, and what freedom!

One of the common phenomena of lucid dreamers is false awakening following a lucid dream. The dreamer truly believes she/he has woken up. This can be so real the dreamer finds himself in his bedroom, getting up, going to washroom, preparing breakfast and going to work.

Various techniques were developed to enable a lucid dreamer to tell apart waking reality from a lucid dream.

Immediately upon awakening into a normal world it is possible to experience a strange phenomenon of seeing, fully formed and appearing real, images within the framework of actual waking space. It should be obvious there is a need to be able to tell the difference between, a vision, hallucination and waking reality.

The world is a dream, death is a dream, the teacher and the teachings are a dream, the result of our spiritual practice is a dream, and there is no place where there is no dream, until GREAT LIBERATION when dreaming becomes an option.

Just as in night-dreams the first symptom of waking is to suspect that one is dreaming, the first symptom of waking from a waking state, the SECOND AWAKENING of religion, is the suspicion that our present waking state is dreaming likewise.

"Mother Tantra" states: If one is not aware in a VISION it is unlikely one will be aware in everyday BEHAVIOR, if one is not aware in behavior one is unlikely to be aware in a DREAM, then one is unlikely to be aware in the LIFE AFTER DEATH.

St. Augustine: "After your death, while your bodily eyes shall be wholly inactive, there shall be in you a life by which you shall live and a faculty of perception by which you shall perceive."

One of the greatest meditative techniques is to train our mind to use every object and situation of waking experience to further increase lucidity and awareness.

Double-arrow attention is a primary technique.

Over 3,000-year-old Hindu "Upanishads" refer to conscious dreaming world, and Tibetan Bon used lucid dreaming meditative techniques 12,000 years prior to Buddhism.

Buddhism tells us we are dreaming ALL THE TIME. The concept of maya clearly states that everything we experience as real is an illusion.

It appears that ONE AND THE ONLY BEING, the CREATOR, the one we refer to as GOD (Clear Light), was so alone "He" split "himself" into infinitely many fragments which have forgotten who they are, and who sort of play eternal hide and seek with the Creator, in a universe filled with dreams.

Being lucid within the dreams is an important prerequisite of any spiritual path. Many high lamas and accomplished yogis have made sleep and dream yoga primary practices, and through them they have attained enlightenment and great liberation.

Any meditation technique which could take decades of practice before substantial results, could easily be adopted in a lucid dream state.

The accomplishment of dream and deep sleep practices also depends on individual's intent, faith, life-force, commitment and patience.

Ordinary dreams have no inherent meaning, the meaning is being projected onto a dream by an individual examining the dream and then is "read" from the dream, (similar to tea cup, or coffee cup "readings").

Ibn el Arabi; "One should learn to control thoughts in a dream, and by this alert lucidity the disciple will produce great benefits for the individual."

Hugh Calloway (aka; Oliver Fox) on becoming lucid; "instantly, the vividness of life increased hundred fold. Never had sea and sky and trees shown such glamorous beauty, even the commonplace houses seem to live and are mystically beautiful. Never had I felt so absolutely well, so clear brained, so inexpressibly free. The sensation is exquisite beyond the words, but it lasted only a few minutes and I awoke."

Normally in dreams we forget our waking lives as much as we forget the dream existence upon awakening. This needs to change if you embark on a lucid dreaming path. In a higher levels of lucidity a dreamer must keep a dream journal and improve dream recall. After a time you will have a good collection of the dreams you're dreaming and you could examine it for the peculiarities. Just like we forget what happened yesterday; it is much easier to forget the dreams. Keep your dream journal right beside you on a night table and immediately about upon awakening from the dream write it down. Just remember, like with everything else in our lives, nothing will happen without the real commitment. Commitment, persistence and the regular practice of Intent are among the most powerful tools any dreamer can possess. Give each dream a title in your journal and record the date and the time of the dream and describe the dream in as much detail as possible. During a normal, ordinary, dream one accepts the events of the dream is being real, that is until person wakes within the dream and becomes lucid, or wakes up out of the sleep.

One technique to inspire lucidity within the dream was for a person to watch his or her hands during the day; examining the palms in the minutest detail, then close the eyes and try to visualize the same. This eventually transfers into the dreams.

Stefan LaBerge first major achievement was to induce Lucid Dreams in laboratory conditions. He was able with his subjects to send messages to the waking world from the dreaming world using the eye movements.

Many meditation techniques, which are easily embraced in a dream, might in a waking state take years, or even decades before results are forthcoming. Lucid dreaming comes naturally to about 5% of population, if they realize the possibility of it.

In the early weeks of newborn's life and he/she had as much is nine to ten hours of REM sleep every day.

About twenty minutes after the beginning of the sleep cycle the slow Delta waves begin to replace the Theta waves. This marks the stage which the psychology considers being a deep plunge into the void of sleep. If subjects are awakened from that stage they often feel fuzzy and disoriented and want to return to sleep again quickly. If a dreamer is abruptly awakened from REM sleep, he sometimes has difficulty moving for a few seconds. This phase of paralysis seems to be controlled by primitive brainstem. The first period of REM sleep usually last about 10 minutes. Dreaming sleep accounts for about 20 to 25% of individuals sleeping life. In our lifetime we end up dreaming somewhere between five and six years, which translates into over 150,000 dream ventures.

Conscious Dreaming is a powerful method which definitely speeds up the whole process of personal development and points you to the right direction on the road to enlightenment. Becoming lucid, entering a dream and waking up within it, does not necessarily ensure a clear vision of the phenomenon being experienced. Each person carries with them great amount of programming, or one's culture, right into the dreaming world and then projects it upon that world. The enormous reeducation is necessary. Ancient texts states that the phenomenal world is nothing but an illusion, nothing but the dream. As said; both the dream and the waking world images are created by the same faculty. We are programmed to believe collectively the world is made of objects and not of infinite interacting energy patterns.

As just stated; lucid dreams occur occasionally in about 5% of population. Fortunately this method can be practiced and greatly enhanced. In these busy times when everything moves with incredible speed we can find EXTRA DESPERATELY NEEDED TIME TO PRACTICE THE SPIRITUAL DISCIPLINES within our dream world.

If it was possible for two or more people to have EXACTLY THE SAME DREAM at exactly the same time what would we call it? Mutual and group dreaming is possible.

Such devices as Dream Light (a lucid dreaming machine) invented by Stephen LaBerge are also very helpful.

One prerequisite to controlling the dreams is the ability

of controlling the thoughts, bringing them into full awareness and using them for positive, loving and virtuous purposes.

In a waking state our conscious mind uses thoughts for thinking, our SUBCONSCIOUS MIND "THINKS" IN IMAGES 24 h per day.

And then there is a deep sleep state, without thoughts, without dreams and images, when we visit with the Creator (Clear Light), nightly.

Clear light is defined as a unity of EMTYNESS and AWARENESS; it is the most fundamental state of ALL existence.

WE ARE THE CLEAR LIGHT!

This is not an object of our experience or some kind of mental state. Clear, unmoving, blissful with no center nor circumference, this is our true reality.

"He" says: There is nowhere I am not. I AM CLOSER TO YOU THEN YOUR JAGULAR VEIN. I am so close to you that you do not see me. I AM CLOSER TO YOU THAN YOU ARE TO YOURSELF.

I AM THAT I AM.

I AM.

The realization that eye movements performed in dreams may affect the dreamer's physical eyes provided a way to prove that actions agreed upon during waking life could be recalled and performed once lucid in a dream. The first evidence of this type was produced in the late 1970s by British parapsychologist Keith Hearne. A volunteer named Alan Worsley used eye movements to signal the onset of lucidity, which were recorded by a polysomnograph machine.

Hearne's results were not widely distributed. The first peer-reviewed article was published some years later by Stephen LaBerge at Stanford University, who had independently developed a similar technique as part of his doctoral dissertation. During the 1980s, further scientific evidence of lucid dreaming was produced as lucid dreamers were able to demonstrate to researchers they were consciously aware of being in a dream state (again, primarily using eye movement signals). Additionally, techniques were developed that have been experimentally proven to enhance the likelihood of achieving this state.

Paul Tholey, an oneirologist and Gestalt theorist laid the epistemological basis for the research of lucid dreams. His work laid the foreground for further researchers to categorize what a lucid dream is.

A lucid dream can begin in one of many ways. Dream-initiated lucid dream (D.I.L.D.) starts as a normal dream, and the dreamer eventually concludes it is a dream. Wake-initiated lucid dream (W.I.L.D.) occurs when the dreamer goes from a normal waking state directly into a dream state, with no apparent lapse in consciousness. The wake-initiated lucid dream occurs when the sleeper enters REM sleep with unbroken self-awareness directly from the waking state.

Some suggest that sufferers of nightmares could benefit from the ability to be aware they are indeed dreaming. A pilot study was performed in 2006 that showed that lucid dreaming therapy treatment was successful in reducing nightmare frequency. This treatment consisted of exposure to the idea, mastery of the technique, and lucidity exercises.

In 1985, Stephen LaBerge performed a pilot study which showed that time perception while counting during a lucid dream is about the same as during waking life. Lucid dreamers counted out ten seconds while dreaming, signaling the start and the end of the count with a pre-arranged eye signal measured with electrooculogram recording. LaBerge's results were confirmed by German researchers in 2004.

Lucid dreaming is the western term used to denote a practice similar to Yoga Nidra. The distinguishing difference is the degree to which one remains cognizant of the actual physical environment as opposed to a dream environment. In lucid dreaming, we are only (or mainly) cognizant of the dream environment, and have little or no awareness of our actual environment. The concept of Yoga Nidra is ancient in Indian traditions such as Hinduism and Buddhism. Krishna is often associated with Yoga Nidra in epic Mahabharata. Similarly, many yogis and rishis have experienced Yoga Nidra throughout their life. In modern times, Yoga Nidra is practised by various Swamis. Yoga Nidra is a state of mind between wakefulness and sleep that opens deep phases of the mind, suggesting a connection with the ancient Tantric practice called 'nyasa'.

Documented since the 8th century, Tibetan Buddhists and Bonpo were practicing dream yoga maintaining full waking consciousness while in the dream state. One important difference is the distinction between the Dzogchen meditation of awareness and dream yoga. The Dzogchen awareness meditation is referred to by the terms rigpa awareness, contemplation, and presence. Awareness during the sleep and dream states is associated with the Dzogchen practice of natural light. This practice only achieves lucid dreams as a secondary effect, in contrast to dream yoga, which aims primarily at lucid dreaming. According to Buddhist teachers, the experience of lucidity helps us understand the unreality of phenomena, which would otherwise be overwhelming during dream or the death experience.

The physician, Galen of Pergamon used lucid dreams in his therapy. Also in a letter written by St. Augustine of Hippo in 415 AD about a story of a dreamer, Doctor Gennadius, refers to lucid dreaming. The dreamer reported that he didn't realize he was in the dream world but the man whom he met in his dream reminded him about this and pointed out that his experience was a proof of life after death.

An early recorded lucid dreamer was the philosopher and physician Sir Thomas Browne (1605–1682). Browne was fascinated by the world of dreams and described his own ability to lucid dream in his 'Religio Medici'; "...yet in one dream I can compose a whole Comedy, behold the action, apprehend the jests and laugh my self-awake at the conceits thereof." Similarly, Samuel Pepys in his diary entry for 15 August 1665 records a dream "that I had my Lady Castlemayne in my arms and was admitted to use all the dalliance I desired with her, and then dreamt that this could not be awake, but that it was only a dream."

When a person is dreaming, the eyes shift rapidly. Scientific research has found that these eye movements may correspond to the direction the dreamer "looks" at in the dreamscape. This has enabled trained lucid dreamers to communicate with researchers while dreaming by using eye movement signals.

In a false awakening, one dreams of having awoken. The room the dreamer falsely awakens in is often similar to the room he/she fell asleep in. They often believe they are no longer dreaming and begin their morning routine. The dreamer remains naïve to the dream either until they realize they haven't actually awaken, or until they really do wake up.

CHAPTER TWO

SLEEPING MIND

Hypnagogic imagery is experienced by many people just before they drop off to sleep. Flashes of images and scenes pass briefly before person's eyes. With diligent practice it is possible to avoid falling asleep, then the images become more solid, and continuous.

A hypnotized mind of a normal person is capable of create a duplicate of another person. All hypnotized person's senses are satisfied that this hallucinated person is really there in the flesh. This fact has very interesting implications when people claim to see ghosts, or spirits. Hypnotized subject who sees 2x Mr. X is unable to distinguish between them, even though he may suspect that one of them is a hallucination. Smart subject mentally ask Mr. X to lift one arm or to leave the room. The hallucinated X at this point raises an arm or leaves the room. Real X of course does not hear the mental request. Hypnotized subject cannot cause apparition to disappear if he could do so than he would not be under hypnosis.

There is also a matter of the minds within minds. Some of the people in the deepest hypnosis or meditation become aware of the hidden observer. There is a part of the mind that sees, stores, analyzes, understands, and act upon the information denied to the hypnotized person's consciousness. **Consciousness and the mind are not at all the same commodity, they are two different things**.

Dreams, once thought to occur only during REM sleep, also occur (possibly to a lesser extent) in non-REM sleep phases. It's possible there may not be a single moment of our sleep when we are actually dreamless. The inability to remember might be related to a type of dreams we are having, like soft white or gold colors, clear light and similar high and low 'images'.

We are not even dreamless during our waking time. The subconscious mind keeps on dreaming 24 h a day.

There is time in our sleep when consciousness sinks really deep, for about five minutes. Body does not even breathe at this time. There is a subject, but no objects of any kind. This is a time when consciousness visits its home.

The record for the longest period without sleep is 18 days, 21 hours, 40 minutes. The record holder reported hallucinations, paranoia, blurred vision, slurred speech and memory and concentration lapses.

REM sleep occurs in bursts totaling about 2 hours a night, usually beginning about 90 minutes after falling asleep. Certain types of eye movements during REM sleep correspond to specific movements in dreams, suggesting at least part of the dreaming process is analogous to watching a film.

Elephants sleep standing up during non-REM sleep, but lie down for REM sleep.

Scientists so far were not able to explain a 1998 study showing a bright light shone on the backs of human knees can reset the brain's sleep-wake clock. British Ministry of Defence researchers have been able to reset soldiers' body clocks so they can go without sleep for up to 36 hrs. Tiny optical fibers embedded in special spectacles project a ring of bright white light (with a spectrum identical to a sunrise) around the edge of soldiers' retinas, fooling them into thinking they have just woken up. The system was first used on US pilots during the bombing of Serbs occupying Kosovo.

Sleeping pills, such as barbiturates suppress REM sleep, which can be harmful over a long period.

Tiny luminous rays from a digital alarm clock can be enough to disrupt the sleep cycle even if you do not fully wake. The light turns off a "neural switch" in the brain, causing levels of a key sleep chemical to decline within minutes. Red LEDs do not do that. The color of the light you're exposed to at night, even while you're sleeping, may affect how you feel during the day—and not in a good way. In fact, certain colors are linked to signs of depression.

Ducks at risk of attack by predators balance the need for sleep and survival, keeping one half of the brain awake while the other slips into sleep mode.

Snoring occurs only in non-REM sleep

Rapid eye movement sleep (REM sleep) is a unique phase of mammalian sleep characterized by random movement of the eyes, low muscle tone throughout the body, and the propensity of the sleeper to dream vividly.

First comes non-REM sleep, followed by a shorter period of REM sleep, and then the cycle starts over again. Dreams typically happen during REM sleep.

What Happens During Non-REM Sleep?

There are at least three phases of non-REM sleep. Each stage can last from 5 to 15 minutes. You go through all three phases before reaching REM sleep.

Stage 1: Your eyes are closed, but it's easy to wake you up. This phase may last for 5 to 10 minutes.

Stage 2: You are in light sleep. Your heart rate slows and your body temperature drops. Your body is getting ready for deep sleep.

Stages 3: This is the deep sleep stage. It's harder to rouse you during this stage, and if someone woke you up, you would feel disoriented for a couple of minutes.

During the deep stages of NREM sleep, the body repairs and regrows tissues, builds bone and muscle, and strengthens the immune system.

Usually, REM sleep happens 90 minutes after you fall asleep. The first period of REM typically lasts 10 minutes. Each of your later REM stages gets longer, and the final one may last up to an hour. Your heart rate and breathing quickens.

You can have intense dreams during REM sleep since your brain is more active.

Babies can spend up to 50% of their sleep in the REM stage, compared to only about 20% for adults.

The REM (Rapid Eye Movement) state was discovered in 1953 by Aserinsky and Kleitman. They noticed that when subjects were woken from sleep during the phase of sleep that was characterized by "rapid, jerky, and binocularly symmetrical eye movements" they recalled the most vivid and elaborate dreams. When subjects were awakened from non REM sleep however, significantly fewer dreams were reported and the reports were less intense and more like memories of dreams. And so, the REM state was named, and has been associated with dreaming ever since.

Early brain monitoring devices were used to find that the electroencephalogram (EEG) recordings of the brain were very different in these periods of sleep than others. In fact, the REM state EEG graphs are almost identical to recordings taken when subjects were awake, as the results indicated that PGO (Ponto-geniculo-occipital) spikes (termed "spikes" because of how they appear on EEG recordings) were occurring during the REM state. PGO waves are bursts of electric energy fired from neurons from pons in the brainstem, through the geniculate body and to the occipital cortex. In waking life, these spikes make up the orientation response, that is, the instinctual response to threat, that can incite decisions for flight or fight, before the animal or human has time to "think".

Primary distinction in the quality of dreams in the various stages of sleep is in the representation of Self. The dreamer can be a simple passive observer, an active participant, as well he/she can have a double role, an altered presence. Distinct representations of Self in dreams, with autoscopic hallucination, also reflects a parallel spectrum of sense of Self in other altered states (hypnosis, mystical or shamanic journeys, meditation) as well as altered states (out-of-body experience, mind-body dissociation, double-Self phenomenon). Indeed, graduated levels of ego development are represented in just this same spectrum of progression from subject to object, from narrow and selfish interest to expanded recognition of one's commonality with a greater whole.

"Our cerebral consciousness is like an actor who has forgotten that he is playing a role. But when the play comes to an end, he must remember his own subjective reality, for he can no longer live as Julius Caesar or as Othello, but only as himself, from whom he has become estranged by a momentary sleight of consciousness." - (Jung, 1964, page. 312)

"The dream is a hidden door in the innermost secret recesses of the soul, opening into that cosmic night which was psyche long before there was any ego-consciousness, and which will remain psyche no matter how far our ego consciousness may extend. All consciousness separates; but in dreams we put on the likeness of that more universal, truer, more eternal man dwelling in the darkness of primordial night. There he is still the whole, and the whole is in him, indistinguishable from nature and bare of all egohood."- (Jung, 1964, p. 144-145).

Humans typically spend about 16 hours of each day awake and 8 hours asleep. Within sleep, they spend about 2 hours in rapid eye movement (REM) sleep and 6 hours in non-REM (NREM) sleep. While we dream, the brain cycles through REM and non-REM sleep stages at 90-minute intervals. "90–95% of awakenings from REM sleep produce dream reports, whereas only 5–10% of awakenings from NREM produce equivalent reports" (Solms & Turnbull 2002, p. 183). The reason for that is the mind has sunk very deep.

The way is not without danger. Everything good is costly, and the development of the personality is one of the most costly of all things. Very effective method upon entering a lucid dream is to pray for the light and seek to enter a meditative state. Prayer meditation will consolidate the lucid dream state. Prayer without the emotion, either in waking or even a dream state is very ineffective. It is the emotion that gives it power. For some reason an individual seems to become more accessible to illuminatory experience when meditating in a dream state than in a waking state.

In a dream, an individual possesses what seems to be a conscious identity but rarely does a dawn upon a dreamer the things in a dream could be other than they are in a normal state. Dreaming individual does not dream in the sense of it being a field or chosen activity. It is an experience which comes to him, which happens to him.

Another characteristic of this level of consciousness is a lack of fine distinction between the dreamer and the images of the dream. It is quite common for the dreamer to be observing a person in his dream at one moment and then to be a identified with that person and next moment.

Carl Gustav Jung says, there is no birth of consciousness without pain. He continues; "nature cares nothing whatsoever about higher states of consciousness, quite the contrary the growth of a critical factor in dreams enables the dreamer to move out of the unpredictability of the inner nature into a conscious relationship to it." Once the state of lucidity is initiated, the dreamer usually experiences a qualitative change in the dream. There is a tremendous sense of personal freedom and independence. The experience suggests that our need for body in a lucid state might be due in part to our identification with a physical body, and our hesitancy to relinquish this identity. The fact is consciousness creates a body on any level it finds itself. It is our job to make these bodies (physical, dream and spirit) fully functional.

"If the doors of perception were cleansed, everything would appear to man as it is; infinite." -William Blake

It is not uncommon for many who are diligently

practicing meditation as well as longing for transformation to feel at a standstill. You may sense that much is happening subconsciously, but for some reason it fails to reach our conscious awareness. Somewhere, we conclude, there must be barriers which stand between our aspiration and the source of our transformation.

The personal subconscious contains all psychic contents incompatible with the conscious attitude. This comprises a whole group of contents, chiefly those which appear morally, aesthetically, or intellectually inadmissible, and are repressed on account of their incompatibility. A man cannot always think and feel the good, the true, the beautiful, and try to keep up an ideal attitude. Everything that does not fit in with that is automatically repressed.

In a state of consciousness we are currently in if we received all the input from existence we would be overwhelmed to the point of burning our neural synapses. Most of the data received goes to a subconscious level. Only a narrow band width is perceived by the conscious mind.

Carl Gustav Jung, the Swiss pioneer of analytical psychology, held that: "Nature is often obscure, but she is not, like man, deceitful. The dream itself wants nothing: it is a self-evident content, a plain natural fact."

Karl Jung - "Our personal unconscious contains the memory of guilt, unacceptable impulses and unresolved interpersonal conflicts. Sometimes an individual starts a premature confrontation with subconscious barriers through impatience or extreme desires. This attitude can be best described as storming of the gates of heaven. This situation is likely to come about when a person has received a glimpse of what lies beyond his self-created enclosure and then longs impatiently to be free. Desire to confront the subconscious barriers is often excessive, even lucidity can prove inadequate to cope with such encounters. If a dreamer wishes to avoid such upsetting and possibly dangerous experiences, he must realize that his conscious desires can set up in motion a deep, inner process, but they must then patiently wait rather than force the natural unfoldment of this inherent capacity. The deeper Self seem to operate on the principle that true growth occurs only over a long period and cannot be rushed."

"Obviously this desire stands in opposition to the humbleness required to receive the Spirit in its fullness. This positive element of longing remains in the background even after the dreamer overcame acquisitive desires. Many metaphysical and religious teachings have held that a dream state and after death state are very similar. Rationally considered, each person's after death experiences are entirely dependent upon his or her own mental state. In other words the after death state is very much like a dream state and its dreams are the children of the mentality of the dreamer."- Evans-Wentz.

"Lucidity may not only lead to transcending the illusory aspects of a dream state, it may also help to overcome the illusory images in the after death state, if the disciple has the power to die consciously, and at the supreme moment of quitting the body can recognize the Clear Light which will dawn upon him then, and can become one with it, all bonds of illusion are broken asunder immediately, the dreamer is woken into reality simultaneously with a mighty achievement of recognition."- Evans Wentz.

But we need not to wait for death to accomplish this.

One method of establishing a firm internal identity is to concentrate on affirmation which serves as a continual reminder of the illusory nature of the experience. An example of such an affirmation is; 'Everything I perceive is a dream.'

Very effective technique is to focus briefly a dream sight on one spot in a dreamscape, like parts of your dream body, and other elements which for the most part remain relatively unchanging like the ground beneath the dreamer's feet. By turning his attention to the ground, the dreamer may strengthen his internal identity. I prefer my hands, it is the best starting point.

Another belief which typically shortens the lucid dream is the notion that the waking state is somehow real in contrast of the unreality of the dream. This stimulates the dreamer to test the dream by waking standards, which quickly leads to re- identification with the flesh body and the senses. It is quite understandable to be satisfied by the virtually unlimited possibilities available in the lucid state. It is only when we have glimpsed intuitively that something may lie beyond the dreams that the lucid dream loses some of its attractiveness.

Lucid dream appears to bring an individual within reach of level of consciousness which was in past associated with deep meditative experiences. It is quite probable that the process of lucid dreaming is closely related to the meditative process. Dreams often provide us with a vivid pictorial representation of the encounter which we face. In addition, the dream allows the individual to view the results of his responses to the obstacle. Does the dream facilitate an objective approach of the obstacle which to meditator is often vague and subjective? When we examine meditation closely, it becomes evident that surrender is one of the most important prerequisites to a breakthrough experience; nevertheless it should be kept in mind that surrender without double-arrow attention could be quite dangerous.

Lucid Dreaming marks the birth of conscious Will in a dream state.

Dream could largely be a reflection of thoughts and memories which are suppressed or overlooked and which seek integration into the conscious self. I consider ordinary dreams as a fiction, but feelings and emotions within it are real.

Not only is the perception determined by one's state of mind but by textual reality itself appears to change according to one's mental set. Conscious dreaming state definitely changes simultaneously with change of thought and underlying emotion.

***

One of the most important abilities of Conscious Dreamers is to perceive energetic essence of the things, and not only the face of it, the surface of it. This is an ability to perceive energy directly of everything that appears in a dream. Whatever we perceive on any level is energy, but normally we cannot directly perceive energy so we use our perception habits to create a familiar patterns. Our own body can be perceived as energy held together by our consciousness. The glow of this energy in a people who are unconscious is diminished and is absent from dead bodies.

At a certain point we need to trust the subconscious or there is no possibility of clearing the garbage from our lives in order to be free. The fact is there is no gain without subconscious. This is one third of our being.

Normally we perceive only about one millionth of the human domain due to the fact that our five senses are not fully developed, and that in most of us another 40 senses are submerged in the subconscious. In a universe of energy there are only individuals assembled by the consciousness and surrounded by the boundless, the fifth element.

In a state of SuperConsciousness everything is understood perfectly.

Lucid dreaming is an extremely sophisticated art of moving from a habitual position in order to enhance the scope of what can be perceived. We are only limited by our own understanding, imagination and discipline. It is possible to cultivate and perform, in the course of sleep and lucid dreams, a systematic displacement of the point of consciousness.

When explaining the dreamscape the dreamers have two options. One is to speak in metaphorical terms and talk about the world of magical dimensions, and the other is to explain the dreaming in the terms of energy.

To set up the dreaming means that you, by the power of

your attention, don't let the dream slip into something else. By the power of your Will you intend the dream you want.

Of course a person needs to start with the small things like looking at the parts of your body and solidifying them and then making the body more and more functional. Lucid dreaming needs to be practiced with integrity and seriousness, and at the same time with laughter, smiles, and lightness of the heart.

***

Strong intent needs a strong life-force. Energy body comprehends immediately that the only way to intend is by focusing your intent on whatever you want to intend.

One goal of lucid dreaming is to intend the energy body.

To become aware you are falling asleep, you need to let your energy body do the work you need to surrender yourself to it. To intend this is to wish without wishing, without thoughts, and to do without doing. With solid determination, without a single thought convince yourself that you have reached your energy body and that you're a Conscious Dreamer. Being in a double-arrow will automatically put you in a position to be aware that you are falling asleep. Usual obstacle is staying awake, remaining conscious without going deeper into a dream world.

The real issue is to become aware one is falling asleep while maintaining double-arrow attention. The body is falling asleep with myriads of its side effects and the mind is staying awake.

A good technique to remain in a lucid dream state is to take a quick deliberate glances at everything present in a dream. You can use a specific dreaming attention on something specific only as a point of departure. From there the dreamers spread out looking at the other items in a dream. Use as many as possible of dream senses and return to the point of departure as many times as possible.

Lucid dream is a process of awakening, of gaining conscious control. This conscious attention must be systematically exercised for it is a door to our dreaming attention.

Within dreams there are real energetic interferences, things that were introduced into our dreams by liminal and subliminal means. Eventually you will need to find them and transmute them. No need to find them all. Once a BIG obstacle is transmuted smaller ones follow immediately.

When you succeed perceiving energy charges within our seemingly solid objects in a dream, sooner or later you will become aware of energy charges coming from extraneous foreign bursts of energy. Our habitual mind then takes these energy currents and turns them into parts of our dreams. Those energy charges could be coming from other human beings or even non-biological objects.

If you succeed entering a dream and remain lucid, conscious, in a double-arrow state, choose one point, for example, your feet and ground beneath it as a departure point. As I said; I prefer my hands, they are 'always' there.

To strengthen the perception shift your gaze to the other items of your dream in very quick glances. Focus briefly your gaze on as many things as you can. When you glance quickly, the images will not shift, the dream will remain under your control. Always come back to your feet or your hands if this is your starting point. Our attention span covers about eight object, so glance at seven points or less.

If you feel you are losing your dream attention, imagine you are spinning your body in a direction natural to you. This will prolong your dream. As we solidify our dreaming we must become able to sustain the sight of any item of dream for a longer period, without it turning into something or someone else. To solidify the quality of the dreams which are, as we know, very subtle, always go back to starting point you have chosen. Every time you remember to perceive the starting point you will increase your power, your energy, to lucid dream. If you feel that, you're losing the lucidity or you're about to wake up you can quickly go back to starting point, in our case, your feet, to prolong a dream. The solidity of the dream body and a dream images is only illusory; its basis is pure energy. Our physical body is also pure energy. The difference is that the energy body in a dream state has only appearance but no mass; since it is a pure energy, it can perform acts beyond the possibilities of the physical body. Our waking state body has a mass.

Lucid dreaming is the act of tempering, solidifying, and making functional the energy body, by gradually exercising it. Through conscious dreaming we fuse and solidify the energy body and the dream body, until it is a unit capable of being perceived by our dream eyes, in a same manner as our physical body.

Just as we can create seemingly solid dream body, we can also perceive the dream world as pure energy, vibrating pure movements of light we can feel.

CHAPTER THREE

FALSE AWAKENINGS

Having the "I am dreaming" card on the night table beside your bed is a must. Every time you think you woke up from a dream you should look at the card and then look at it again. If you're still in a dream world, the card will never read the same way. This way you will not mistake false awakenings for waking reality. Another good technique is to close one eye, observe the environment, then close the other eye, if the images are not identical you are still dreaming. Levitating and flying is another one.

Common phenomenon is a false awakening which follows a lucid dream. The dreamers believe they have awaken. This can be so real that the dreamer is quite convinced that he or she is getting up to have a shower, prepare breakfast, and leave for the office, while in actuality she is still dreaming. Lucid dreamers learn to test reality in several ways; pain, gravity, reminder card, if you can fly it is certain you are dreaming. If you're in pain, you can be fairly certain you are awake, but that is not quite true on deeper realms of a dream world. Subconscious mind can evoke a memory pain.

False awakening is when the subject examines his/her environment at length and not being able to see that, what he's looking at, is any different from the physical world, despite a nagging background feeling that something is not quite right.

Yogic Dreaming is an experience of becoming conscious while in a dream state; knowing you are dreaming.

False awakening is when a dreamer thinks he is awakening from asleep only to discover later upon actual awakening he was still dreaming.

Strong case can be made for the need to regard lucidity as an opportunity to cooperate with or forgive the dream elements, rather than an opportunity to exercise control over them. The importance of this approach is evident when we regard some conscious dreams as having two discrete parts, the symbolic content, and the dreamer's response to it.

Always try to determine whether an awakening from a dream is actual or false; there are several techniques available. When you discover it is false, you can immediately participate in a lucid dream. Flying dreams are usually the precursor to lucid dreams; in fact lucid dreamers have many more flying dreams than the ordinary dreamer. However pleasurable the flying is, it's only one of the thousands of things that can be done in a conscious dream. Lucid dreamer can perform any activity of his choice. Dream yogis state that the total control of the sleep state, including dream and dreamless states, is possible. Conscious dreamers know even the character in a dream can be changed or transformed.

Sometimes into the awakening to normal everyday world dreamer sees a fully formed completely substantial images of people within the framework of actual waking space. These are hallucinated images most probably caused by inability of the brain to switch instantly from a dream state to waking state. In case a wild and disgusting monstrous nightmares the greatest weapon you have is love, smiling attitude, and even laughter. Fear is your greatest enemy. One of the most important prerequisites on a spiritual path is to become conscious while dreaming.

The more one has lucid dreams the more one will experience false awakenings.

Often the scene might be of your bedroom and you might have a false awakening. If you find you have woken up do not move, let your body be perfectly motionless and let the sympathetic system that has awakened to a degree fall asleep again. There is a very good chance you will pop into REM sleep again and you have a great opportunity to enter the dream consciously. So lie totally motionless do not move a muscle, try not to think, relax and slow down your breath and wait for the dream to return. If you are successful in having lucid dream that doesn't mean you will succeed next time. When in the lucid dream lucidity is easily lost just by taking too much interest in the dream details. Reminding yourself this is a dream could be helpful in the beginning until you become proficient at your dreaming. To a greater degree the dream events taking place in ordinary dreams are fiction, but our feelings and emotions are always real. So when you become fearful in a dream and even when you become lucid your fear may not disappear automatically, because certain body chemistry has been created, fearful body chemistry has been created.

***

Despite having healthy eyes, Maryann finds it impossible to see more than one object at a time, while being blind to everything else around her.

Look around, what do you see? Children playing outside, your office or a bus full of people, perhaps? To perceive these complex visual scenes, your brain has to process each individual object; a friend's nose, a colleague's ear, the door, a seat, a shoe; and then stitch huge number of info all together to create a meaningful world.

But not everyone can do this. There are people in the world whose brains cannot place the pieces of the puzzle together; instead they only process one object, or a part of an object, at a time. It is called simultanagnosia, and it clearly illustrates power of subconscious to release just a selected input.

What was amazing was that Maryann lived alone and was functioning well around her house. She wasn't bumping into walls and she could find the peas and the carrots and the chicken and make herself whole meals. But how was she doing it?

There was only one logical conclusion, her brain must be

subconsciously processing information about her world that her conscious mind doesn't have access to.

Our ability to subconsciously process a lot of what goes on around us frees us up to use our conscious mind for the most important stuff at hand. It's a gift we rely on, even though we hardly give it a second's thought.

There are many other intriguing examples of how our brains can process information unconsciously. For example a condition in which people are blind, yet they can walk around an obstacle course.

We all have different attentional windows at different times. This is why the practice of double-arrow attention is so crucial. If you're walking down a busy street, for example, your attentional window is large; you are aware of lots of things around you. If you suddenly spot a dog by your feet, your attentional window becomes smaller as you focus on the animal. At this point, the other aspects of the street fade into the background.

This is a trick that magicians use to make objects disappear; they divert your attention from the whole scene to just a tiny part of it by clicking their fingers or waving a wand while they remove the object in an area outside of your attentional window. Our subconscious mind plays that trick on us all the time. This division has to end if we are ever to be free, to be truly awake.

On top of that we have three very different brains. First there's the most primitive of our brains, sometimes referred to as the "reptilian brain" because we share it in common with reptiles, like snakes, alligators and komodo dragons. The reptile brain has a singular focus: survival. It doesn't think in abstract terms and doesn't feel complex emotions. Instead, it's responsible for fight-or-flight, hunger and fear, attack or run.

The second brain is mammalian the one we share with the animals that came along after reptiles. The mammalian brain, sometimes referred to as the Limbic Brain because it extends around and off of the reptilian brain in a dog-leg shape that resembles a limb, handles complex emotions like love, indignation, compassion, envy, and hope. Anybody who's worked with animals or had a pet knows mammals share these emotions with humans, because we share this brain. While a snake can't feel shame or enthusiasm, it is natural for a dog or cat. And, like the reptile brain, the mammalian brain can also be stimulated indirectly by words, and is also non-verbal. It expresses itself exclusively as emotions although these are more often felt in the heart than the gut.

The third brain - the neocortex ("new" cortex) - is something we share with the higher apes, although ours is a bit more sophisticated. Resting over the limbic brain (which is atop the reptilian brain), our neocortex is where we process abstract thought, words and symbols, logic and time.

CHAPTER FOUR

INNER VISIONS OF DREAM SHAMANS

Shamans of old recruited children which showed paranormal sensitivities and groomed them to become next generation Shamans. Now day's system "treats" them with pills.

Let's take a closer look what mental illness is. When the door to subconscious mind opens for whatever reason (stress, trauma, drugs, alcohol, meditation, religious practices, Satanism, electronic techniques, sexual abuse, PTSD, etc.), even a bit, the psychological problems commence. The degree of the problem depends on how wide the door is open. Please note; there is no literal doors nor boundaries between our subconscious, conscious and super-conscious minds. They are separated by different frequencies.

Subconscious mind "thinks" in tri-dimensional, virtual, live, moving pictures, 24 h a day. It is huge in scope and can affect all five of our senses; also thinking and emotions. Subconscious, for one reason or the other, starts to affect conscious mind. The reasoning power and empathy diminishes, and in extreme cases disappears. Mental hospitals are full of people whose Ego has completely disappeared–got swallowed up. Brilliant doctor Anita Muhl, way back in 1930s, noticed that even in most extreme cases of disassociation, Ego surfaces at least for one minute in every 24 h period. If we grabbed it at that moment and worked with it, the periods of consciousness could be gradually increased. But than you would have to know the methods for expanding consciousness. Yes, but who will bother with that; it is much easier to wrap these people in strait-jackets and pump them up full of drugs.

In 1950 the number of split personalities worldwide was estimated at 200 (two hundred). By 1980s it was about

140,000. Now days it is into millions, some estimates state one out of every hundred.

Shamans of old were dealing with normal and natural population, which is not a case now days. Programmed, split and multiple personalities abound. Some of them are demonic. Most of the Shamans are not used to this kind of dis-associations. Some of them are totally petrified by them.

Not only is our subconscious affected from a liminal level, but also subliminal. We are bombarded with subliminals on a daily bases.

Recently there was a showing of a horror movie in a Toronto theatre. Many attendees got violently sick. Not only did the Hollywood creeps project disgusting images on the screen, they used infrasound at gross moments to affect people, not only on a mental level, but also physical. Infrasound was felt in the gut and the head. You cannot hear infrasound but you can often FEEL it. In the bones, eardrums, stomach and head. Cities are full of artificially produced infrasound. All machines do it.

***

They call themselves the Elder Brothers. We can learn to live in the spiritual world that this lost tribe lives in? (see: "From the Heart of the World, The Elder Brothers Warning.") Kogi tribe in the mountains of northern Colombia call the Mirror World 'Aluna' (world of the subconscious, world of cerebellum?). Selected male children are taken from birth and put in a dark cave for the first nine years of their lives to train to become Shamans. The children live in the dark; they may not see the outside world and in this way they come to see the multi-dimensional Mirror World- Dream World. After nine years of training the children exit the cave, going out into the real world to become the future visionaries and spiritual leaders of the tribe.

The Kogi people trace themselves back to the pre-

Colombian Tyrona people who were contemporaries of the Inca. Like the Inca, the Kogi built stone stairs and platforms in the mountains that have not eroded in a thousand years. They are a mystical people with a power that no one else possesses, the power of accessing supposedly multi-dimensional world.

The Kogi world is a 26-D (presumably) hidden in a 3-D world. Their ideas are very pure and wonderful. In the tribe's long history they have never had a homicide. Of course, they are primitive and we are civilized. Everything about their history and religion is passed down through oral instructions and their lives are run by the spiritual leaders or Shamans named "Mamos." All Kogi Mamos are chosen from birth and spend childhood in a cave in total darkness, learning the ancient secrets of the spiritual world, or Aluna. Later they are the priests and judges who control Kogi society. All major decisions and shamanic work are done by divination. All is the world of Aluna, so the Mamos see a reflection of the physical world first in the spiritual world. If Aluna is the Mother, then the Kogi listen to the Mother by divining. This lost technique of divination is what keeps the Kogi world in balance and order.

Of unique importance is that the Kogi are a peaceful tribe that have never killed one of their own and rarely intermarry. They never grow grey hair and have no facial hair. They can spend nine days awake- without sleep during their ceremonial rites. The Kogi or Cogui or Kagaba, translated "jaguar" in the Kogi language are a Native American ethnic group that lives in the Sierra Nevada de Santa Marta in Colombia. Their civilization has continued since the Pre-Columbian era. The Kogi language belongs to the Chibchan family. They live in Aluna, an inner world of thought and potential. From Aluna they astral travel or remote view to places both on and off the physical planet. Their sacred lands are perceived as a metaphysical symbol of cosmic forces within the whole world - an oracle of the natural balance and health of the planet. Kogi focus all their energy on the life of the mind as opposed to the life of a body or an individual (just look how we venerate our athletes even as 90% of them are on steroids). The Kogi say without thought nothing could exist (here they must be talking about super-conscious thoughts). This is a problem for so called civilized world, because we are not just plundering the earth, we are dumbing it down, destroying both the physical structure and the thought underpinning of existence.

In the deepest recesses of the jungle along the border of Peru and Ecuador to the Amazon basin, one of Earth's harshest and most unforgiving ecosystems, a land of punishing humidity, floods and all manner of deadly reptiles, poisonous plants and insects live many Native tribes. The fact that the Achuar have not only managed to survive but have actually thrived in the jungle for more than 5,000 years is proof, they say, of their ability to commune with and receive guidance from the spirit world while dreaming.

The Achuar go so far as to equate "reality," what they consider their "true life," with the state of dreaming rather than the state of wakefulness.

Nightly during dreaming, and also during visions, the soul departs the body and enters a dream multiverse where anything is possible and anything can be learned. Terrifying dreams or visions, those that we would characterize as nightmares, are considered the most profound of Achuar experiences because they result in personal growth. Children are taught to "move toward" the dream threat or obstacle. If they can successfully grasp it while conquering their fears, then the frightening vision will collapse and reveal its true nature and message. To run away is to reject a gift and to miss a golden opportunity. They will go out and pick wild jungle tobacco, one of their most sacred medicines, and they'll also make ayahuasca or maikua (powerful hallucinogens) and go out in the forest and fast. Neighboring tribes are the Shuar and Shiwiar.

We either idolize them or put them down as primitive.

One thing is for certain; through the use of ayahuasca and its male counterpart yagé, other hallucinogens and chewing on coca leaves, they become adept in the inner world.

***

Attention between the eyebrows is a direction to focus upon the third eye, or what is now understood to be pineal gland. If you close your eyes and focus between the eyebrows, you will feel a strange pull as if you're exerting a whole new range of small muscles. If you persevere with focus on this, pressure will increase and will be felt like a powerful pull. It should feel as if you are looking into the center of your head. Eventually it will feel like you're seeing inside your head. Initially as if you're looking with periphery of your eyes, pressure on the eyes will soften and become very relaxed. This eye roll-back in your head is sort of cross-eyed, it will become fixed, locked on the invisible third eye. The body has to disappear, the thoughts have to stop, all the emotions including that of expectation have to disappear, eyes have to become motionless, then the images come.

Better focus is behind the eyes in the center of the head. Even better is to focus about 2-3 feet in behind the head.

Attention takes the energy from our eyes, turns it inward, activating the third eye into life. But let me qualify this. Pineal gland, or so called Third Eye, is just a physical focus in the center of the head. The truth is that inner vision is going on in our subconscious mind every millisecond. Nothing needs to be activated. Our subconscious mind dreams 24 h a day in a virtual, tri-dimensional, live pictures. All we have to do is shut our outer world, like we do every night when we fall asleep. The difference being now we are falling asleep consciously, dreaming consciously, and waking up consciously.

If one become the master of dreaming, not only can one direct the course of the dream but one can cease to dream all together.

Dreaming self can radiate beautiful energy and light but it is still a dream, just as much as an Ego in most cases is a dream, a mental construction. Upon becoming more proficient in a dream world the dreamer must use double-arrow and keep strengthening the witnessing consciousness which is a true goal of the spiritual path. Self-consciousness, double arrow, leads to the freedom from death. A lack of consciousness, lack of self-reflection leads to death. Those who are super-aware do not die; those who lack self-consciousness are already dead, they just did not realize it yet.

'Christ' description of Heaven; "there shall be time no longer." It is to be noted that both time and space in a dream world are also being dreamed. The dream world is not really that much different from waking reality. Both are created by our mind's creative faculty.

Socrates declares; "...it is even open to dispute whether we are awake or in a dream."

Among the San tribes of Kalahari Desert the question which is a dream and which is reality is summed up by their understanding of the Great Dream.

And then there are Australian aborigines and their Dream Time.

Here is an interesting Amazon Shaman method. Shaman finds suitable place by the red ant hill to initiate his apprentice. Apprentice first smokes copious amount of powerful jungle tobacco. Meanwhile Shaman constructs a seat on the bottom of a vine he cut. Apprentice seats in the seat, Shaman winds the vine as much as possible and then lets it unwind. Fast spin, tobacco infusion and Shaman's intent send the apprentice into a dream world- Shaman's dream. Here Shaman proceeds to dismember the apprentice and then puts him back together, and proceeds to teach him age old secrets. Once the initiation is completed, Shaman takes the apprentice and throws him into the ant hill to facilitate quick return to waking reality. How would you like to be that apprentice?!

Or this initiate? Saint John (who baptized 'Jesus') was baptizing new Christian initiates in the river Jordan. He had 2 helpers. They would lead a new initiate to the river. Two helpers would hold initiate's arms while St. John submerged initiates head under water and held him there. When an initiate started running out of air, he began to struggle, and then struggled violently fighting for his life. Finally he would 'realize' he has been fooled, he would give up and accept death. At this very moment St. John would pull him out and baptize him in the name of the Holly Spirit. This was now a new Christian. Compare now days' watered down baptizing. Weak method and weak effort lead to no results.

Siberian Shamans would submerge newborn baby into the ice-cold water for a few seconds. These seconds are very long time for the baby because how it processes the time. As a result, this child by the time it grows up will have great resistance against cold weather. Today this method would be considered child abuse and Shaman would end up in jail.

Ojibwa women dealt with the concerns of childbearing and childbirth in their dreams. Pregnant lucid dreamers can do the same. If you can change dream behavior, your waking behavior will change to. When one dream image attacks another, you the dreamer is literally attacking part of yourself.

In a Mirror Gazing method meditators perceive many faces coming and going; even stepping out of the mirror. Gaze steadily at your reflected image without blinking. Place in a dark room a lighted candle nearby, so you face is illuminated but the candle is not visible in the mirror. If you are not prepared properly, this technique could be very disturbing to some practitioners. Ultimately the mirror images disappear and you are looking in the mirror where there is nothing reflected. Close your eyes ; you are now inside the subconscious mind.

The same technique can be used in a dream world; its

effectiveness is unbelievable.

Mystics of all persuasions have stated over the centuries that both past and the future are nonexistent, for only here and now, this very moment, is real and existing. Everything happens in an eternal now. Only in now time can something take place, and only in now time can something change. When a person enters into now- time past and the future disappear, thoughts stop.

In the world of quantum physics there appears to be no time, no before nor after, so questions as to when or where have no meaning.

Those who have learned to navigate the dream with awareness sooner or later begin to discover that a dream world, and so called waking world, are very similar. Intending something in waking reality can have precisely the same effect as it does in a dreaming. Undertaking a determined action will determine if it will.

***

When perceiving grotesque and so-called evil apparitions the first thing the dreamer needs to remember is that all of them are just a dream images created by your own mind. Light, love, smile, laughter and hugs are the best weapons against such subconscious 'entities'. Having a sense of humor in a dream is one of the best tools a dreamer can have. Embracing the monster and accepting it usually brings an immensity sense of relief; 'monster' instantly flips around into its opposite. It has been in prison and darkness and repressed for years and decades. Talking to a demonic dream image and asking who it is, is very helpful. The name could often reveal surprises. Ask why it is trying to trick you, and what it is trying to do. Volunteer to help while at all times being in a double-arrow attention. As mentioned; if lucid dream is beginning to fade spinning or whirling is very effective way increasing consciousness and prolonging a dream. Mavlevy dervishes and Sufis use whirling in this waking world as a very effective technique of increasing consciousness.

Certain Tibetan orders believe the entire universe to be a product of the mind, created by the collective stuff of the thoughts and the emotions of all living beings. The Tibetan Book of the Dead is not only a guideline to the after-death journey, but can also be a guideline for the dream world. Unfortunately it is a bit outdated and culturally biased.

Beliefs are most of the time secondhand, someone else's ideas, or the ideas of some social group. Some beliefs are original, like in a case of Wright brothers and their idea of flying. Any belief should be turned into a full-fledged knowledge, and if that is not possible it should be abandoned.

Most of us are imprisoned within our own description of the universe. The dream Ego is not creating a dream for he/she does not know how to create dream images. Dream Ego itself is being dreamed. In normal circumstances the dreamer's mind, awake or asleep, will always be split into the dreamer and dreamed. And then there is a third side as we are being told by sages and mystics over the centuries.

Strong powerful act of intending is the key to both the dreaming and the waking world. The good technique is to treat all phenomena is if they are a dream. A very useful rule of thumb is to get into the habit of checking the reality of each event.

As said; research has established that each one of us dreams for over two hours a night ranging from a ten minutes in the beginning of sleep all the way up to over an hour in the morning. However many people do not remember their dreams at all. Some people claim they dream in black and white, and then some people have very vivid dreams and good memory of them. And of course, there are some people who are lucid in their dreams and are perfectly aware they are dreaming.

We can transform all fear producing dream enemies

into dream friends. The most impressive most important principle in our dream is to face and 'conquer' fearful images and danger. Yogis and gurus develop fearlessness of dream images and dream situations. Even a feeling of everyday happiness often can result from dream experiences. Dreams, like everything else that we do and experience, produce a particular chemistry. The average adult during the average night's sleep has about five REM periods, which emerged from deeper stages of sleep. This typically occurs every 90 minutes during and last anywhere from 10 minutes to over an hour.

Lucid Dreamer can experience every night the same expanded and limitless personal power, feelings and emotions sought by drug users, without the same risk. One helpful practice or lucid dreamer is to carry on the conversation with the characters that appear in your dream. However always remember, all your dream images and dream actions are you. The power to will changes in a dream content is a skill that can be acquired and is the secret to mastering nightmares. When the creative dreams appear do not evaluate the ideas at the same time is generating them. A dreamer should accept and appreciate all friendly gestures in his dream and transmute the scary ones with his power of love.

If you're aware enough to pay attention to the strange happenings inside your dream, you will notice cues from a SuperConscious; "become aware you're dreaming."

When attempting to enter the lucid dream state from our waking, a good technique is to keep your mind on one image, even if it is not a clear image; or on one thought. This will usually produce pale beginnings of a dream state.

Lucid dreams are more than a life like. If examined in detail, they can almost be the way that Tetrachromats see. During Lucid dreams pay special importance to emotional detachment to prolong the experience and remain self-aware. Sinking deeply into a positive and especially a negative emotion will lose a degree of consciousness.

Conscious Dreamer must be able to comprehend the nature of the dream state through dream images and dream content, realize the dream state is an illusion; and eventually he must be able to meditate inside a dream world. Very advanced meditator will maintain unbroken continuity of consciousness throughout waking, sleeping and dreaming states.

CHAPTER FIVE

MUTUAL AND GROUP DREAMING

Mutual dreaming (also known as shared or group dreaming) is the paranormal claim two or more people can share the same dream environment. The concept was popularized in a movie 'Inception', where lucid dreamers could link up via technology and roam around the unconscious of a single dreamer.

In reality, no such device exists. But how might we go about proving the hypothetical existence of mutual dreams?

The best mechanism we have for initiating mutual dreams is through the act of lucid dreaming. Though they can sometimes incubate specific dream themes, it is hard for non-lucid dreamers to plan their dreams in advance to alter the course of the dream in progress, and impossible, without becoming lucid,.

But lucid dreamers can make these influences and perform all kinds of in-dream experimentation.

The definition implies one of at least two paranormal explanations: that we have the capacity for telepathy in dreams - or the dream world itself is an external construct, an alternate reality that could stem from an artificial stimulation or other shared astral realms.

As said elsewhere; it is possible for two or more individuals to share the same dream at night although physically they might be distant from each other. The principle is same as in the waking reality. Participants has to be in the same space (dreamed, visualized like in deep hypnosis) at the same time.

"If a man could pass through Paradise in a dream, and have a flower presented to him as a pledge that his soul had really been there, and if he found that flower in his hand when he awake - Aye, what then?"-Samuel Taylor Coleridge

Some people dream to sleep. Others sleep to dream.

Problem with mutual and group dreams is not so much the place, which is visualized. Study the agreed upon 'meeting place'. You need to draw it or paint it to the minutest detail. It needs to be imprinted in your mind. It than becomes just a matter of Intent when you are in the dream world. Please distinguish between ordinary visualization which is blind and a real visualization in which you see, just like you are seeing these words. The big problem is the time. For not only are you to be at the same place but you have to be there at the same time. Problem of 90 minutes of unconscious sleep presents itself before dreaming period begins. The solution is to enter consciously from waking world into a dream world and remain conscious. Dreaming period commences almost immediately, so it becomes easy to synchronize the time.

Always 'confront and conquer danger' in dreams. If an animal looms out of the jungle, go toward it. If someone attacks you, 'fight' back with hugs and love.

Always move toward pleasurable experiences in dreams. If you are attracted to 'someone' in a dream, feel free to return the love, but do this in a double-arrow mode only, with some noble goal in mind. If you are enjoying the pleasurable sensations of flying or swimming, relax and experience them fully. Swimming is fantastic; water looks like kwicksilver and feels great.

Always make your dreams have a positive outcome and extract a creative product from them. Best of all in this regard, try to obtain a gift from the dream images, such as a poem, a song, a dance, a design, or a painting, or even a new spiritual technique.

I noted that some of the early claims about REM sleep and dreams turned out to be slightly wrong (e.g., the eye movements do not always correlate with the dreams, dreams sometimes occur in non-REM sleep towards morning, and people do not become crazy if they are deprived of REM sleep, at least for some time).

It is said the Swiss psychologist Carl Jung in his lifetime analyzed over 80,000 dreams. Dreams for Jung played an important complementary role in the psyche. The general function of a dream is to restore our psychological balance by producing material that re-establishes, in a subtle way, the total psychic equilibrium. Jung approached dreams as living realities that must be experienced and observed carefully to be understood. He considered Freud's method of "free association" as incomplete. Jung- "Free association will bring out all your complexes, but hardly ever the meaning of a dream. To understand the dream's meaning, I must stick as close as possible to the dream images." During analysis, Jung kept asking the dreamer, "What does the dream say?" Analyzing ordinary dreams is useless. We need to learn to enter them consciously, learn to navigate them and make them useful.

"The stigma that has accompanied dreams into our century can be thought of as quite unfortunate. In our society, dreams are often thought of as unimportant or as pure nonsense."- (Gackenbach, 1997.) "This stigma accompanies many dreams, including lucid dreams. There is a small body of research that indicates the possible therapeutic uses of lucid dreaming. We can see how hard it would be for our society to accept this kind of therapy if they view the key element, dreaming, as nonsense. Society needs to change the attitudes around dreaming due to the possible benefits that dream therapy could have on problems such as post-traumatic stress disorder. I plan to demonstrate the benefits that lucid dream therapy could have for the treatment of post-traumatic stress disorder and show why society needs to embrace dreaming as an important and useful human resource."

Lucid dreaming has been noted in history numerous times. Aristotle mentioned lucid dreaming. Even the philosopher Thomas Reid spoke of using lucid dreams to control his nightmares. Some have disputed lucid dreaming and said there is no such thing. Green and McCreery offer an explanation for the dispute: "If people doubt lucid dreams they do so because they have never experienced one." This is an interesting argument and quite possibly true. Stephen LaBerge explains why some dispute lucid dreams and why this dispute is faulty: "One might object that lucid dreamers are simply not attending to the environment; rather than being asleep, perhaps they are merely absorbed in their private fantasy worlds. . . .if subjects claim to have been awake while showing physiological signs of sleep (or vice versa), we might have cause to doubt their subjective reports."

The question that now must be raised is: what is considered a lucid dream?

As defined by Green and McCreery "Lucid dreams are those in which a person knows he is dreaming." (1994, p.1.) Despite the exclusive language, this is a clear and simple definition. Those who have had a lucid dream but are unfamiliar with the terminology could easily recognize their dream as "lucid." Hobson outlines some possible characteristics of lucid dreams and lucid dreamers: "(a) that lucid dreamers will frequently awaken from REM sleep once dream consciousness is achieved and (b) that lucidity will be easiest to induce at times in the night when the system is likely to be changing from REM to waking." (1990, p.38.) This quotation makes lucid dreaming sound quite disruptive to sleep. It is perhaps a relief that LaBerge says "Lucid dreaming is normally a rare experience." (1990, p.109.)

I strongly believe lucid dreaming and Transcendental Rebirthing has a connection to the treatment of post-traumatic stress disorder. General symptoms of post-traumatic stress disorder include feelings of fear, guilt and detachment, etc.

From a scientific perspective, REM dreaming has a pretty specific neuro-phenomenology. Activation of the limbic system brings strong emotions, and this is combined with enhanced access to long-term memory and a depression of short-term memory, so we don't tend to question who or where we are. The parts of the brain that bring mental imagery are also actively firing away, creating symbolic structures for all this content. In a nutshell, dreaming is a potent mix of visual-emotional-linguistic metaphors that link to our deepest memories and experiences. So being aware during this intense process, a little activation of the prefrontal cortex, does not necessarily pull rank.

California Institute of Integral Studies, recently collaborated with noted ayahuasca researcher Luis Eduardo Luna to research the electrical output of the brain while under the influence of an aya brew. They discovered an amazing effect: a strong synchrony in the frontal lobe over multiple frequency bands, specifically the high beta and gamma range. This same effect has been found recently by dream researcher Ursula Voss in lucid dreaming: a strong blip around the 40 Hz (gamma) wavelength that is not present in ordinary dreams. Other researchers have found a correlation between gamma and high levels of meditation.

Native American healer Rolling Thunder suggests that lucid dreaming is a preferable way to access the hidden realms of reality, provided the practitioner knows the intent and direction of the journey.

Ominously enough, the US military has done extensive research into remote viewing, which is the application of deep imagination, trance or dreams to discover information about a place, person or event. Shamans call this technique soul-flight, and it's also known as out-of-body experience and astral travel. The movie The Men Who Stare at Goats is a loose adaptation of the remote viewing. Work that went on in the US intelligence community for over twenty years to determine the usefulness of remote viewing to receive information about a target.

This work is now declassified. Officially the US government professed in 1995 there is no benefit to remote viewing. However, the various programs, with names like "Stargate," "Gondala Wish," and "Sunstreak" had some convincing documented successes, according to ex-

Stargate chief Dale Graff in his book 'Tracks in the Psychic Wilderness', including the location of a downed Soviet TU-22 airplane by remote viewing

And as Robert Waggoner recently pointed out, mutual lucid dreaming opens the door to not only shared dreams, but also real dream intrusion a la Inception; without the need for a narcotic drip line.

Here's an example of what could be called an initiatory lucid dream that begun as a sleep paralysis nightmare, shared by a woman dreamer who lives in the Middle East, published in the eBook 'Sleep Paralysis: A Dreamer's Guide'.

"I was reading for a while, then I noticed that the wall (about 6 feet from the end of my bed) started to sort of wobble. My body was paralyzed, unable to move. My breathing was kind of non-existent, though I desperately needed more air. Suddenly, it opened up into a black void. Like a 9 ft black hole, vaguely the shape of a figure. "O my god," I thought, "I am dreaming. This can't be true." The black-hole oozed into the room. I was beyond terror. I still don't understand how my heart didn't collapse. The blackness started molding itself into a recognizable shape. It became a 9 ft. tall Japanese devil or devilish-looking Samurai. Viciously grinning he said, "You are not dreaming. You thought you could integrate me." He then, in one sweeping movement, stretched out his enormous black hand, grabbed me, stuffed me into his blood-red mouth, and swallowed me. Then I fell into unconsciousness for a moment, now a vortex pulled me down into an abyss of no dimensions. All of a sudden, I was spat back out into his hand. Somehow, I had crystallized into a red ruby. I WAS a ruby; I felt like a ruby. So there I was, in the big hand of a giant, looking at him, and he looking at me. In that moment-seeing each other-something happened. We looked at each other, became truly aware of each other, and then, there was love. I know what the mystics talk about/can't talk about. There is believing, and then, there is knowing."

If she had enough presence, energy and intent to make

herself large and him small, grab the samurai, put him in her mouth and then spit him out, this would be amazing. Then 'they' could hug each other and laugh and laugh.

Shared dreaming, also referred to as mutual dreaming, recently received unprecedented attention in paranormal psychology. Studies now reveal that shared dreaming happens not only spontaneously or involuntarily, but may actually be induced or initiated by the individuals concerned. It is thus possible to make use of shared dreaming for two individuals to communicate with one another, or to share their dream experience with one another. Because of the communication involved in shared dreaming, it can be considered one form of telepathy."

Mutual dreams are called different names; collective dreams, group dreams, shared dreams.

In many indigenous cultures around the world, dreaming is practiced as a shamanic art. Lucidity is not often discussed directly, but most times, the lucid-control dimension is evident in the dream reports collected by anthropologists. For many of the first people on the planet, being aware of being aware is not a trick for its own philosophical novelty, but a prerequisite for undertaking a dangerous dream journey. These dreams, marked by clarity, intense imagery and emotions, are invariably known as Big Dreams, and in most cultures are treated and interpreted differently than the dreams that reflect anxieties and every day-life concerns.

"Jesus"; 'Where there are two or more in my name there is Kingdom of God.'

***

Every human being has three minds. The Ego mind brings us order, directness and purpose. Subconscious mind brings us conflict, self-assertion, doubts and hopelessness. The third mind is perfect; our SuperConscious mind. Our subconscious mind is a product of all our life experiences, the one that rarely speaks because it has been defeated and delegated to obscurity. The Ego mind is artificially created from our life experiences. Once across a certain threshold it is the nature of the SuperConscious mind to put a blueprint in front of us, to put up map in front of us, so we can chose a direction and move.

Intent is a force that exists in us; true intent always accomplishes what is set out to do.

Spirit Voyager needs to learn how to perceive energy directly as it flows in the universe and also to perceive human beings in the same way. Direct perception of the energy flow is definitely possible. Our awareness, our consciousness is also energy; it is in constant flux, a luminous vibration that is never stationary.

The Spirit Traveler should have neither deviance nor gross remorse. Dreamer takes nothing for granted. Ever!

***

Energy fields of the universe are converted into sensory data, and the sensory data is then interpreted and perceived as the world. What turns this universal energy into sensory data is our consciousness. What we call senses in ourselves is nothing but a degree of awareness, a degree of vibration. When a childhood memory arrives and opens, it is experienced as a vibration in a particular part of the body; and a total tridimensional live view of a long forgotten event of our childhood comes up. We can even perceive it visually as if it is happening in now-time.

Never judge people; all the human beings are prisoners and it is that prison that makes all of us act in such a miserable way. Your challenge is to take people as they are and leave them alone. The goal of Conscious Dreamer is to gain certain abilities and acquire efficient tools to continue with his voyage, which by the way will never end. The energy body is the mirror image of the physical body; when visually perceived it is our dream body. Our physical body and energy body are like two pieces of paper compressed and glued together. By constant practice we can bring our energy body and our dream body closer, so it resembles physical body. Normally the 'distance' between these two is enormous. With discipline and continuous practice the Spirit Traveler can forge the replica of the physical body that is to say tridimensional 'solid' Dream Being. At that point humans can claim to have two bodies.

To see energy directly is the bottom line for every human being. Spirit Voyager should have a love for knowledge in whatever form it is presented. Procrastination is one of the major problems and a self-discipline is the antidote. Spirit Traveler never complains. They take everything the way it exists. It is a challenge, something to learn from and to become stronger.

Spirit Traveler understands discipline; it is the capacity to face with serenity and perfect understanding the laws that are infinitely stacked against us. Discipline is an art, the act of facing infinity with no fear. Not because they're strong or there is nothing to fear, but because they're filled with awesomeness of the existence itself. It is that kind of discipline that increases awareness immeasurably. Spirit Travelers are the beacons, the possessors of energy and consciousness that are the means by which universe becomes aware of itself.

The Spirit Voyagers should be able to create an energy barrier around themselves, the energy barrier impenetrable to anything. From total silence, just by Intent, this barrier is constructed. It is possible only if internal dialogue is completely stopped.

Spirit Warriors fight elegantly, fearlessly for their existence. They are humble and efficient, acting with no expectations and withstanding anything that lies ahead of them. Once the Spirit Warrior enters infinity he or she cannot rely anymore on external sources to bring him/her back. To come back they must clearly state their Intent to do so. Spirit Voyager must have something he is willing to die for, before he can think he has something to live for. If you have nothing to die for how can you claim you have something to live for? Life and death are two ends of the same stick.

Astral Warrior can always count on one being, one on which they can focus all of their Love; this fantastic planet, Mother Earth, the Original Matrix that gave us this body. The center of everything we are and everything we do, the very being to which all of us return, the very being that allows Spirit Voyagers to leave her on their final journey and then return again.

'Forget' the self, forget the Ego and you will fear nothing in whatever level of awareness you find yourself to be in. Part of the making a dream body functional is to project the focused thoughts in dreaming in order to accomplish the production of any object or structure, or landmark, or scenery of dreamers choice.

To become able being in mutual dreams or a group dream, the dreamers practice gazing at the simple object and memorizing every detail. Only when they pass this point successfully they move on to visualize more complex objects and spaces. So in startup phase, visualization has to be so powerful that the two objects in a dream, the physical and dream object become identical. From a simple object the dreamers can graduate to more and more complex items. The end aim is for the group of dreamers to visualize identical particular space or even a total world and then dream that world and so create a new reality. Here question begs to be asked, is it possible that this world, our waking world was created that way? If two or more dreamers are capable of dreaming identical space at the same time, they enter that particular vision which becomes consensual reality.

If you are able to visualize (clearly see) someone's face in your dreams and that person is at that moment also conscious in his dream, he'll know you're calling him; this is like a visual and audio: Dream Skype.

Somebody mentioned I am divulging too much. How could I; I know nothing. It does not matter if the greatest secret is presented on paper. Unprepared will not understand it nor be able to do anything about it. The True Secret protects itself.

The goal of lucid dream work ultimately to wake up within the dream, but this waking up is not just within the dream, it can initiate Second Awakening in what we all know as our waking life.

Words are used to convey the ideas, but when the ideas are grasped, men forget the words.

We are dreaming all the time whether we are awake or asleep. Same creative faculty involved in creating the dream world creates our 'waking' world.

CHAPTER SIX

DREAM BODY

In a dream world there are no shadows. There is light; clear light emanating from every object making it visible, but nothing has a shadow. Let me qualify that, strong dreamer can dream darkness and a shadow, intentionally. Our dream body can jump over the trees, high buildings, fly through the air, become large or small and take a shape of any animal or a bird, or anything else for that matter. It can become aware of people's thoughts or become a thought, or cross impossible distances. Nothing is impossible for the dream body. Dream body is not in any way affected by the laws of the physical world. The physical body is controlled by our intellect while our dream body is controlled by our Intent. There is no way to think about it or to understand it rationally. You have to feel it; the physical body has to feel as if it is sound asleep, you quiet it down deliberately by removing your awareness from it. When your body and mind are at rest, your dream body breaks out and takes over. You are asleep and yet you are fully conscious.

Intent is a layer above the thoughts. We need to look beyond the thoughts; Intent is so far away from the thoughts we can't even talk about it, we can't even feel it, but we can certainly use it. Only by intending, intending, and intending it gets stronger. But when you Intend something make sure it is a success.

Dream body is definitely inside our physical body but it doesn't have to be. Storing sexual energy is one step in the journey toward the spirit body. Sexual energy is needed to sustain pressure or extending awareness past its current limits. It is sexual energy that governs dreaming.

Gazing, stopping the internal dialogue, and dreaming all stop the usual patterns and conditional energy fields. By stopping the normal flow of your attention you can enter into the dream world. For that to happen you need to stop your ordinary, waking world.

Gazing technique is one avenue to the energy body. It destabilizes your energy fields and refocuses your awareness along the lines of your Intent. Look at the single object and gently cross your eyes until you have two identical images, then direct your perception between those two images. By practicing this technique it then becomes easier to gaze without crossing your eyes. At first gazing seems to be an optical exercise however you eventually expanded it so that your gaze with your entire physical body. Fire gazing, a candle gazing, or a water gazing is also very helpful.

Gazing suspends perception and brings you closer to perceiving the energy. Each person is a huge conglomerate of energies. Scalar storms rage throughout our body. A path with heart, with feelings, gives you direction and purpose. If you encounter a fearful situation place your hands two inches below your belly button; if you're a man right hand against the skin and left hand on a top, if you're a woman left hand on top of the belly right hand on top of the left.

Spirit Travelers have to learn to focus their attention with infinitely more force and precision. Travelers have only one option open to them; to succeed in whatever they do. The dreaming Self can become aware and perceive this waking world. Your body and your mind are accustomed to it but your dream body is not. When you enter the absolute darkness where there are no distractions; the dream self takes over, the third eye opens and sees a dream world. The conscious awareness of daily life is what you want to shift from the body to the dream body.

One of the greatest human misconceptions is belief that health is in the realm of physical body while it is actually in a subconscious world.

Don't automatically act on your thoughts. Instead use your feelings and pay attention to your instinct and intuition.

Sometimes it happens you wake up inside a dream body but you cannot see anything or hear anything. You can intend to see and give yourself a permission, and sometimes this malady clears up on its own.

To enhance a sense of touch of your dream body you need to touch the objects very gently. Generally speaking all physical like senses operate better in a dream body then in a physical body because they are limited by your imagination only. So the question arises; does the dream body exists all the time or does it disappear as you wake up? Well there are 3 possible answers. Dream body exist even when you wake up, for subconscious dreams in pictures 24 hours a day. Because everything that happens is recorded in memory dream body cannot ever disappear. Second answer; dream body disappears when we awake. And the third one; it falls asleep when we enter this reality, just like physical body falls asleep when we enter a dream world. Take your pick. Remember; every coin, be it physical, mental, emotional or spiritual has three sides, equally true simultaneously.

The difficulty of enhancing your dreaming power is that it is very easy to get lost in a magic of dreaming and so lose a deeper connection, connection with consciousness and supra-consciousness. While in your dream body you can travel slowly, rapidly, or instantaneously you can also change your relation to the dreamscape so that the environment speeds up or slows down. In a conscious dream, super-lucid dream, you can control the entire dreamscape. If you want to change a building into a tree, simply intend it. Or if you want to experience a new location, just Will it and a dream will change course. We are talking here about already powerful Intent and powerful energy.

Dream Voyager needs to live impeccably. We have an innate sense of what is good and what is bad. If you have doubt, push the question into the extreme. If we ALL start killing each other, the end is obvious; if we ALL started destroying instead creating, etc.

Dreaming is energy producing; we are sensing a different frequency in our body during a transition from a dream world to waking world. For those who are unprepared this might be unsettling. You can sometime hear squeaks, cracks, pops and perhaps sounds resembling ocean surf, or a freight train in the distance, distant waterfall, etc. All of these sounds are natural when accessing the dreaming field. As you progress sometimes you might experience these things when you are awake. Be aware of it but don't pay much attention to it.

Yogic Dreaming is a learnable skill, like studying a foreign language or a musical instrument, it requires time, energy, and dedicated practice to master it. Most communication in a dream body is nonverbal. It is "telepathic". Communication from so called another entity often sounds and feels as if it comes from right inside your head. Jolts of energy occurs regularly when the second field is stimulated; these are felt in your physical body When there are indications of a moving energy always respond with strength and abandon rather than fear or morbidity. In a dream world speaking in a beginning is a bit difficult but with the progress this speech impediment will change since dreams reflect your thoughts.

You can perform imagination exercises throughout the day of your dream body imagining, your dream body performing certain acts. Good technique is to regard your daily life as a dream and examine it in that manner. See that each and every action you undertake either subtracts or adds to your dream power then act accordingly. The dream body is an intent within the Intent of your entire being; it just needs actualization and development. The procedures to awaken the dream body are exactly the same procedures as to awaken the real one. Therefore developing the dream body is a major step in developing Intent.

Transferring your awareness from your physical body to your dream body teaches you how to handle that Intent. You must initiate Intent to make this transitions, and you must hold the Intent steady to remain aware of the dream body.

As you work with dreaming exercises, pay attention to the force which moves and then stabilizes your consciousness that forms Intent. The more you exercise it the more you learn how to handle it. Once you're in your dream body, your Intent is to exercise it in every way possible. As with any intent you intend by intending. You just feel it. Good analogy would be when you were learning to walk. You try, you fall, you get up and try again, fall again and try again, and finally you succeed. Look how long you took to make your physical body fully functional. You know you want to navigate the dream world so you Intend. The hardest part is cooperating with the forces that are much greater than yours and are beyond your control, like that of super-conscious mind. If you ever find yourself trapped in an unpleasant situation, stop, relax and ask yourself why is it when I react in a negative way this automatically generates the negative energy? Always think in positive terms.

During the transition into the dreaming body you may experience a variety of internal sounds like ocean surf, a hum bells, ringing in your ears and many others. Dreaming lends itself to a variety of moods. Always stay on the positive side of your feelings and emotions.

At the core of the Intent is Silence. The ultimate power has no movement and no form. Intent lies beyond thoughts, beyond the feelings, beyond emotions but it can be used. Every person in existence is connected to the pure spirit and to the Fifth Element at all times. So the job at hand is not to reestablish the connection. This is already so! We just need to remember it, to perceive it. The average person's Intent is practically dead. Spirit Voyagers realize they begin with the nonfunctional intent. To begin awakening intent Spirit Traveler starts by performing a single action that is deliberate, precise, and sustained, like meditation, repeating the act long enough to produce unbending Intent. Accessing Intent occurs in a heightened consciousness. The good way to start your awakening is to practice as many meditative exercises as possible. Also stay alert for the glimmering of something waiting to unfold. The further you travel the more you will sense something looming, something waiting to break into full awareness. This is the unknown ready to become known. By wishing without wish, and doing without doing, the Spirit Voyager hooks onto Intent directly. At the base of the deep inner silence is Dreamer's Intent which matches that of SuperConsciousness. Whenever this match occurs, you have manifested your goal.

How can Intent be understood? Question, the human mind can ask; "Can a God make a stone so heavy "he" cannot lift it. Whatever the answer, we are faced with the problem. If he can, he is not Almighty if he cannot he is not Almighty. But the problem is in OUR dualistic thinking. Triune thinking is necessary to understand the existence. So the correct answer is yes God can make a stone so heavy he cannot lift it, no God cannot People will do anything, he cannot lift it, and none of the above, ALL AT THE SAME TIME. Again, humans do what is possible, God DOES the impossible.

Intent is the state of mind with which an act is done. Intent is a wish without a thought, the act of intending to do something, or for something to happen (Ultimate intent can be made at Zero-point energy level). A good definition for intention is: "to have in mind a purpose or plan, to direct the mind, to aim."

Lacking intention, we sometimes stray without meaning or direction. But with 100% pure Intent, all the forces of the universe align to make even the most impossible, possible.

Intention plays a crucial role in anyone's spiritual path. In fact, I would say in some ways it is the most important part of the entire path, because it is the beginning of it. You have stepped through the entrance gate to your spiritual path when your wants turns into intention. Intention begins with a recognition, no matter how faint, of something within you that feels good and right, even if it is only for a moment.

When you begin your spiritual journey with intent, it

might seem that it is similar to beginning a journey toward a destination, but that is actually not the case. And one of the causes of suffering that many people experience is precisely because they think there is a destination on their spiritual path, and therefore get frustrated when they never seem to get any closer to that destination, or even feel they got lost on the way. Intention-journey is without destination.

This is the most wonderful and liberating thing about Intent: you already are who you truly intend to be. All you need to do is to realize it. To realize it through the entire structure of your being. Here is the thing: that Clear Light (Inner Light) is already within you. All you need to do is to shed the various layers that block it and cause it to be so rarely seen.

Law of Intention and Desire is based on the fact there is always an infinite amount of energy and information present to create whatever you truly desire.

At the quantum mechanical (this sounds so dry and lifeless) level the entire universe is the movement of energy and information.

Personal change is brought about by conscious attention and intention. Attention gives energy to the Law of Attraction, which then pulls your desires to you.

Whatever you put your awareness on, it increases.

Whatever you remove your attention from disintegrates and disappears.

Intent transforms your quantum information and energy into what you put your attention on, by organizing it, using infinite correlation till you manifest your desires. This is how the Law of Attraction pulls your desires to you like a magnet.

When you place your attention on the object of your intent, it will orchestrate an infinite number of events to materialize your desires. But this is only in a case of 100% pure Intent.

We experience proof of this infinite organizing power daily in our bodies. Every second, every cell in the human body must perform trillions of functions to maintain life. Our mind-body system produces over a quadrillion chemical reactions every second. What KNOWS what chemicals to produce and how? What power moves the chemicals into the right place and for the right thing? The intelligence needed is stupendous.

Human body is capable of hearing music, thinking, killing germs, growing a baby, driving a car, being aware, talking on the phone, breathing, digesting food, having an emotion, and circulating blood, all at the same time! This miracle of infinite organizing powers can be consciously trained by you to manifest your desires or wipe out your F.E.A.R. (False Evidence Appearing Real).

Intent lays the groundwork for Effortlessness, spontaneous expression of your desires.

Where is the energy for a perfect Intent going to come from? At our deepest level we are pure infinite energy. Practice Transcendental Rebirthing and REAL meditation to initiate becoming familiar with it.

Desire without action usually happens when your intentions are laced with negative attachments and aversions.

Intent is desire with strict adherence to the Law of Detachment!

Your intent is for the future, but your awareness must be in the present! Your attention must be focused on the actions you can take today that will manifest your intentions for tomorrow!

Only the present which is conscious awareness, is real and eternal!

A positive affirmation can produce a neurotic achiever identity if you are attached to the outcome. Always surrender the outcome to Existence, then focus your attention on the daily actions you need to do, to manifest your desires.

Detached, effortless intention will prevent you from struggling against the present in the pursuit of manifesting your future! You must accept the present as it is and intend the future as you would have it to be.

If we want to know our state and to purify our intentions we can reflect on what is happening around us, for the outside world can be a mirror to our inner state.

Law of Attraction or the Power of Intention is pure and simple. The Law of Attraction is this: You don't attract what you want. You attract what you are.

'Hua Hu Ching', written by Lao Tzu says; "Those who want to know the truth of the universe should practice the four cardinal virtues. The first is reverence for all of life. This manifests as unconditional love and respect for oneself and all other beings. The second is natural sincerity. This manifests as honesty, simplicity and faithfulness. The third is gentleness, which manifests as kindness, consideration for others and sensitivity to spiritual truth. The fourth is supportiveness. This manifests as service to others without expectation of reward."

Intent means "purpose." Being purposeful, we will often make choices and look for opportunities to achieve; it provides that anchor in our thinking and decision making.

As the old saying goes: "If you don't know where you want to go, any road will take you there." Passivity, the inability, or unwillingness to make the big choices in life and act upon them, keeps many people "stuck in first gear." Understanding the principle of intention means realizing that choosing something as a focus of your energy means not choosing lots of other things. Some people can immobilize themselves with the fear of making a wrong choice. Others may be apprehensive about the options they will have to give up. But ultimately, not deciding is actually deciding.

One can start with small decisions. Make them consciously, own them, and commit to them. Appreciate that they generally work out fine. Keep the bigger ones on your decision list and train yourself to "just do it." A well-formed statement of intent, the outcome you seek to bring about, can help you focus your attention and energy on the things that really count in your life.

Learn to intend and let the universe handle the details.

Your focused Intent sets the infinite organizing power of the universe in motion. Trust this infinite organizing power to orchestrate the complete fulfillment of your desires. Don't listen to the voice that says you have to always be in charge. In the spiritual world, it is the intention that gives the value to the action itself; intention is followed by action.

What we owe to ourselves and everyone around is to examine the reasons of our true Intent. Our goals need to be generous and humane for the intention to work.

What is Ego intent? Intent is will plus desire. When you have a clear, strong desire and you put your will behind it, you have intent.

Will is one of the most fundamental qualities of our Divine Self. When you tap into and develop your Will, you tap into all the power of creation. True Intent-Will is not a thought, or an object, or a wish. Intent is what can make a man succeed when his thoughts tell him he is defeated. It operates in spite of the Spirit Voyager indulgence. Intent makes him invulnerable. Intent sends a sage through 'space', to infinite eternity and back.

***

When people believe, they decide they merrily agree with far greater subconscious power. This decision was already made seconds ago; it already occurred in a subconscious mind. We just execute it, never even suspecting the decision was not ours.

Your body always knows if you made the right decision; be aware of the feelings. If you make a wrong decision you will feel tense, ill at ease. With the right decision the body relaxes and stands ready for the next decision. At a later date you will FEEL when you make right Intent, yow will feel an energy flow someplace in your body; like a gentle pleasurable breeze.

Remove yourself from personal thoughts and emotions. Spirit Travelers desire nothing, even though in a spirit world they can get anything they want. Advanced Spirit Travelers only spin worlds of energy. Like a clear water-filled balloon placed in the ocean you are one with it, yet you are in your own world. Freedom in a dream world means you can manifest the impossible, something which has no reference or foundation in everyday life.

Spirit Voyagers eyes shine and reflect the Intent. Not only do they reflect the Intent, they summon the Intent. You must be unconcerned with the outcome of your undertakings.

As a form of energy thoughts are as real as anything else, but the bodily knowledge and verbal language exist independent of each other.

Proper timing occurs when you are aware of the forces around you and you are in tune with them. Waiting is also a force. The discipline of awaiting provides a stepping stone for handling Clarity. Spirit Traveler needs to learn to be patient, to wait, to let go and let the consciousness flow. A personal Will means you have the capacity to Intend, to choose a new direction in life and intend new dreams. Learning does not mean to just accumulate new thoughts, new ideas, but you must acquire the ability to act and do. You must be willing to innovate, to experiment, and be brave. Trust in the SuperConscious otherwise you virtually have no chance of becoming a person with REAL spiritual knowledge.

In an everyday world our aim is to elevate our perception into constant state of a double-arrow, higher awareness, of higher consciousness.

Occasionally a Dreamer needs to recapitulate the

accumulated time and remember his/her experiences. This doesn't have nothing to do with intellect. It has to be done through the body through the feelings. Our waking energy field is supported through reasoning power, and the dreaming field is supported through action and eventually they support each other. Spirit Travelers learn to act with no expectations.

The real knowledge is not gained through thinking. The trick is to think clearly without ordinary thinking, to be meditating 24 hours a day, to be in double-arrow attention seven days a week for the rest of your dreaming and waking life.

Proper timing is to be somewhere between laziness and hurry. If you are neither lazy nor in some kind of hurry, you stand a better chance of feeling your balance within waking world and the dream world. Additional skill for refining the timing is relaxation. You need to feel your body, its needs, and its directions. Body operates in now time and so does the energy that powers it. Time is often paradoxical. Fifth Element emanations are constant and they are eternal and unchanging, yet at the same time they are always in a constant flux. Energy frequency within the emanations of a Fifth Element determine the nature of your timing.

There is no doubt that all forms carry power. Different forms carry different power, and this is valid for the dream world forms as well. Be careful what forms you summon.

The intellect and the thoughts can take you only so far; for the total freedom the entire energy body must be developed.

And they allowed Apollonius to ask questions; and he asked them of what they thought the cosmos was composed; but they replied; "Of elements."

"Are there then four?" he asked.

"Not four," said Larchas, "but five."

"And how can there be a fifth," said Apollonius, "alongside of water and air and earth and fire?"

"There is the ether," replied the other, "which we must regard as the stuff of which gods are made; for just as all mortal creatures inhale the air, so do immortal and divine natures (he is taking about you) inhale the ether."

"Am I," said Appollonius, "to regard the universe as a living creature?"

"Yes," said the other. - 'The Life of Apollonius of Tyana', Philostratus, 220AD

CHAPTER SEVEN

MAKING A DREAM BODY FUNCTIONAL

If the dream is of minute objects, first transform them into the large object; or if it is or large object transform it into the small object. If a dream is of single thing transform it into many things, or if it is of many things, the dreamer shall transform it into one thing. As you develop consciousness inside your dream, you can produce any change you wish. Potential of that skill is truly limitless. The ability to transform the images and impose changes upon the dream should be regardless of whether the images are threatening or not. Dreamer must raise his consciousness to a level high enough to remember in a dream that the fearful image cannot hurt you unless you let it. If your consciousness inside your dream state is high enough, you can dispose of a fear of any dream image.

Once the Dreamer realizes the illusory state of dreams the Dream Traveler is ready for further advances on the path; a fully conscious dreamless state where there are no images of any kind.

As an exercise you can move the objects without contact, you can make them lighter of heavier, you can make them disappear, it is all a matter of intent and the amount of energy you possess. You can also materialize objects.

Dreamed action can produce effects on the brain and the body, sometimes as much as if your experience the corresponding events in a waking state.

When lucid dreamers hold their breaths or breathe fast in a dream, the body really does hold its breath or breathe fast. When you consciously move your dream eyes in predetermined fashion, the physical eyes move in the same pattern.

You could sing in a dream which engages the right hemisphere, and you can do simple mathematics in a dream which engages the left hemisphere.

Lucid dreaming takes effort and therefore lot of energy.

A true yogi will remain fearless even at the enormously powerful archetypal images that might appear at the time of his death or in his dream.

Ability to concentrate attention and hold it on the desired point confers tremendous power to the processes of individual in a lucid dream or in a waking world. If you increase your skills of concentration and meditation, you will definitely increase control of dreams.

We should understand that our body is composed, built, out of 60 to 70 trillion cells, and at the time of the death they are all still alive. We should know in after-death-state tremendous visions will appear. The knowledge how to deal with these powerful and frightening dreams and frightening images is crucial. At that point of time possibly soul saving.

Flying dreams and lucid dreams are strongly related. When you find yourself flying without benefit of aircraft or air balloon ride, it is a great dream sign. Start suspecting your dreaming.

Once you get more proficient, play with your senses one at a time as you explore the dream world. Once you have mastered to a degree enhancing your five senses, we are all familiar with, then use other so-called paranormal senses that are now sublimated in a subconscious world. When you achieve a degree of proficiency of lucidity, create a futuristic television with most fantastic live colors and incredible surround-sound, then use a dream hands to dial-up and enhance further both color and sound; or use the mind to accomplish it. Make this television set truly magical where you can experience fantastic tastes, and smells, sounds sights and even touch. Then make that television set tridimensional with live images. Once you accomplish this, dispose of the dream television, and accomplish this with all of your dream senses.

Lucid Dreaming is not in itself the goal of the practice, but it is an important development along the path of Dream Yoga. We can accomplish psychological tasks in our lucid dreams or overcome energetic difficulties. The effects of those dreams will definitely extend into the waking life. In higher lucid dreams the dreamer practices transforming everything that is encountered. There are no boundary to experiences that cannot be broken in a dream. Ordinarily we do not think of us as having multiple selves, or multiple identities, but we can accomplish this in a dream. We can create ourselves simultaneously in two different dream bodies. We can multiply anything in a dream.

In a dream world always aim for the highest and seemingly most difficult and most elusive goal. This will automatically take care of the lesser stuff. There are many categories in which our minds are restricted by previous beliefs; like size, quantity, quality, speed, accomplishment, transformation, emanation, journey, seeing, hearing, feeling, taste and all our senses including the paranormal, and all experiences. We can change the size in a dream we can become small like an insect or even like a bacterium, or as large as we wish. Take one object in a dream and transform it into thousands using awareness. Navigate the dream rather than be driven; dream rather than let yourself be a dreamt. We can change our emotions in a dream when you're angry change the emotion to love. It's only energy we have attached the meaning to. That energy we can easily change. The qualities of fear jealousy, anger, greed and helplessness in dreams can be changed. All negative emotions are not helpful; all of them can be changed, transformed, and transmuted. Changing the emotions inside the dream enables you to change your emotions in waking life. Often we can change the speed of the dream, we can slow things down to a slow-motion, or we can visit hundred places in one minute. The only boundaries in a dream or the boundaries in your imagination. Whatever we cannot accomplish in our life, we can accomplish in a dream, plus thousand times more. We can practice anything.

Once you get a bit more proficient, ask the subconscious mind to show you the king/queen of the dream world. Just keep repeating a thought like a mantra; "Show me the king of the subconscious." Repetition will turn into intent. Be prepared for the huge surprise. Once it shows up, immediately ask: Show me how we can become friends.

Everything in astral world has its own light, its own brilliance, and therefore there are no shadows. If awareness is tied up to the dream body we are not affected by the laws of the physical world. The dream body can jump over the moon, fly, become large and small, it can transport itself through the large distances; also be telepathic. Dream body is not controlled by our intellect but by our Intent. It has to be felt.

If you wish you can write a book, swim across the ocean, and complete what needs to be finished. We can learn to transform our body into anything we wish; like a butterfly or a dog, a horse and mystical bird Phoenix. We can transform ourselves into a loving person, a saint or an angel.

We can multiply our body and break through the limitation of experiencing yourself as a single, separate Ego in a dream world. Dreamer can travel anywhere; we can visit the streets of Zagreb, surface of the moon, or even other galaxies, and go to the bottom of the ocean. Nothing is preventing you to travel to the center of the sun, you can see inside your body, you can see and feel your heart pumping, you can go to the cave in Himalaya and visited a sage and learn from him. Definitely ask for teachings. Use a dream state to experience something you have not done before. You can experience any mystic state, any spiritual state, you can breathe water like a fish, or walk through the walls, or fly like a bird. You control the universe and travel on the beam of light. All these experiences will be deposited into your memory. Go to the heaven but also don't forget to visit the hell; and remember it's only a dream. Meet god herself and asked her to change most unwanted trait of your own nature. The possibilities in a dream are unlimited. We can make whatever changes to dream we wish but it is of outmost importance that the change everything towards positive good and loving, the only direction that will the best serve our spiritual path. Actions taken in a dream affect us internally just as actions taken in our waking life. There is tremendous freedom in a dream, but there is no freedom from the cause and effect. So we need to be very careful not to undertake any malevolent actions within our dreams. If you believe you cannot do something either in your dream or your waking reality, you will never be able to. The moment you say you can do something, and you strongly believe it, you have already failed. Treat your dreams with most respect and use them to develop freedom from all limitations, to overcome all obstacles, and finally realize your true nature and a true nature of all phenomena.

So dream wisely.

In a dream you can go to distant places; it is also possible to just intend a change of dream scenery.

You can intend to see tri-dimensionally 360° around you and all six directions, but at the beginning this undertaking is not easy because how our mind is pre-set. However if you have enough energy, enough consciousness and developed Intent, this can be accomplished. Anyone searching for ultimate meaning of life must take this inner journey. On a psychological and a spiritual level it's a dream voyage, a dream quest, for your true self, for your missing parts; your subconscious and a SuperConscious mind.

Whatever we do in a waking state creates the growth of the new neural patterns in our brain. Lucid dreams might be even more effective, because of its vividness of imagery and possibility of using so-called transpersonal senses, in establishing new neural patterns. Any actual skill in the waking reality can be enhanced by repeating it in a lucid dream; any performance, physical or mental can be enhanced.

So basically lucid dreaming can become a rehearsal for lucid living. Remember doing anything without double-arrow attention is not worth doing; you are just strengthening already very strong subconscious patterns.

Once in a lucid dream, and able to sustain it, a dreamer can intentionally turn his Will towards the questions he might have, or what he might want to create. In lucid dreaming state the conscious and subconscious mind meet face-to-face. Lucid dream requires the ability to process the conflicting, strange and very improbable information presented by the dream, flexibly enough to conclude that your experience in the dream is illusory. In dreams we have conscious access to the contents of the unconscious or the subconscious mind. Through lucid dreaming we can bring the extraordinary creativity of the dream state under conscious control.

If a dreamer develops the sense of courage and love toward frightening figures, its threatening nature immediately transmutes into benevolent or even divine. If a dreamer on the other hand allows himself to fear the threatening nature of the dream figure, of a dream image, fear will just increase and 'entities' will become more threatening. One technique that works very well is to remember to ask a threatening image 'who are you' and say; 'I am your friend, is there anything I can do to help you', or 'is there anything you can help me with?'

Lucidity is not necessarily confined to the dreams. There is a close relation between dreams and hallucinations. A dream could quite well be described as a hallucination which occurs during sleep, and a hallucination occupying the subject entire perceptual field could be described as the waking dream. We can also raise our level of lucidity, of consciousness, to a higher level throughout all our senses.

Accomplished Lucid Dreamer should remember his physical body is asleep in a certain place. He should also be aware, or she/he should know the place and the time of the day when he laid down. It is important to establish that connection.

In ordinary dreams generally laws of physics are not often violated while in lucid dreams a dreamer should do it as often as possible.

If a stronger emotional conflict arises even though the dreamer is lucid it will usually end in the termination of the experience and waking up.

It could happen in a more powerful dreams that person wants to wake up but cannot, which in its inexperienced dreamer could end up in a great fright.

Dreams, remembered or not, and especially nightmares, often cause corresponding emotions upon awakening; sometimes for the rest of the day and sometimes for a lot longer than that.

Your breathing for the most of the time is going on unconsciously, but when you become conscious of your breathing you have a choice. You can change your breathing pattern deliberately. This is so with your dreams as well. When fully lucid you realize the entire dream world is your own creation and with this understanding my come exhilarating feeling of freedom. Now you know no laws of society, no laws of physics, nothing external would constrain your experience. If you have enough consciousness, a powerful Intent, and sufficient amount of energy you can do anything your mind could conceive.

A dreamer can get proficient and even increase his energy through dreaming as time goes by. The person, or a dream Ego that experiences being in a dream is the same one as in our waking consciousness. There is also a dream Self, a king or queen of the subconscious world; if you're a man, it is feminine and if you're of a woman, it is masculine.

They say if you die in your dream, you will really die. If this was true, how would anybody know? This is hogwash, for thousands of people have dreamt they have died and then awoke just fine. Dreams and visions of death were quite common with Shamanic methods.

If you do not have excellent dream recall your chances of having lucid dreams are not great. As you record more dreams in more and more detail, you will remember more, and your chances of becoming lucid will increase. Don't wait until you get up in the morning to make your notes on your dreams. By morning you will forget most of it if not all. Always record your dreams right after they happen; with each dream include the date and the time it happened.

A part of your mind has a job of reality testing, determining whether something is of the internal or external origin. There is a witness that never sleeps that is always conscious.

Flying in a dream is a very reliable test if you are dreaming or not. Many lucid dreamers jump into the air, and if you're able to levitate or fly, you can be certain you're dreaming. Beside you on night table there should be a card with the text that says 'I am dreaming' and it should always be used when person wakes up or thinks he has woken up. Look at the card read it, then look away and read it again. If you're still in a dream state in 99.99% of the cases, the card the second time you read it will read differently. So concluding; any time you find yourself seriously suspecting that you just might be dreaming, you most probably are.

Lucid dreaming hardly ever occurs without our intending it. If you want to have lucid dreams more frequently, you must begin by cultivating the intent to recognize when you are dreaming. Thoughts like "next time I am dreaming I want to remember that I'm dreaming" are helpful but silent wordless intent is even more helpful.

As you are falling asleep and your senses are closing your thinking is getting foggy. The last thing you remember should be intention to remember, to recognize the next time you're dreaming. Your last thought should be I want to remember that I'm dreaming.

CHAPTER EIGHT

OBE

In out-of-body experience (OBE or sometimes OOBE) is an experience that typically involves a sensation of floating outside of one's body and, in some cases, perceiving one's physical body from a place outside one's body (autoscopy). About one in ten people claim to have had an out-of-body experience at some time in their lives. Some work by neurologists suggests that such experiences are generated by the same brain mechanisms that cause lucid dreams.

Despite some similarities in their phenomenology and induction methods, EEG studies do not suggest an equivalence between OBEs and lucid dreams. Lucidity is strongly associated with REM sleep but OBEs are far less consistent, producing EEG traces that can variously resemble shallower sleep, a waking, eyes-closed state or other uncategorized states. However, while this may suggest that perceived OBEs are a type of lucid dream which takes place in a dream environment that mimics the actual environment of the dreamer, this falls short of supporting the idea that some conscious form of the dreamer actually leaves the body and perceives their external environment while still in a sleeping state.

Twelve-year-old boy has a nightmare and wakes up screaming just past the midnight. He dreamt five young people he knew had a car accident on a bridge in his town. All of them died. Boy was highly distressed, and it took his parents some time to calm him down and convince him it was just a dream. In the morning everybody was shocked by terrible news. Accident happened on a bridge few minutes after midnight. How is this to be explained?

Wikipedia: "The idea is rooted in common worldwide religious accounts of the afterlife in which the soul's journey or 'ascent' is described in such terms as an ecstatic, mystical or out-of- body experience, wherein the spiritual traveler leaves the physical body and travels in his/her subtle body (dream-body or astral body) into 'higher' realms." Hence the "many kinds of 'heavens', 'hells' and purgatorial existences, believed in by followers of innumerable religions, may also be understood as astral phenomena.

The astral body has various names in different cultures: Hebrews call it ruach, in Egypt, it was known as ka, the Greeks knew it as eidolon, Romans called it larva, in Tibet it's referred to as the bardo body, ancient Hindus called it pranamayakosha. Buddhists referred to it as the rupa and Linga sharira, Germans called it is Jüdel, Doppel-gänger, or fylgja, ancient Anglo-Saxons gave it various terms: fetch, waft, tisk, energy body or fye, in China it was than khi.

Adepts at such a practice could allegedly project their avatar across many miles and appear in two places at once, a concept known as bilocation.

Though the Eastern yogis are most known for tales of teleportation, it's also present in the Christian tradition.

In 1774 St. Alphonsus Liguori is said to have gone into a trance while preparing for Mass. When he came out of his meditation, he reported that he had visited the bedside of the dying Pope Clement XIV. His presence was confirmed by those attending the Pope, despite his being four days travel away, and not appearing to have left his original location.

In Autobiography of a Yogi, Paramahansa Yogananda describes how, as an adolescent, upon asking his guru, Swami Pranabananda, to locate a family friend, the swami went immediately into trance. Not understanding, the young yogi sat politely while his guru sat engaged in deep meditation.

Thirty minutes later, the swami emerged from his trance state and announced that the family friend would be arriving shortly. Astonished when the friend did indeed shortly arrive, young Yogananda asked his guru how this could have happened. The swami explained that he had simply 'gone' to where the friend was bathing in the Ganges river and told him Yogananda wished to speak with him. As far as the friend knew, he had simply run into the swami at the Ganges.

Dreams are; they exist so there must be three sides to them, just like with everything else. No two accounts of the Astral World are the same. This points out we are dealing with a Dream World and its many levels, ranging from dark and foreboding to light and sublime.

An externally generated experience will present itself the same way across the population. This is not quite true; take an example of Tetrachromacy and many other extrasensory abilities. If astral projection is real, we'd all see the same beings, the same gods, the same angels, irrespective of our cultural and religious views. It would depend on reality, and not on us. It would also be really easy to prove.

An internally generated experience will be highly subjective. It depends on your mind, and as in a lucid dream it is driven by conscious and subconscious expectations. Spiritualists see angels and UFOlogists see aliens because that's what they expect to see.

If there's one reliable principle in lucid dreaming, it's that your expectations play a leading role in your experience. This is just one way we can establish for ourselves that it's an internal and personal experience. Equally, during an apparent astral projection experience, you might travel to different astral planes, see layers of ethereal realities shaped by energy and light. Yet one key similarity remains: in astral projection, your thoughts, emotions and intent guide the experience. In the same way, if you imagine a friend's house on your astral travels, you will likely zap there in an instant. If you imagine your body back in bed, you will quickly return to it.

The core experience of astral projection, out-of-body experiences, sleep paralysis and wake induced lucid dreams are very similar. All of these slightly different exit methods were all internally generated dream states.

This often occurs as part of a near death experience. This is where a person is knocked out of their body because of some kind of severe trauma, i.e. car accident, surgery, heart attack, etc. OOBE'ers know of things happening in the real world, in real time; such as conversations and events centered around, or near to, their physical body. Because hearing, touch and other senses can be active and mind creates the images.

It begins when you are half-asleep in bed. You may feel partially or completely paralyzed. You are aware of lying in bed, yet there are some very unusual sensations going on.

As you shut down sympathetic, active, nervous system and dissociate from your body, you begin to feel as if you're floating, sinking, etc. (See my eBook; 'Transcendental Rebirthing' for complete list). Your mind shuts off awareness from your physical body. As long as you are awake, and your body falls asleep, you will naturally transfer your awareness to a more flexible replica body; a dream body.

You could describe this as a spirit or astral body. Or you could call it your lucid dream body. It's all about perspective.

As lucid dreamers, the expectation principle often works in our favor. We can use it to manifest dream figures and objects, change the scenery, and fulfill our greatest desires. Even if things turn sour and we experience a lucid nightmare, we remain aware that none of it is real and we are safe.

In lucid dreams, there is no need to fear negative dream figures. In fact, you can embrace them and have a personal breakthrough. Given the choice, would you rather fight off a twisted spirit or embrace it as part of your subconscious self and let the fear melt away forever?

Believe it and it will be so.

In the beginning it is best not to react to the dream characters in any way, especially physically.

But everything is a mind travel. This universe is of a mental nature. The trick is not to get bogged down in your own personal dream world, but to meet other fellow Spirit Travelers. Otherwise it is a very lonely existence; this is the reason The One fractured itself into infinitely many.

The first layer of the body is the outer layer; the physical level, which operates on chemistry; to be clear, over a quadrillion chemical reactions per second. Underlying it is energy level that produces and moves all this chemistry. Then there is mental level; dream level. The fourth one is Etheric- Akash - Fifth Element level and fifth one is Spirit Body, consciousness level, super-intelligence that directs all this energy.

In the Astral body we can have 360 degrees vision and can see all sides at once, but it cannot, most of the time, be assimilated by the brain, all at once. This goes against the mind's lifelong habit of frontal vision. Spherical vision is like being one huge multi-faceted eye that can see in all six directions, up, down, left, right, front, back, but all at once! Like everything else, in the astral body even sensory organs are an option.

Spherical vision will often cause you to think you are in a mirror image dimension, or a reversed copy of reality. This means your house, under the influence of the cerebellum, might appear to be reversed, back to front, or side to side. This is caused by you losing your original natural viewpoint during projection. At some point during the projection you have become disoriented and taken a different viewpoint from normal, i.e., you have rotated or turned upside down or inside without thinking. This reverses your natural left right, up down viewpoint.

If you want to look behind yourself you don't have to turn around, or move at all. You just intend it.

The subconscious mind has vastly greater powers of visualization than the conscious mind. Images are just like in waking world except much brighter. Because of the direct perception dream world appears more real.

It is like comparing a quantum super-computer to a child's calculator. In the astral dimension, during any conscious projection or lucid dream, where the conscious mind is aware, this difference can cause great confusion.

To avoid the problem: Concentrate on what you are intending and doing while you are projecting and don't let your mind wander.

Exercise your dream mind; exercise your dream body. Make it fully functional.

If YOU DO NOT DO THINGS, your subconscious mind will, and you might not like it very much.

One of the earliest references to personal experiences with lucid dreaming was by Marie-Jean-Léon and Marquis d'Hervey de Saint Denys.

The person most widely acknowledged as having coined the term is Dutch psychiatrist and writer Frederik Willem van Eeden (1860–1932). In a lucid dream, the dreamer has greater chances to exert some degree of control over their participation within the dream or be able to manipulate their imaginary experiences in the dream environment. Lucid dreams can be realistic and vivid. Higher amounts of beta-1 frequency band (13–19 Hz) brain wave activity is experienced by lucid dreamers, hence an increased amount of activity in the parietal lobes making lucid dreaming a conscious process.

Skeptics of the phenomenon suggest that it is not a state of sleep, but of brief wakefulness. Others point out that there is no way to prove the truth of lucid dreaming other than to ask the dreamer. Lucid dreaming has been researched scientifically, with participants performing pre-determined physical responses while experiencing a lucid dream.

"We are asleep. Our life is a dream. But we wake up, sometimes, just enough to know that we are dreaming." - Ludwig Wittgenstein

***

Ordinary dreams are false; they are a con job, they are hiding something. There is no need to interpret them; that is a waste of time. However, the feelings and emotions in a dream are real. So if you become lucid, pay attention to the feelings. Having said that, you should know there is an exception to every rule. While dreams are false, that is not the case with mutual or group dreams. Also inspirational dreams where the solution arrives, or a message from another Dreamer.

Upon waking up we hardly remember our dreams, so we conclude that they are not important. By the same logic, when we are dreaming, we do not remember the waking world at all, so it would appear that waking world carries even less importance, or no importance at all. So it seems in evolutionary terms sleeping consciousness came first, it was primary, primordial, and preceded waking consciousness.

Women dream more than men and children dream more than adults. Newborn babies dream even more. So dreaming has been part of our psychological equipment from the earliest evolutionary time.

History of Australian aborigines says the man has two souls, one is eternal dreamtime soul which existed and will exist eternally. The other one is the one that appears in dreams.

We talk to young children about the land of dreams, the land of make-believe, the fairy lands, as if there were actual places that exist. Many fairy-tale stories and the magical tales usually begin with a journey of one kind or the other. These journeys are of many kinds, usually being a process of going into a cave, secret passage, a forest, high mountains, sometimes there are marshlands, the canyons and similar things.

Narrowness and difficulty are often prominent feature of this entry into the land of make-believe.

***

Be aware of bodily feelings when your body is falling asleep. Here is what it might feel like when vibrational frequency is changing from a conscious mind to subconscious. Feeling of dislocation, heavy or light body, sense of falling, caving in, sensitive to the minutest sound, light flashes in head at even a slight noise, out of body, drumming of the heart, etc. Use double-arrow; it is difficult exercise, for mind needs to stay awake while body must fall asleep.

Let's go step by step. As body is slowly falling asleep, it is producing chemicals to tranquilize it. Patience here is essential. Body must disappear! Now you are facing the thoughts. As long as you are thinking you will not fall asleep. Use Ooooooo-Hoooooo mantra, with incoming and outgoing breath, with double-arrow, to prevent thinking. As thoughts are subsiding, let the mantra become just a rhythm. Lot of practice is needed, but one day there will be no thoughts in your mind, now you face emotions. Be super-aware to recognize subtle impatience, expectation, worry, etc. If your awareness is sufficiently developed, you will experience falling down into the world of subconscious. When visuals are provided, you are spiraling down the pale, whitish, tunnel in a counter clockwise direction. Depending to what degree the time is altered this could happen quickly or slow.

At 'the bottom of the tunnel' you are now facing a wall of darkness that seems tridimensional and live. It is crucial to remain without thoughts here; just remain a Witness. Soon sprinkles of gold dust, or play of light and fleeting images will appear. But you still did not bridge the gap. Then in a millisecond you enter a dream world, the world of subconscious mind. You have jumped over the gap.

When you enter dream world in this manner lot of energy becomes available to you. Now you can Intend things. Remember; both dream world and the waking world end up in your memory bank.

Once you become proficient, and once you are aware of your subconscious, you will never sleep in the same way again. The body will sleep, but you will be awake, one part of you will go on knowing, on being aware, on being conscious. When that happens dreams become impossible, day dreams also become impossible. Then dreaming is brought under conscious control, and you can dream if you wish.

This is rare, but sleep paralysis might happen. On awakening, mind awakes but body might stay asleep. You cannot move. Do not panic. If you succumb to fear, your subconscious might provide images and you might see aliens torturing you, or something ridiculous like that. In the middle ages it would be incubus and succubus. Not only see, but hear, touch smell; all the senses are involved. This is an excellent opportunity to expand your consciousness; use it. Gradually your body chemistry will change and you will be able to move your body.

Opposite of sleep paralysis, when mind is awake but body is asleep, is the condition where the mind is asleep, but body is partially or fully awake. In this case body actually reacts to a dream; it is not sufficiently tranquilized.

George was a carpenter. He must have loved his trade very much, for he was doing carpentry work even in his dreams, every night. The problem was, he was sitting up in bed and kept on hammering, and sometime he would hit his wife. He ended up sleeping in adjoining bedroom.

And then there is a case of family in Lethbridge, Alberta, Canada. One member came home at 2:00 AM and found four members of his family sitting around coffee table asleep. They all sleepwalked from the second floor bedrooms, and when he woke them up, they did not have the slightest idea what was going on. It is peculiar that sleepwalkers do not show any rapid eye movement and they report no dreams when awakened.

Some guerrilla circles would tie up a long line of warriors together. Only the front man would be awake, marching through the jungle and the mountains in the nighttime. The other guerrillas would walk and sleep.

This is similar to Indian file where front person is leading and everybody else is following in exactly the same footsteps, at very close distance. This would put people following in a trance. When this is done in a running mode, the front man exchanging every once in a while, huge distances could be covered without any tiring.

***

The feelings and emotions you experience in your dreams are real and actual. So the cerebellum might not have any real emotions, but only a sensation of the movement into the space. It may be argued that in waking consciousness we do experience the real emotion. However, that experience is a projection of the emotion, much like the Self experience is a projection of the movement? Of course the real emotion is going on somewhere deep. The conscious mind can bring these emotions under its own control with a bit of practice.

Cerebellum is the size of the clenched fist, located right behind and below the cerebrum. Like the cerebrum cerebellum also has two upper hemispheres. In the developing human embryo brain structures arise from the brainstem. These are brain, the midbrain and the hindbrain. Human embryo repeats in nine months the entire process of evolution.

By day, under normal waking conditions, the cerebellum functions as an auxiliary of the cerebrum, but at nighttime when we go to sleep it takes its own share of life. The word cerebellum actually means little cerebrum. When cerebrum sleeps then the cerebellum can live. Our dreams are their expression of the life and consciousness of the cerebellum. When we fall asleep the electrical activity of the cerebrum shows predominantly long small waves. In about an hour after this condition, deep sleep is setting. Suddenly the cerebral cortex is activated and goes in a manner very similar to that displayed in the waking state; but in fact the organism is more asleep than ever.

The muscles of the body are paralyzed; dreaming has begun. The eyes now move beneath a closed eyeleads, watching entranced the activities taking place in the cerebrum. At this point the cerebellum is using the contents of the cerebrum for its own purposes. The cerebellum is conscious, and works not only at night in our dreams, cerebellum is active 24 h hours a day, in virtual subconscious world.

The parasympathetic nervous system is the main source of so-called paranormal activity.

If a person is in the coma for years, he will dream all the time, and not even for a single moment suspect whatsoever he is doing is just a dream. And if he then dies, he will never realize that last few years of his life were just a dream, that it was never real. So for the mind there is no difference. Meditative sleep is a deep relaxation with no unconsciousness, person is fully aware that he is dreaming, his body is relaxed there is no tension at all.

Dreaming begins with mammals. Reptiles do not dream (or do they on a deeper level?).

When you dream, for the extent of the dream, the world that is created within the dream, and the people and events in it, are real. When you wake up that reality disappears. The worldly plane of the universe is considered by meditators to be like a dream. It is real within its own context, and it has purpose. It is called maya, an illusion, neither absolutely real, nor absolutely nonexistent. Maya, or this dream of worldly life, is very instructive. We are constantly learning from it. That which is subject to time, space, and causation, to change and relativity, to pain and pleasure, to sorrow and misery, is maya, samsara. It has value but not permanence. As a dream helps, you work through emotions and desires, the worldly dream, maya, creates opportunities for you to grow and work through habits and desires. You wake up from it, and it disappears. You wake into realizing the Absolute, and this plane of existence disappears into a memory.

To develop lucid dreaming to the full potential, we need to make a Dream Body more functional. Its attributes of memory, will power, awareness, and the use of all five senses is developed, followed by developing extra-sensory perception.

Lucid dream world is so rich, incredibly detailed, tri-dimensional, vividly colored and alive; it is a small wonder we mistake it for waking reality. Dream personality lacks a reasoning power and often accepts the most ludicrous situations as real.

In a dream world the sun shines, the stars cover the night sky, the grass is green, and if you look in a mirror you look, well, like you; you walk on the ground held down by the "law" of gravity. But if you are lucid enough to know dream gravity is a mere convention, you are FREE to take it or leave it, flying at will, teleporting. Lucid dreamers regard ALL "laws" of the dream world as the self-made rules that can be changed.

We should never forget that the reality and solidity of our waking world is created by the same "organ of perception" that creates our dreams.

There are some turning points in your consciousness. At these turning points you are nearer to the center than at other times. When you're changing gears, you must pass through the neutral gear. That neutral gear is closer to our real being in the morning, when sleep is still going and you are feeling half awake, just at the midpoint you're in a neutral gear. There is a very small point when you are not asleep and when you are not awake. Here is where your consciousness changes from inner to the outer. Your body frequency changes. If you watch carefully, you can feel body vibrating. Between dream state and waking state there is no mechanism; there is a gap. In that gap you can have a glimpse of your being. Exactly the same happens at night when you are falling asleep. So you are going to sleep, relax, be in a meditative state. Close your eyes and wait, the sleep is coming. Just wait don't do anything, just pay attention to your body. Body is falling asleep it is relaxing, it is becoming heavy, or light, dislocating, feels weird.

Feel everything. Forget about thinking process. If you think, you will never fall asleep. Sleep has its own mechanism, it is starting to work on your waking consciousness. Remember the transition moment will be very subtle, very small. If you're not 100% aware you will miss it. It is not the long period, a single moment, a tiny gap and you will change from waking to sleep. It might take months, even years, to bridge that gap consciously. The gap is a millisecond right in between consciousness and unconsciousness. This moment happens every day, but you're not normally aware of it. If you get stuck in the gap, do not be afraid, you will become aware that you are neither awake nor asleep you will feel very weird, because you never experienced this before. From there you can enter the dream world consciously. Now you are Conscious Dreaming.

You cannot truly know a person unless you know what he or she is doing in his or her dreams. Dreaming world is full of your own desires.

In a deep sleep you exist in nature's deep womb. All objects are gone. Remember this while walking, moving, eating, working, etc. Remember yourself as a Clear Light, as a pure consciousness. Allow this remembering to penetrate your entire being. Advanced meditators never sleep. Don't misunderstand me, body sleeps, while the mind is awake.

CHAPTER NINE

SLEEP PARALYSIS

REM sleep does not always turn off immediately about upon awakening, this is why you may experience waking up and not being able to move. For some, sleep paralysis can be a terrifying experience, but it is quite harmless and can be very useful for inducing further conscious dreams.

Neurotransmitters gamma-amino-butyric acid and glycine cause REM sleep paralysis.

It feels like your body is undergoing extreme distortions, or shakes with strange vibrations, or it becomes completely paralyzed, all of these unusual body states are related to process of a sleep onset, and particularly REM sleep. There is nothing to be afraid of, nothing at all. These strange experiences are the result of your active, sympathetic, nervous system gradually shutting down. Sometimes nervous systems don't turn off or on at the same time. You may wake up partially from REM sleep before the paralysis system turns off so that your body is still paralyzed even though you're otherwise fully awake. Sleep paralysis can also occur when people are falling asleep even though this is rare. For uninitiated this is scary, and terrified people typically struggle in the fruitless effort to move, or to fully wake up. This is wrong approach. Person needs to relax and enjoy it and propel himself into another dream state, or use it as a meditation. If you experience sleep paralysis relax your mind. You're actually in the same state for 7-8 hours every night during deep sleep. It will do you no harm at all; and it will pass anywhere from few minutes to 20 minutes. Whenever you experience sleep paralysis, you're on threshold of REM sleep. You have, as it were, one foot in a dream state and one foot in a waking state.

During sleep the body paralyzes itself as a protection mechanism to prevent the movements that occur in the dream from causing the physical body to move. However, this mechanism can be triggered before, during, or after normal sleep while the brain awakens. This can lead to a state where the awakened sleeper feels paralyzed. Hypnagogic hallucination may occur in this state, especially auditory ones. Effects of sleep paralysis include heaviness or inability to move the muscles, rushing or pulsating noises, and brief or extended hypnagogic or hypnopompic imagery.

For inexperienced dreamers and meditators dream paralysis could be terrifying. In a typical case a person awakens but then finds he cannot move his body. It may feel like a great weight is holding them down and making it very difficult to breathe. Here it is very, very important not to panic. Tranquilized body needs very little energy, therefore it doesn't need to breathe or it breaths in micro-breaths. You might be even breathing fully but you cannot feel it. So pay no attention to your breathing. Take the opportunity and see if you can enter a dream world again. Hallucinations may appear, often loud buzzing noises, vibrations in the body, flashes of light, or people, and threatening demonic or extraterrestrial figures may appear. Even more frightening is when you either believe, or actually have, your eyes open and your apprehending these figures. A dreamer may feel things done to his/hers body, body distortions, or electricity running inside him/her, and assign this to all kinds of causes. As the fearful experience progresses, the surroundings may begin to change. Some people create the image of being taken aboard UFO. Some people may feel they are leaving the body and they are dying. Sometime floating up or sinking through the bed. The experienced dreamer should realize that he still dreaming and wait patiently for chemistry that immobilized his/her body to wear off.

All these side-effects are easily produced at Transcendental Rebirthing workshops.

Sleep paralysis experiences are likely to cause some of the strangest night phenomena, such as visitations by extraterrestrials, demons, incubus and succubus. They don't necessarily need to be terrifying; it depends in your mind. They could be saints and angels. Your attitude towards either should be the same, neither fear nor attachment. You need to remember all of these images that are happening, all of them are being dreamt by you. When people panic in the state of paralysis, and try to cry for help, or try to force themselves to move, in order to awaken the body, this usually makes matters worse. This is an excellent opportunity to practice the Internal Smile.

Keep in mind subconscious can bring up the memory of you being under anesthetic if you ever were.

Out-of-body experiences often give us the compelling impression there are two distinct and separate bodies, the physical, earthly body and a dream body - the astral body. But we can, and do, easily dream all of that. Always watch for signs of strange sensations vibrations and distortions of your body image. You can feel them last thing in the morning when you wake up. Do not move, observe your body and you will feel that the body's vibrating at different frequency. Relax look inside and 'try' effortlessly to enhance it.

While having out of the body experience a dreamer should remember everything around you is just a dream, including your supposed physical body you are looking at. When your body falls asleep and the active, sympathetic, nervous system is shut down, the body will become imperceptible; it will not be there. When asleep the brain requires very little information from waking senses. It uses information that's already inside the memories like expectations, fears, desires, thoughts and myriad of experiences. Strong emotions change behavior and influence perception. We can definitely work with emotions inside our dreams.

***

Every electro-magnetic charge we create, every thought, action and deed is instantly recorded and stored in Akash, the Fifth Element. Because our whole mental experience happens in the now, the Akashic Record is a compilation of zillions of 'nows', and any past event can be re-visited in the Now, in other words... seen as it is happening.

As Steiner says: "The one who has acquired the ability to perceive in the spiritual world comes to know past events in their eternal character. They do not stand before him like the dead testimony of history, but appear in full life. In a certain sense, what has happened takes place before him."

"Neither shall they say, Lo here! Or, lo there! For, behold, the kingdom of God is within you." -Luke 17:21

The Gnostic Gospel of Thomas; disciples asked him; when is the Kingdom of God going to come? Jesus replied; "It will never come waiting for it. It is not a question of here or there because the Kingdom of Supreme Father is spread throughout the Earth but people do not see it."

Lucid dreaming is a trip to sub-consciousness, which follows completely different rules than our brain during waking state. As such, our subconscious mind occasionally plays various tricks on us, especially during sleeping and dreaming. One of these "body-mind tricks" is sleep paralysis - a state of complete muscle weakness.

It is a condition where people are paralyzed at the onset of sleep or upon waking. Mentally awake, but physically asleep and paralyzed. It is a disorientating condition that may also proffer vivid and terrifying hallucinations.

The feeling of total body insensitivity during sleep paralysis is often associated with other symptoms, such as sense of suffocation, decreased heart rate, presence of evil person in the room, sense of being dragged around, etc. Obviously, this is not the most pleasant type of dream experience. But is sleep paralysis dangerous? No. Why? Because it is an ordinary human condition. It's a protection mechanism, which prevents us from acting out in our dreams as we sleep. After falling asleep, the brain's signals to muscles are blocked, and therefore we do not move our physical body as we dream.

Here are some steps to help you identify and cope with sleep paralysis.

Learn to recognize the symptoms and interpret them properly. Sleep paralysis can affect you in many ways. There are, however, some commonalities that people experience, including: An inability to move the trunk or limbs at the beginning of sleep or upon awakening.

Brief episodes of partial or complete skeletal muscle paralysis.

Visual and auditory hallucinations (people often sense an evil presence, or feel a phantom touch, or hear an unidentifiable noise in the room.)

A sense of breathlessness (or chest pressure).

Confusion. Helplessness. Fear.

What to Do During Sleep Paralysis?

Do not force anything! Don't fear. Don't panic. Be cool. Smile (internally).

If you really need to, focus on eye movement. Your ability to open your eyes and look around is generally not hindered by sleep paralysis. Please understand; you can also dream your eyes are open and your body is paralyzed. Now do you realize the importance of a reality check! Some people recommend rapidly moving your eyes back and forth to break the paralyzed state. If you are afraid, fear energy will often create scary images, demons, extraterrestrials, etc. by the bed side. (Imagine for a second your subconscious mind using a memory of your tooth extraction, if you had one, and ascribing it to extraterrestrials.) If you can generate a positive deep emotion it could be angels, saints, Jesus, Buddha, etc.

Some people intentionally induce a sleep-paralysis state to induce what they believe to be out-of-body experiences.

Imagining oneself moving effortlessly from the body may be a pleasant alternative to sleep paralysis.

Sleep paralysis can terrify but it isn't really dangerous or harmful. It's actually the panic that causes so called "psychological injury".

You might feel the urge to break free of the paralysis by trying to sit up or moving a lot. Doing this can often cause you to be paralyzed further and the pressure to increase. The best way is to relax and recognize that you are in no danger and the feeling will soon pass. The worst feeling is that of suffocation. Body is paralyzed, it does not need much oxygen to start up with. So breathing is very slow and shallow. Key is not to go into a fear mode. Instead trying to awake the body, go into the opposite direction. Put your mind into the meditative mode and 'exit' the body. This is a superb opportunity.

You might find yourself still dreaming while experiencing paralysis. This is the time when sleep paralysis is most confusing. For example, you might awaken to see the outlines of your bedroom, but at the same time you might see an intruder in your dream. These sorts of dreams are common in conjunction with sleep paralysis, and they are known to be exceptionally frightening. When dreaming your room you believe you have your eyes open and are perceiving the actual room.

Remember; just as you can enter the subconscious, it can enter waking world.

Rule one: Never fear.

Rule two: Never fear.

Rule three: Never fear.

Your fear is the only weapon "he" has against you.

The following is medical - psychological explanation. Same thing, different wording.

"Paralysis is a phenomenon in which a person, either

falling asleep or awakening, temporarily experiences an inability to move, speak or react. It is a transitional state between wakefulness and sleep characterized by complete muscle atonia (muscle weakness). It is often accompanied by terrifying hallucinations (such as an intruder in the room) to which one is unable to react due to paralysis, and physical experiences (such as strong current running through the body). One hypothesis is that it results from disrupted REM sleep, which normally induces complete muscle atonia to prevent the sleeper from acting out his or her dreams. Physiologically, sleep paralysis is closely related to REM atonia, the paralysis that occurs as a natural part of REM (rapid eye movement) sleep. Sleep paralysis occurs either when falling asleep, or when awakening from a sleep. When it occurs upon falling asleep, the person remains aware while the body shuts down for REM sleep, a condition called hypnagogic or pre-dormital sleep paralysis. When it occurs upon awakening, the person becomes aware before the REM cycle is complete, and it is called hypnopompic or post-dormital. The paralysis can last from several seconds to several minutes, with some rare cases being hour or longer, by which the individual may experience severe panic symptoms, if not properly educated. As the correlation with REM sleep suggests, the paralysis is not complete: eye movement is still possible during such episodes; however, the individual experiencing sleep paralysis is unable to speak.

Hypnagogic and hypnopompic visions are symptoms commonly experienced during episodes of sleep paralysis. Some scientists have proposed this condition as an explanation for reports of alien abductions and ghostly encounters. Some suggest that reports of alien abductions are related to sleep paralysis rather than to temporal lobe lability. There are three main types of these visions that can be linked to pathologic neurophysiology. These include the belief that there is an intruder in the room, the incubus (succubus), and vestibular motor sensations."

Many people who experience sleep paralysis are struck with a deep sense of terror when they sense a menacing presence in the room while paralyzed. This hypothesis could account for why the threatening presence is perceived, in most cases, as being evil.

A similar process may explain the experience of the incubus presence, with slight variations, in which the evil presence is perceived by the subject to be attempting to suffocate them, either by pressing heavily on the chest or by strangulation. A neurological explanation hold that this results from a combination of the threat vigilance activation system and the muscle paralysis associated with sleep paralysis that removes voluntary control of breathing. Several features of REM breathing patterns exacerbate the feeling of suffocation. These include shallow rapid breathing, hypercapnia, and slight blockage of the airway which is a symptom prevalent in sleep apnea patients. According to this account, the subject attempts to breathe deeply and finds herself unable to do so, creating a sensation of resistance, which the threat-activated vigilance system interprets as an unearthly being sitting on her chest, threatening suffocation. The sensation of entrapment causes a feedback loop when the fear of suffocation increases as a result of continued helplessness, causing the subject to struggle to end the episode.

The intruder and incubus experiences highly correlate with one another, and moderately correlate with the third characteristic experience, vestibular-motor disorientation, also known as out-of-body experiences. A neurological hypothesis is that in sleep paralysis, these mechanisms which usually coordinate body movement and provide information on body position become activated and, because there is no actual movement, induce a floating sensation. The vestibular nuclei in particular has been identified as being closely related to dreaming during the REM stage of sleep.

It is amazing how one group of people can be excited

about body paralysis and the other terrified.

***

Our body chemistry is astounding. Here is some more information to digest.

Right drug for right disorder, in the right amount, at the right time is medicine; wrong drug for the wrong disorder, in the wrong amount, at the wrong time is poison. Tell me who is so competent to decide. As said; our mind-body system produces over a quadrillion chemical reactions every second. It can create any drug in the universe instantly. Trust your inner intelligence!!! Spirit Traveler should have a good understanding of his/her body chemistry.

The endo-cannabinoid (inner cannabis) system regulates almost EVERYTHING in the body. The endo-cannabinoid system has been recently recognized as an important modulatory system in the function of brain, endocrine and immune tissues. It appears to play a very important regulatory role in the secretion of hormones related to reproductive functions and response to stress. In humans this system also controls energy homeostasis and influences the function of the food intake centers of the central nervous system and gastrointestinal tract activity. It controls lipids synthesis, tissue as well as glucose metabolism in muscle cells. It is also involved in physiological processes including appetite, pain-sensation, mood, and memory. Endo-cannabinoid system is also involved in sexual behavior and expression.

The inner-cannabinoid system, with its complex actions in our immune system, nervous system, and all the body's organs, is a bridge between body and mind. By understanding this system we begin to see a mechanism that explains how states of consciousness can promote health or disease. Endo-cannabinoids directly influence a person's open-mindedness and ability to move beyond past situations and limiting patterns of thought and behavior.

Cannabinoid receptors are similarly found in every animal species down to the sponge and lowly amoeba. Endocannabinoids and their receptors are throughout the body; in the brain, organs, connective tissues, glands, and immune cells. In each tissue, the cannabinoid system performs different tasks, but the goal is always the same: homeostasis - the maintenance of a stable internal environment despite fluctuations in the external environment.

The endo-cannabinoid system is a group of endogenous cannabinoid receptors located in the mammalian brain and throughout the central and peripheral nervous systems, including every cell.

But cannabis couldn't get us high or have some of its therapeutic benefits if our bodies didn't already contain a biological system capable of interacting with its active chemical compounds. This holds for every other drug like LSD, DMT, various endorphins, etc.

Human body produces its own endogenous (internal) cannabinoids (chemicals otherwise unique to the cannabis plant). These cannabinoids fit neatly into a series of specialized receptors located throughout the human body, with their greatest concentration in the hippocampus (which regulates memory), the cerebral cortex (cognition), the cerebellum (motor coordination), the basal ganglia (movement), the hypothalamus (appetite), and the amygdala (emotions).

Something much more complex to understand is the fact our body is made by colonies of billions of cells. Average person has about 60-70 trillion. Each cell is independent, has its individual needs for energy sources and has its own biochemical process. The endo-cannabinoid system is formed by both cannabinoid receptors and endo-cannabinoids that interact in the same way as a lock and its key. **Every single cell of our body has keyholes through which inner drugs enter.**

The name "endo-cannabinoid system" makes reference

to the fact that this endogenous system is the one affected by the intake of phyto-cannabinoids (external ones), which act as a false key, able to fit the lock of cannabinoid receptors, producing a different effect to the one produced by the perfect key which is represented by the endo-cannabinoids produced by the body. Other words, external drugs have slightly different molecular configuration then internal ones, which are perfect. On entering through cell membrane keyholes these external drugs cause substantial damage. This is why you feel stoned and have other side-effects. With internally produced drugs, even though they are 100 - 1000 times more powerful, there are no negative side-effects.

The biggest producer of endogenous pot is the brain. Neuropeptides such as serotonin, melatonin, cortisol, internal cannabinoids and melanin, are even made by the skin, in response to environmental stressor.

To produce the proper amount of endogenous cannabinoids, the body requires a sufficient amount of Omega-3 fatty acids. Omega-3 are the precursor to endogenous cannabinoids. Condition known as "Endo-cannabinoid Deficiency Syndrome" can lead to a variety of symptoms and related conditions, including irritable bowel syndrome, fibromyalgia, migraines and many other disorders. Remember, cannabis contains hundreds of cannabinoids and so does our mind–body system. Homeopathic micro-doses of cannabis cannabinoids causes body to produce more endo-cannabinoids.

Internal THC is also involved in voluntary exercise and is related, for example, to runner's high in human beings. Pushing the limits of physical activity, breath, sounding, various meditations, yogic dreaming, and consciousness also produce plethora of internal drugs.

CHAPTER TEN

KARMA

Karma is the Sanskrit word for action. Ignorance of its laws is no excuse. It is equivalent to Newton's law of 'every action has a reaction.'

When we have an emotion, think, speak or act we initiate a force that will react accordingly. This returning force maybe modified, changed or suspended, but most people cannot eliminate it. This law of cause and effect is not punishment, but exists for the sake of education or learning.

A person may not escape the consequences of his actions, but he will suffer only if he himself has made the conditions ripe for his suffering.

We all remember: "As you sow, so shall you reap." Whatever we put out in the Universe comes back to us. But that includes subconscious wishes and generational Archetypal super-programs.

Aging people should know their lives are not mounting and unfolding but that an inexorable inner process forces the contraction of life. For a young person it is almost a sin, and certainly a danger, to be too much occupied with himself; but for the aging person it is a duty and a necessity to give serious attention to himself.

Every civilized human being, whatever his conscious development, is still a primitive man at the deeper levels of his psyche. Just as the human body connects us with the mammals and displays numerous relics of earlier evolutionary stages going back to even the reptilian age, so the human psyche is likewise a product of evolution which, when followed up to its origins, show countless archaic traits. (Some people are born with tails, some with primate's hair, and some with not being able to walk upright.)

If what we want is happiness, peace, love, friendship...

then we should **be** happy, peaceful, loving and a true friend..

Wherever we go, there we are; and that is our biggest problem. For us to grow in Spirit, it is we who must change, and not the people, places or things around us. Whenever there is something wrong in our life, we can be pretty sure there is something wrong inside us. We must take responsibility what is in our life.

Spirit Traveler understands, even if something we do seems inconsequential, it is very important that it gets done, as everything in the Universe is connected.

Each step leads to the next step - past-present-future they are all connected. Old thoughts, old patterns of behavior, old dreams, prevent us from having new ones. History, the past repeats itself in infinite variations until we learn the lessons we need to change our path. Unless we are willing to change we are dead already, we just did not realize it yet. You get back from something whatever YOU have put into it. Lack luster effort have no impact on the Whole. All Rewards require initial investment. Rewards of lasting value require patient and persistent effort.

Law of Karma states: If you believe something to be true, then sometime in your life you will be called upon to demonstrate that particular truth. Turn your beliefs into experiential knowledge ASAP.

As stated; karma means action, it is our actions that determine our future; even the actions we have undertaken in our past remain in our memory and influence our future. It is helpful to think of karma as the process of cause and effect because this leads to the recognition that the choices made in responding to any situation internal or external have consequences. Karma is certainty that whatever you do comes back to you. If you react to some situation with negative emotion, trace left in the mind will eventually ripen and influence the situation in life negatively. For example; if someone is angry with us and we react in anger, we leave a trace, a recording that makes it more likely for anger to arise in us again. Angry people encounter situations that seem to justify their anger while happy people do not. But if we suppress the emotion like anger, there is still a negative trace, just as powerful. The best response to rising negative emotion is to allow it to self- liberate by remaining in a double- arrow awareness, watching the energy and the feeling that is arising in the body and let it spread out and implode all over the body. This is the real alchemy. The negative emotion was just transmuted into pure energy. You have just harvested the emotional energy, and you have become emotionally more powerful. Your consciousness has increased. We should as often as possible remind ourselves emotions we are experiencing are simply imprints from previous actions undertaken.

Yogic dream methods give us means of formulating the future karma. If you are conscious during your dream states, you can slowly transmute your negative emotions. Traces of our actions and our imprints are at the root of all of our dreams. When they transform body chemistry changes; for the energy changes consciousness and pure light of awareness surfaces. Then there is no dream, only the luminous 'form', the mental nature that is absolute reality; the Clear Light. We can say the enlightenment, in a sense, is the end of the dreams and is known as awakening. From that moment on the dreaming becomes optional. When a dreamer identifies himself and is swallowed by negative emotions, it results in corresponding body chemistry, murky ugly chemistry.

Anger and fear are very detrimental. They come in many variations such as the words, tension, resentment, criticism, argument, and even violence. The cure for anger is pure unconditional Love which arises from higher awareness.

Mind plays tricks. Its main trick is to identify itself as the subject and then take everything else to be separate from that subject. All life needs to take some form, and if we don't shape it, it will take a form dictated by karma and your genetic inheritance, which we may not like very much. We can integrate all positive emotions including pleasure and bliss with awareness; we can train ourselves so that pleasure itself is a reminder to come to full consciousness, to bring awareness to the present moment, to the body, to the senses, and let go of distraction. Not identifying with anything can be done in any dualistic situation in which there is subject and object. When pleasure is used as a door to the practice it is not lost; we need not be anti-pleasure.

When both the subject and object dissolve in a Clear Light, the Union of emptiness and clarity is experienced and there is joy.

The approach to negative emotions like hatred is similar. If we observe anger rather than participating in it, or identify with it, or being driven by it, then the dualistic obsession with the object of anger ceases and the anger dissolves into emptiness. If awareness, presence, is maintained in that emptiness, then the subject will also dissolve. The consciousness inside that 'empty space' is the Clear Light. By observing the pure presence it is not meant that we remain as an angry self, observing the anger, but that we are conscious of the space in which the anger is occurring. When observed in this way the anger dissolves into 'empty' essence. Please note; every emotion contains energy. It is of utmost importance that a person learns to harvest that energy. Suppressing or expressing emotions consumes additional energy.

This does not mean that a person should now be emotionless forever. Emotions are now under conscious control, and we can use them when need arises.

When emptiness and presence are integrated with anger than anger is no longer obscuring the Clear Light. If we observe thoughts this way, and if observer and observed both disappear, then there is experience of consciousness. (It is worth repeating - 'God': "I am closer to you than you are to yourself. I'm closer to you than your jugular vein. There is nowhere I am not. I am so simple you cannot understand me.

I am so close you cannot see me.")

Sages say; the more wisdom is present the less thoughts there will be. Lack of thoughts is an indication of the progress on the spiritual path. As meditators, it is important to be fully responsible for our everyday life. When bad things happen, take care of them, when something is wrong we must address it. But if we do not see something wrong, let's not go looking for it.

Don't get addicted to negativity. It is very easy to say we are integrated when things are going well, but when a strong emotional crisis comes, it is the real test. When being challenged in such a way by existence we can discover for ourselves how integrated we really are and how successful our practice is, just by paying attention to how we react to situations that arise in our daily lives. Generally, we lose a lot of energy and self-consciousness is removed throughout the day.

There are many moments in our lives when we are particularly exhausted, we have lack of energy and we are partially conscious. We have to bring ourselves to that which is always awake, then we can wake up what is exhausted and sleeping. Distraction of our daily life and the unconsciousness of sleep are just two sides of the same coin. This is why we created meditative practices. It is best not to divide practice into periods of meditating, dreaming, sleeping, and so on. Ultimately we must be present, conscious, in all moments, waking and sleeping. We should practice every millisecond of our lives. The experience of Clear Light, the pure consciousness, is reached through meditative practices, but once it is reached the practice is not necessary anymore.

***

Without experience all the teachings become only abstract philosophy and/or dogma.

If any knowledge, no matter how great, is not being used,

it is useless. Our everyday mind is constantly busy with feelings, thoughts, memories, images, internal dialogues, judgments, meanings, emotions, and daydreams. It is the Ego, I, me, and my experience. Ego takes itself to be a subject in a world of objects. It likes some experiences and dislikes the others. Ego is highly reactive but even when it's extremely calm and subtle like in a deep meditation, or intense concentration, it maintains the internal posture of a one entity observing the environment and continues to expect dualism.

The Ego bound by duality of the subject and the object arises from the moving mind. From this mind all suffering arises. We live in memories of the past and fantasies of the future, cut off from the direct experience of the beauty of life. The fundamental reality of the mind, the mind behind the Ego, is pure non-dual awareness.

The teachings refer to this mind as a primordial mind. It is like an ocean, while ordinary mind is like rivers lakes and creeks that share in the nature of the ocean and return to it, but temporarily exist as apparently separate bodies of water.

Clear Light is emptiness; and awareness combined with so called emptiness is clarity. I have no choice but to use language full of dualities; but I will stress here there is no such a thing as emptiness anywhere in the existence. Ultimately there is neither subject nor objects, nor any other duality or distinction.

Enlightenment is not taking a drug or some kind of high experience. It is not something found by performing an action or by changing oneself. Enlightenment is not a trance or a far out vision or supernatural light. It is what we already have, what we already are. When there is an expectation of enlightenment it cannot be found. The expectations are about fantasy, about future. What can be expected from pure emptiness? Nothing. If there is expectation of any kind only frustration will follow. Expectation is a super-powerful barrier on the road to liberation.

The experience of meditative emptiness is like experience of space, the recognition itself is the light. Space is pure potential. It has no up or down, in or out, boundaries or limitations. Those are all qualities we conceptualize in space that are not qualities of the space itself. There is not much we can say about the space to describe it, even though it is the essence of everything that exists. Nothing can be said about it because it is beyond all qualities, attributes, or references. If you do not know the base area right now, then you cannot find it until you stop looking for it.

On one level, a delusion does not exist and never has. On another level it is a completely different story. What we search for is closer to us than our own thoughts, than our own experience, because Clear Light is the ground of all experience. Clear Light is not an experience at all but rather it is a space in which everything is experienced, space in which all experiences occur, and out of which all experiences arise. You might think it is your experience. Ego is quick to take the ownership. But it is just space, just consciousness in which experience arises recognizing itself. It is pure awareness knowing itself; this pure awareness is never lost, and it is never not conscious. This is the original ground, the well of the existence, the primordial awareness.

When we are involved in internal processes, we are not in this awareness; for consciousness has no process. Process is a function of the conceptual moving mind; awareness is effortless. That awareness does not actually have any qualities or attributes.

Without understanding 'emptiness', pure consciousness, it is difficult to cut to the roots of the self and to find liberation from its boundaries. Our mind can create a dream and identify with one being it places in a dream. Every moment of life, waking dreaming and sleeping, being a pure non-dual awareness, in a double-arrow mode, this is the certain road to enlightenment and the path that all realized masters have taken. This is the essence of the dream and sleep yoga. You can receive so many teachings you head will hurt. Nothing will change when one does not directly know the nature of the mind, the teachings can be difficult to understand. They may seem to refer to something impossible, they may seem like a science-fiction because the nature of a fully conscious mind is beyond the conceptual mind and cannot be comprehended by it. Trying to grasp the nature of the mind through the concepts is like trying to understand the nature of the sun by studying shadows. Continue learning and receive teachings but develop a deep enough understanding you can take from the teachings only what supports you. If you continue to practice without the results, with no positive changes in life, practices are not working. Abandon it. If some practice is not working experiment with it. Experimentation should be done to find what the purpose of the particular practice is.

The ultimate recognition that your practice is successful is in the process of death. The capacity to remain at point in a non-dual awareness is your passport to the life after death. If you have never experienced the Clear Light during sleep, during dreams, and during deep sleep, it is very difficult to die consciously. If you can become one with the Clear Light of sleep, dreams and deep sleep then you can integrate through the Clear Light with all the beings who achieved enlightenment. They have described the road for you, the road you need to travel. Try to get a sense of the entire teachings and take a close look where you are and where you are going. You need to be clear on direction. Then you will know how to apply the teachings, what techniques and methods to use and what the results will be. The teachings are like a map that can tell you where to go and where to find what you're looking for. The map clarifies everything; without it you can become lost.

***

Prayer filled with the energy of the emotion is very powerful; intention is developed and what you pray for moves to a realization. Practice Mona Lisa smile and Internal Smile always.

Laughter Yoga is the latest craze. But in many situations it is inappropriate to laugh; in some medical conditions cathartic laugh can even be deadly. Laughter yoga sure will not be of much help when death arrives. In contrast, you can always smile. Maintain the positive experiences of peace and joy. Generate gratitude and appreciation during every moment of your life. The Clear Light is ultimate mystical experience, the highest joy, the greatest peace. So take joy and peace as qualities to maintain. Feel this qualities in your body, see them in the world, and wished them for others. Dedication and continuation is the key to integrating life and practice. With awareness and intent, continuity is developed. When it is your life will be different, you will become a positive influence on the surrounding life.

Every practice that brings more awareness into your life is beneficial, but it takes long sustained intent and practice to realize the ultimate goal. Do not allow yourself to grow discouraged; you can only get discouraged if you expect something. You're projecting into the future. **Do things, do the practices with no expectation whatsoever.** You will soon realize your life is changing in positive ways.

A good technique is to throughout the day remain in the awareness that all experiences are like a dream. Imagine that you are in a lucid dream during the entire day. Do not allow this to be merrily an empty word repetition. Each time you tell yourself, this is a dream, become more lucid more conscious, more aware. Involve all of your body and all of all your senses, become more present and be in the now time. Every time you are smelling, tasting, touching hearing, thinking or having an emotion be in a double- arrow mode. Be clear what double-arrow is.

In a lucid dream realize that all the emotions, or judgments, all preferences and the aversions are being dreamt, all your reactions are a dream. Before going to sleep review the day and see how your awareness practices have been. When you wake up in the morning reflect how your dreaming practices have been. During the day or evening it is good to pray for success in practice. Generate a strong intent. Once you're able in a dream state to intend things, intend the body of light, which nothing can touch. Upon each awakening at night become conscious. First thing in the morning become aware, become self-conscious, being in a double-arrow. Review the night, generate intent and continue the practices during the entire day. There are thousands upon thousands of practices you can do. Main practice is maintaining awareness of now time, being self-conscious, being self-aware.

Here I would like to add something very important. While you progress on spiritual path, under no condition you are to neglect everyday life. This is your base; this keeps you grounded.

CHAPTER ELEVEN

DEMONS OF THE DEEP

The higher the tree the deeper the roots.

Closely examine your dreams; are you running from anything inside your dream? Are you doing anything inside your dreams that goes against any moral principle you have? All these aspects can be changed.

In a lucid dream state we can have a conversation with another dream character. Just ask questions like "who are you, who am I, why are you here, why are you acting the way you are, why is this happening in this dream, what do you want from me, what you want me to do, what questions would you ask of me, what do I most need to know, can you help me, can I help you ", while at all times being conscious, every dream character is you. Stefan LaBerge had this list of the questions you can ask another dream character. The most powerful approach is that of opening your heart accepting any dream figure is a part of yourself. Give it a hug and project a feeling of love. The effect is astonishing and instantaneous if you can find in your heart to genuinely love your dream enemies, they will become your friends.

Or you can say something like this when a dream demons a dream monsters appear looking them straight in the eye; I'm not afraid, I want to be your friend. What can I do to help you? Almost instantly the coin will flip around and the monster will become friendly. If you become fully lucid in a nightmare, you will realize that the nightmares cannot hurt you, and you need not escape it by awakening. Once you stay with it your dreaming power will increase exponentially. Your only real enemy in a dream is your own fear; even at a higher level of dreaming this is still true.

One of the very effective ways of inner healing is to see and seek the 'demons' of the subconscious and reconcile with them. They are 'located in a southerly, dark direction, down, below.' Emotional balance is obtained through this process. It is easy to find them; to find the demons of the subconscious just move from the area of light to the area of darkness, from the higher places to the lower ones, deep ones and from the present deep into the past. You need to be super aware and hold your double-arrow awareness and have your heart open. You must be fearless, for all of our lives the creeps have made us fear dark places. Just look at most TV programs and movies.

Not only is the lucid dreaming useful for mental healing but it could even have the physical effect. Dream state and waking state both use the same perceptual processes to arrive to mental representations or models of the world. William James the founder of American psychology, wrote that you should keep alive in yourself the faculty of making efforts by means of little useless exercises every day; for example standing on a chair for 10 minutes once a day for 10 days.

The dream is thought to be unreal as opposed to the real waking life; but the dream has its own reality. Increased consciousness can be applied to the dreams just as well is to the waking reality.

All the emotions are provided by Mother Nature as tools. They are necessary for the full range of human experience; and that includes the emotions of anger, fear pride and jealousy and so on. Without all these negative emotions we would have no choice. We would be like robots. All the emotions have their place and their time. None of the emotions are negative in themselves. They become negative when you possess them or run away from them. You need to think in the terms of energy. The energy of negative emotions can be harvested and imploded. All the experiences, waking or dreaming, have an energetic base. Everything in the universe be it physical, mental, emotional, or spiritual have the energy or prana as the base.

The average person experiences emotions at death, and the dominant emotion determines the lights and colors that manifest. Often there is, at first, only an experience of colored lights of which one color is primary, but it may also be the case that the few colors are predominant and that there is a combination of many colors. The light then forms different images as it does in a dream, of houses, people, entities, space, time, etc. This and everything else creates a dream world. When we are dying, we may relate to such visions as entities, in which case we are governed by our reactions to them and moving toward our next birth. Or we can have meditative experiences, which allow us opportunity of liberation or at least the possibility of consciously influencing our next birth in a positive direction.

Visualizing the images in a dream state definitely changes our body chemistry. Visual images are symbolic supports and are like maps used to focus the attention on patterns of energy that exist inside our body. Images created by Tibetan and Hindu masters are used as visual metaphors to teach people. These visual metaphors become a language used to articulate the experiences of the energy centers in the body. When meditative practitioners visualize the right number of petals, at the right spot in the body, with the right color, then the power of the mind affects that particular energetic point and is influenced by that point. When this occurs we say mind and prana are unified in a particular chakra.

Prana is sometimes compared to a blind horse, and the mind to a person unable to walk. Separately they are helpless, but together they make a very functional unit. Every dream offers an opportunity for healing and spiritual practice, every dream without exception. It takes an enormous practice to recognize the illusory nature of a dream state while asleep but we also must realize the illusory nature of waking life. The process by which experiences arise is the same whether we are dreaming or awake. In a dream world the teachers and the teachings are a dream; the results of our practice within a dream are also a dream. Everything is a dream until pure consciousness arises; we continue dreaming ourselves and our lives in both the dream and physical dimension.

Not knowing how to work with thoughts, one is controlled by them. Thoughts need to be brought under conscious control and used for positive purpose and positive action. We must understand the essence of everything that arises is empty, even though it doesn't seem so. The world within and without are our own manifestation, then we know there is no inherent existence either in ourselves or the world, then whatever arises in the experience has no power over us. When we know the true empty nature of existence we are about to become free.

Ordinary sleep is like a dark room. Mother Tantra says awareness is a flame of a lamp. When the lamp is lit, the darkness disappears, and the room is illuminated. Instruction by symbols, metaphors, parables, similitudes, ciphers and allegories is the one of the most powerful ways to communicate spiritual teachings. Even though the real spiritual experience cannot be communicated through any language, metaphorical images are used in teachings for they are perceived not only by a rational mind but also our subconscious mind. Of course, if understood properly.

The goal of conscious dream practices is liberation. Our intent should also be to experience what is beyond the dreams. We do not need always to go that far; dreams can be beneficial in our everyday life. Dream of a clear light is a dream free from images thoughts and the emotions. Developing capacity for a Clear Light dreaming is similar to developing a capacity for a double -arrow attention during the day. Even when dream images are present, they shine with clear light from within.

Pure consciousness is not bound by space, time, or personal history. In dream practices the dreamer can meet with the real beings, receive real teachings from the real teachers. The greatest value of the lucid dreams, conscious dreams, is found in a context of a spiritual journey. If we pay attention to dream content, we can definitely judge our own maturity in the practice. If practice becomes very strong, the results of the practice of manifesting intended dream give us confidence in our efforts. In a dream world, or through the dream world, we can heal our psyche, heal emotional difficulties we were not able to overcome previously. We can remove energetic blocks that may be preventing the free circulation of energy in the body.

***

We accept that a piece of plastic or a metal can hold a huge amount of information and that this information is transferred to another inert material and people. But for some incomprehensible reason we do not think a sperm and an egg transfer all the information to a new being. This process has taken place all the way back into infinity, and ALL THE INFO IS AVAILABLE today.

Whereas the personal unconscious consists, mostly, of 'complexes', the content of the collective unconscious is made up of powerful (universal human) archetypes.

Archetypes produce certain psychic forms with all of its accompanied sense of visual, hearing, olfactory, touch and smell experiences, including presently sublimated senses.

If you have a dream about tomorrow, and tomorrow comes and everything happens just as did in our dream, this does not mean the future is fixed and cannot be changed? No, it just means you did not change it. Many Yogic Dreamers have used dreams as an important wisdom door through which they have discovered many teachings, made connections to other masters, otherwise distanced in time and space. Many masters developed dreaming practices as capacity to help others. Ultimately, you want to use dreams not only to liberate ourselves from all the relative conditions, but also to improve them.

***

Concentration:

Place the object of concentration so that the eyes can look straight ahead, neither up nor down during the practice. Try not to move not even to swallow or blink while keeping the mind one pointedly on the object. Thoughts here are useless, let them go. Even if the tears should stream down your face, do not move do not blink. Let the body breathe by itself. Strange sensations arise in the body and many strange visual phenomena appear; you may find your mind doing strange things. These experiences are a natural part of the development of concentration and the result of active sympathetic nervous system shutting down. So be neither disturbed nor excited by them. Keep your mind on the object, do not allow the thoughts of the past or the future, do not daydream, do not let your mind be taken away by some fantasy, or a sound, or a physical sensation, or any other distraction that arises. Do not lose the awareness of the object even for a second let the body breathe and let breathing become more and more subtle until the sense of breath is lost. Slowly allow yourself to sink more deeply into quiet and the silence and calm. Make certain that your body is completely relaxed. When it is hundred percent relaxed, it disappears you cannot feel it. You have successfully shut down sympathetic nervous system, but you should not allow yourself to fall into a trance, into fog. You need to be super-aware. There is no need and no use for any thinking. Just be pure awareness. When mind gets distracted and goes away from the object effortlessly bring it back to the object and leave it there. The stability of the mind developed through the concentration is a foundation of Dream Yoga and all other meditative practices. Change the way you relate to the objects and people in waking life and you will eventually change the experience of the dream. After all you live in a dream of waking life. It is the same you that lives in a dream of sleeping life.

As a technique a person could remind themselves that this supposed reality of waking life is just like a dream. There is no stronger method of bringing consistent lucidity to dream state than by being continuously aware and in a double-arrow attention during the day. Every situation and reaction to it should be recognized as a dream. In preparation before going to sleep, and subsequent lucid dream, person can use a technique of remembering, of recalling the memories of the day remembering that everything was like a dream and try to connect to dots the points of awareness you had throughout the day. Just how many times were you in a double-arrow attention and for how long? Do this every day just before you fall asleep. When you wake up in the morning review the night. Do not move, look back and remember the dreams you had. How many dreams can you remember, how many details can you remember? Intend to do better next time. Record all your dreams. When you finish remembering; before you get up generate a strong intention to remain aware, to remain self-conscious, and be in a double-arrow throughout the day.

Meaning in dreams is not inherent in a dream. It is being projected onto the dream by the individual examining a dream. This approach is useless. Accomplishments in lucid dream and sleep yoga will depend on individual's faith, intent, commitment, patience and double-arrow practices. Every breath can be a practice, every perception, experiences of the senses can be a practice. Every step you take, every thought you think every emotion you feel, every word you say, connect your awareness to it. Your body operates in now time, so should your mind. Connecting mind, body, and feeling is one of the most important things we can do to ensure our progression on the spiritual path.

Breath is a bridge between the body and the mind. Breath changes with a strong emotion. When we are afraid breath becomes quick in shallow. In sadness the breathing is often deep and punctuated by sighs and crying. Rather than waiting for experience to alter the breath, we can deliberately change the breath to change our experience. TR is a very effective method to achieve that goal with.

When we fall asleep with mind and body disconnected, they each go their own way. The more we hold onto the stress and tensions accumulated during the day, and the mind also continues as it was during the day, running from one place to another, one time to another, ungrounded and lacking any steadiness, and anxious unconscious state, with little awareness; in this situation we lack power and consciousness, and dream yoga will show very little progress.

Your devotion to the practices and a consistent effort are powerful assets on the spiritual journey. A technique of going without the sleep for three to five nights can enhance the dreaming in a person who finally goes to sleep. This technique should not be done without experienced sage looking over it. Other very useful technique is a dark room retreat for extended period.

Know prayer has the power, but is not in the words; it is in the emotion you put into the prayer. Develop strong intention and place it in a prayer, develop strong emotion, but the emotion which is under your full control. Important point is to feel strongly the intent and desire in the prayer and to put our heart into it.

***

The term 'archetype' has its origins in ancient Greek. Root words are 'archean', which means 'original or old'; and 'typos', which means 'pattern, model or type.'

Archetype is individually or collectively inherited unconscious idea, pattern of thought, image, etc., that is 'universally' present in person's psyches. Plato's 'ideas' were "pure mental forms that were imprinted in the soul before it was born into the world."

Jung states in part one of 'Man and his Symbols' "My views about the 'archaic remnants', which I call 'archetypes' or 'primordial images,' have been constantly criticizes by people who lack a sufficient knowledge of the psychology of dreams and of mythology. The term 'archetype' is often misunderstood as meaning certain definite mythological images or motifs, but these are nothing more than conscious representations. Such variable representations cannot be inherited. The archetype is a tendency to form such representations of a motif, representations that can vary a great deal in detail without losing their basic pattern."

A more or less superficial layer of the subconscious is undoubtedly personal. I call it the "personal subconscious". But this personal layer rests upon a deeper layer, which does not derive from personal experience and is not a personal acquisition but is inborn. This deeper layer is called the "collective unconscious"; the term "collective" because this part of the unconscious is not individual but universal; in contrast to the personal psyche, it has contents and modes of behavior that are more or less the same everywhere and in all individuals.

The assumption that the human psyche possesses layers that lie below consciousness is not likely to arouse serious opposition. It is a well-known fact. But there are layers lying above consciousness. The conscious mind can only claim a relatively central position and must put up with the fact that the subconscious psyche transcends and, as it were, surrounds it on all sides. Subconscious contents connect it backward with the physiological states on the one hand and archetypal data on the other. But it is extended forward by intuitions which are conditioned partly by archetypes and partly by subliminal perceptions, depending on the relativity of time and space in the subconscious. Remember; the road to SuperConsciousness leads through subconscious mind.

Every archetype is capable of endless development and differentiation. The conscious mind allows itself to be trained like a parrot, but the subconscious does not - which is why St. Augustine thanked God for not making him responsible for his dreams.

But what is the Ego, our-Self? Ancient sages taught that

every human being has a mortal lower self, called the Eidolon and an immortal Higher Self (Soul) called the Daemon, the term I will use here to differentiate with the now days term 'demon'- meaning inherently evil. Eidolon is the embodied self, the physical body and Ego personality. Keep in mind this Ego personality is not solid but is fractured, other words composed of many 'I', each pulling in different direction.

Daemon is the Spirit, the inner Self, which is each person's spiritual connection to God - SuperConsciousness. Mysteries were designed to help initiates realize that one's Eidolon is an artificial self and that one's inner identity is the 'immortal' Daemon. The quest for Self-knowledge leads the ancient or Gnostic initiate on a remarkable journey of discovery. At first initiates experience themselves as the Eidolon, the embodied personality - Ego, and see the Daemon as a Guardian Angel or Heavenly Twin. The more mature initiate, experiences the Daemon as a higher manifestation of their own Higher Self or Soul. To those blessed with the final vision of complete Self-knowledge or Gnosis, the Daemon is more awesome still. It truly is the 'divine I, the SuperEgo, the Essence' that has no appearance and yet takes all kinds of appearances in the world of creation.

Valentinus puts it like this: "Although it appears as if each person has their own Daemon or Higher Self, the enlightened initiate discovers that actually on the axial Pole of Being there is one Daemon shared by all - a universal Self, which inhabits every being. Each Soul is a part of the one Soul of God. To know oneself therefore is to know God."

Make sure when you are reading this not to mix the terminology (demon vs Daemon).

The sage Sextus writes: "If you would know Him by whom you were made, you would know yourself." Similarly, the Christian philosopher Clement writes: "It is the greatest of all disciplines to know oneself; for when a man knows himself, he knows God." (Not the almost universally accepted meaning of the word God.)

The only constant in this infinite universe is change. So never fear, never fret, no matter how powerful the happening is. Be patient, it will pass.

***

Frederick Leboyer:

"A baby's life passes through two stages in the womb, two seasons of equal duration, which oppose each other like winter and summer. The first is the golden age. The embryonic stage, when the infant is like a small plant, growing and blossoming. Anchored. The embryo becomes the fetus, the plant becomes animal. Movement comes to it, beginning at the trunk, spreading out toward to the extremities. The fetus stirs, takes pleasure in its limbs. And in his freedom.

Supported by waters all around it, the fetus is weightless, light as a bird, agile as a fish. Its contentment and freedom are limitless. As is its kingdom, whose boundaries it brushes against from time to time.

For in this first half of the pregnancy, the egg the membrane which contains the fetus, and the fluids in which it is bathed, grows more rapidly than the child. Fast as the infant develops, its kingdom grows faster. So the baby never suffers a sense of confinement. Yes, its contentment is unlimited. And the photographs we have of it at this stage show completely relaxed expression. A vision of serenity. This is the golden age. But it doesn't last. In the depths of the womb, the infant has been overtaken by a natural law. The law of universal evolution, which stipulates that everything must become its opposite.

Midway through the pregnancy everything changes. The infant continues to grow and to develop rapidly but the egg that contains him grows only slightly by comparison. His tribulations begin. The baby begins to feel closed in, slowly the universe is contracting. What was once unbounded space becomes more confining each day. Gone is the limitless ocean of earlier and happier days; that absolute freedom is no more.

And one day the baby finds yourself a prisoner. And in such a prison. The cell is so small that a prisoner body touches the walls, all of them at once. Walls that draw nearer all the time. To the point when one day the infant's back and the mother's uterus seem to be fused together. For a long time the little creature want to accept it.

Struggles.

Protests.

In vain.

Inexorably the prison closes in. The child accepts, is there any choice? The spine curls up, the head bends, the whole body makes itself small.

Perhaps some instinct suggest that none of this is permanent that good can come from misfortune. Each day the baby grows larger inside the shrinking prison. And huddles up. Crouches. Submits.

Then one day the prison comes to life. No longer merrily to keep the infant huddled in submission, it begins, like some octopus, to hug and crush. Terrified, infant endures it. The contraction cases, returns, goes away again, then there is another. Not strong, playful.

So that once the infant has recovered from its initial fright, it comes to like them. To wait for the contractions, to hope for them. When they come, embracing the infant, hugging it, it surrenders to them, arches its back, quivers with pleasure at this sensual game.

And these "caresses" are going to last a whole month, the ninth.

Painless for the mother they prepare the child for the contractions of actual labor, which will be 10 times more intense.

One day, these contractions are no longer a game. They

crush. They stifle, they assault.

One day labor status the delivery has begun. An intransigent force, wild, out-of-control, has gripped the infant. A blind force that hammers at it and impels it downward. Is no longer enough for an infant to bend its back. overpowered, it huddles up as tightly as it can. With its head tucked in and it's shoulders hunched together, it is hardly more than a little ball of fright. Prison has gone berserk, demanding its prisoner's death. The walls close in still further.

The cell becomes a passageway, the passage, a tunnel with heart bursting, the infant sinks into this hell. Its fear is without limit. Then suddenly fear changes to anger and rage, the infant throws itself against the barrier. At all costs, it must break through. Free is self. Yet all this force, this monstrous unremitting pressure that is crushing the baby, pushing it out toward the world, and this blind wall which is holding them back, confining it. These things are all one; the mother. She is driving the baby out.

At the same time she's holding it in, preventing its passage. It is she who is the enemy. She who stands between the child and life.

Only one of them can prevail; it is a mortal combat.

The infant is like the one possessed. Mad with agony and misery, alone, abandoned, it fights with the strength of despair. The monster drives the baby lower still, and not satisfied with crushing, it twists it in a refinement of cruelty.

The infant's head and body execute a corkscrew motion to clear the narrow passage of the pelvis. And the infants head, bearing the brunt of the struggle until it is almost forced between the shoulder blades down into the chest; why doesn't the head give way?

The baby is now at the height of his travail. The effort required is too great, and the end is surely near. That seems certain. The monster bears down one more time and it is then that everything explodes. The whole world bursts open. No more tunnel, no prison, no monster."

Leboyer continues:

The child is born. And the barrier? Disappeared. Thrown away. Nothing! Except avoid with all its horror. Freedom! And it is intolerable. Where am I? Everything was pressing on me, crushing me, but at least I had a form. My mother, my hated prison, where are you? Alone, I'm nothingness, dizziness. Take me back, contain me again, destroy me but let me exist.

The infant is crazed with pain. And for a simple reason, suddenly nothing is supporting his back. And it is in this paroxysm of confusion, in despair and distress, that someone seizes the baby by the foot is suspended over the void. The spinal column has been strained, bent, pushed, and twisted to the limit of its endurance, and now it is robbed of all support. And the head, so supremely involved in the passage outward, now it is also dangling, twisting. And this, at the very moment when in order to calm this vast terror, this panic, what is essentially is a coming together with mother; a reuniting."

It is very important at this point to understand the newborn does not process time in the same way adults do. For the mother the delivery might last two hours. For the baby it is eons. Newborn's time is so slow, slow, slow.

Add to this alcohol, caffeine, microwaved foods, irradiated and genetically modified foods, food preservatives, artificial coloring, artificial sweeteners, aluminum cookware, all drugs, all highly processed foods, all carbonated and sweetened drinks, foods sprayed with fungicides and pesticides, refined salt, and refined sugar, anesthetics and painkillers, vaccinations, etc. Top it off with mother's stress, other legal and illegal drugs, forceps, mother's inability to give a natural birth, and above all archetypal inheritance going back through evolution.

A shot of alcohol consumed by a pregnant woman can cut off the baby's oxygen supply for at least 45 minutes medical researchers say. The baby is doubly affected because the alcohol enters the mother's blood and the fluids in which the fetus floats. Original birthing pain is not some kind of mental abstraction. It is a sensation, a feeling. The birth trauma hurts physically and in particular places, like the head, the neck, the shoulders, the chest etc. Birth experiences can lay a foundation for later chronic conditions, like asthma. Drowning in amniotic fluid is one, being too drugged to take proper breaths is another. Often in a person relieving a birth trauma, even after many decades, original injuries materialize themselves again, exactly at the same spots. A person doing 'rebirthing' often goes through many symptoms that were not present just moments before. Even though he/she is laying on his/her back motionless, the blood pressure can rise to 200 or more. Breathing changes, brainwave changes. This includes sensations of choking, gagging, fatigue, localized pains, dizziness, weird pressure, and feelings of being crushed or suffocated. Raising the birth trauma into consciousness is often very hard. When a person gets close to these imprints, his/her vital signs skyrocket. Feeling extremely cold (fear) or extremely hot (anger) is common.

Even the earliest environment in the womb is recorded in memory. It still lives in us, all the sounds smells, feelings and sensations are still there. Original trauma creates a huge electromagnetic storm in the brain.

Pain is a bio-electric force. If we understand that we are talking about sensations frozen in time, the actual physical pressure, then the source of chronic migraines, chronic asthma, chronic heart problems and any other disorders, is no longer a mystery. Birth trauma cannot be adequately imagined, it has to be relieved. An adult cannot imagine how it feels to be squeezed for hours by massive contractions, to be blocked in an unyielding canal, to be suffocated by an overdose of anesthetic, to be drowning in the amniotic fluid, to be fighting for air, to be squeezed by a doctor's metal forceps around the head and yanked out, or to be held upside down in a cold room with blinding lights and spanked.

How do the painful experiences of birth get transformed into what we call the subconscious? It is done by neurochemical processes of suppression. 99.9% of us cannot remember what our births felt like, and for good reason. There are chemicals in the brain that are triggered by pain that prevent the memory of the trauma. Remember, these chemicals do not get rid of the trauma itself; they only prevent us from being conscious of it. Nothing can change the actual imprint of the trauma. We must face it sooner or later, even if it is when we exhale our last breath. For many of us, birth is the closest we will come to death for the rest of our lives.

I recall a young man, who after taking ayahuasca, without presence of a qualified Shaman or experienced facilitator, described how Satan attacked and tortured him; twisted him in an impossible ways for over four hours. In a room all by himself he took ayahuasca two more times with same results. I commend this man's incredible courage, but resolution is not possible through erroneous belief. Birth is imprinted in each one of us; in our bodies, in our minds. It needs to be consciously re-experienced, properly understood, and filed in a memory bank.

Not only do we have the memory of our own birth imprinted; we also have all the birth imprints going back through all of our ancestors. Not only do we inherit our ancestor's physical characteristics but also energetic, mental and emotional. These imprints form super-powerful archetypes which are very, very, hard to overcome. On top of that life has piled up, both through liminal and subliminal means, awful lot of bad crap. In cases of extreme trauma perpetrated on children by evil people, makes it almost impossible to liberate themselves.

***

Carl Gustav Jung's 'psychosis' began when he was 38 years old, when he found himself haunted by visions in his head and heard voices. Jung himself worried about this "psychosis" — things that today we'd might say were consistent with symptoms of schizophrenia (a term he also used to describe himself during this period). He so enjoyed the unconscious mind he had unleashed, he summoned it whenever he wanted. Most people who have psychosis or hallucinations seek to minimize their symptoms, to drown out the visions and hallucinations. After first experiencing these visions, Jung did just the opposite. He found the experience so exhilarating and full of unconscious content that could be further examined, he didn't just wait for the visions to come on their own. Instead, he encouraged their appearance throughout the day, for years. Each night and in-between seeing patients during the day, Jung spent time in his study inducing the visions and hallucinations. He did this not through the use of any kind of drug, apparently, but instead through his own personal methods that allowed his subconscious mind to become open and flowing forth.

Nikola Tesla did it similarly, transforming the knowledge of the use of the electricity and fundamentally changed the world.

New York Times describes the Jung's testimonials told by the Red Book:

"The book tells the story of Jung trying to face down his own demons as they emerged from the shadows. The results are humiliating, sometimes unsavory. In it, Jung travels the land of the dead, falls in love with a woman he later realizes is his sister, gets squeezed by a giant serpent and, in one terrifying moment eats the liver of a little child."

While Jung described his visions as a type of "psychosis" or "schizophrenia," those terms meant something different a hundred years ago than they do today. Today, the terms describe a specific constellation of symptoms, one of which is the meaningful and significant interruption the disorder makes upon a person's ordinary, daily life.

Also, Jung reportedly found a way to bring on his unconscious stream of thoughts and visions at will, something most people today who experience psychosis or schizophrenia, can't do. Nor can they do the opposite, make them go away by just willing it.

Jung talks about the archetype (also called "primordial image", primordial complex) as of biological patterns of behavior (inborn behavior patterns). Archetypes are inborn tendencies which shape the human behavior.

Basically an archetype is nothing else but a pre-shaping possibility or an innate tendency of shaping things. We can say archetypes resemble the instincts in that that they cannot be recognized as such until they manifest in intention or action.

Archetypes make up the structure of the collective unconscious, they are psychic innate dispositions to experience and represent basic human behavior and situations. Thus mother-child relationship is governed by the mother archetype. Father-child - by the father archetype. Birth, death, power and failure are controlled by archetypes. Religious and mystical experiences are also governed by archetypes.

The most important of all is the Ego which is the archetype of the center of the psychic person - his/her totality or wholeness.

Archetypes manifest themselves through archetypal images (in all the cultures and religious doctrines), in dreams and visions.

The collective unconscious, originally defined by Carl Jung and sometimes called the objective psyche, refers to a segment of the deepest unconscious mind not shaped by personal experience. It's genetically inherited and common to all human beings. Sexual instincts are a good example.

"But what is the Archetype? An innate tendency which

molds and transforms the individual consciousness. A fact defined more through a drive than through specific inherited contents, images, etc.; a matrix which influences the human behavior and our ideas and concepts on the ethical, moral, religious and cultural levels. The great problems of life, like sexuality among others, are always related to the primordial images of the collective subconscious. These images are really balancing or compensating factors which correspond with the problems life presents in actuality. This is not to be marveled at since they are deposits representing the accumulated experience of thousands of years of struggle for adaptation and existence. The sexual instinct is something questionable, and will always be so whatever a future set of laws may have to say on this matter. It belongs, on the one hand, to the original animal nature of man, which will exist as long as man has an animal body. On the other hand, it is connected with the highest forms of the spirit. But it blooms only when the spirit and instinct are in true harmony. If one or the other aspect is missing, then an injury occurs, or at least there is a one-sided lack of balance which easily slips into the pathological. Too much of the animal disfigures the civilized human being, too much culture makes a sick animal.

Archetypes are primordial conglomerates imbedded in our body. As stated; we readily accept a piece of plastic can hold a huge amount of memory, but we are very reluctant to accept that our first cell held the memory of the entire evolution and history of the existence. Sex Archetype; Eros is a superhuman power which, like nature herself, allows itself to be conquered and exploited as though it were impotent. But triumph over nature is dearly paid for. Nature requires no explanations of principle, but asks only for tolerance and wise measure. "Eros is a mighty Daemon"- as the wise Diotima said to Socrates. We shall never get the better of him, or only to our own hurt. He is not the whole of our inward nature though he is at least one of its essential aspects. "

"The discussion of the sexual problem is only a somewhat crude prelude to a far deeper question, and that is the question of the psychological relationship between the sexes. In comparison with this the other pales into insignificance, and with it we enter the real domain of woman. Woman's psychology is founded on the principle of Eros, the great binder and seperator, whereas from ancient times the ruling principle ascribed to man is Logos. **The woman is increasingly aware that love alone can give her full stature, just as the man begins to discern that spirit alone can endow his life with its highest meaning.** Fundamentally, therefore, both seek a psychic relation to the other, because love needs the spirit (higher consciousness), and the spirit love, for their fulfillment." - "Woman in Europe" (1927). In CW 10: Civilization in Transition. P.254

Love needs SuperConsciousness and consciousness needs Unconditional Love.

Finally, the archetype is psychoid (psychic-like); it shares both psychic and material aspects and acts as well on a psychic and/or material plane. Archetypes are inherited multigenerational super-powerful programs, tendencies and instincts on how you do and react to things. Not only do we inherit physical characteristics of our parents, grandparents, and so on back into infinity, but we also inherit all mental, energetic and spiritual (consciousness) tendencies. All of them reside in our subconscious and because subconscious thinks in images these Archetypes sometimes present themselves as virtual, live, tri-dimensional images which are very, very difficult to overcome. Difficult, dangerous, but not impossible. Just the way it should be. (Samo na muci se poznaju junaci.) There is no coming to higher consciousness without pain and discomfort.

Possession, psychologically speaking, is to identify with a subconscious program, and become taken over by it, such that we act it out in and through our lives.

We all had moments where we've been possessed by

something, where we felt "not ourselves," where we are no longer identical with ourselves. Some of us spend our whole lives living someone else's life instead of our own. We've all had moments where "something" has gotten into us, where we feel out of sorts, beside ourselves. When deeper, primordial archetypes seize us. Jung writes "They easily catch hold of you and you are possessed as if they were lions or bears, say, primitive forces which are quite definitely stronger than you."

To arrogantly think we as modern-day rational people, are too sophisticated to believe in something as primitive as demons is to have fallen under the spell of the evil spirits we are imagining are nonexistent. What the ancients call demons are a psychic phenomenon which compel us to act out behaviors contrary to our conscious intentions. Jung; "the psychic conditions which breed demons are as actively at work as ever. The demons have not really disappeared but have merely taken on another form: they have become subconscious psychic forces."

Jung says; "…the complex forms something like a shadow government of the Ego," in that the complex dictates to the Ego. When we are taken over by and in internal conflict with and because of programming, it is as if we, as natural rulers of our own psychic landscape, have been deposed, and are living in an occupied country. We are allowed our seeming freedom as long as it doesn't threaten the sovereignty and dominance of the ruling power. As soon as a person succeeds in expanding his/ her consciousness subconscious makes a bid for it." Jung comments, "…a man does not notice it when he is governed by a demon; he puts all his skill and cunning at the service of his unconscious master, thereby heightening its power a thousand-fold."

The Gnostic text 'The Gospel of Philip' says:

"So long as the root of wickedness is hidden, it is strong. But when it is recognized, it is dissolved. When it is revealed, it perishes. As for ourselves, let us each dig down after the root of evil which is within each of us, and produces its fruit in our hearts. It masters us. We are its slaves. It takes us captive, to make us do what we do not want, and what we do want, we do not do. It is powerful because we have not recognized it."

Man's personality is divided between the familiar Ego and the unfamiliar dark and hidden side the Self, the alter-ego, doppelgänger, Mr. Hyde and Dr. Jekyll ('Two spirits dwelled within my breast each seeks therein its separate existence.'- Goethe-'Faust'). If it is true that we are two creatures in one body, then it is true that we are ourselves and doppelgänger; then the question arises is the other a friend or an enemy? If we treat an aspect of our self as an enemy then it should be clear what the consequences will be.

Why is the consciousness afraid of the subconscious and vice versa? The answer lies essentially in the opposite natures of the two systems; when one exists the other has to be absent.

Here another question arises; is there a way where both of them can be present at the same time? O yes there is!

It is well known that dreaming is an essential part of our human mental health. If deprived of dreams the subconscious will enter the outer world; the day consciousness is attacked. So any denial of night dreaming time is met by counterattack on the normal waking time. We could say mental illness is a permanent or temporary intrusion of the subconscious Self into the Ego waking consciousness.

The source of the demons lies within ourselves.

If the demons are not integrated, neither is the human mind, which is to say embracing and integrating our demons is critical to the evolution of the soul. Jung asks: "How can evil be integrated? There is only one possibility: to assimilate it, to raise it to the level of consciousness." Raising the demons to the level of consciousness takes away their independent existence as they rejoin the profound unity of the psyche. Jung states: "Then the opus magnum (the 'great work' of alchemy) is finished. Human soul is completely integrated."...Not quite; there is another 1/3 left out, our SuperConscious mind.

When an archetypes are not completely integrated, and consciously understood, one is possessed by it and forced to its imminent goal. The daemonic expresses itself by enlisting us to its cause and forcing us to unconsciously act it out, to give living form to itself in the third dimension.

Jung writes, "If we don't see the negative side of what we do, what we are, we are possessed...Only through understanding of unconscious aspects, as a rule, can we liberate ourselves from possession." Jung comments, "...the demon that is always with you is the shadow following after you, and it is always where your eyes are not." The spirit of the subconscious impersonates us, fooling even ourselves, as it cloaks itself in our form. This fickle spirit has "put us on" as a disguise, appearing as ourselves, or at least who we imagine ourselves to be.

Many people, including sometimes ourselves, who zombie-like, compulsively and mechanically enact their habitual patterns with no spontaneity or creativity, like a programmed robot?

So anybody possessed by an archetype develops inhuman qualities. When we become taken over by an archetype we become inflated, subconsciously identifying with God-like powers while simultaneously forgetting our humanity. (see my eBook 'SuperConscious Meditation')

People who are possessed by their subconscious have a very magnetic, charismatic and "possessive" effect upon others' subconscious.

Jung: "When someone is able to perform the art of touching on the archetypal, he can play on the souls of people like on the strings of a piano."

Connecting with the archetypal is like plucking a higher-dimensional chord of our being, which activates a resonance in the collective subconscious in whoever hears it. The person who is channeling the living power of the deeper, archetypal force can entrance others. This power can be used for the highest good, helping people to awaken, or it can be used for the deepest evil to manipulate, dis-empower and enslave people. Being archetypal, this energy is neither good nor bad, but can manifest itself on either side of the coin.

The emergence of the daemonic in our world is both potentially and actually the doorway into and revelation of the light. Being a function of our consciousness, how the daemonic materializes–as the deepest, destructive evil, or as creative genius, depends upon nothing other than how we dream it. Jung comments, "The archetype is spirit or anti-spirit: what it ultimately proves to be depends on the attitude of the human mind."

We all know people like this, people who are under a spell so that there is really no talking with them, as they perversely take in and interpret whatever reflection is being offered of their unconsciousness as evidence of the rightness of their deluded point of view. Psychologically, they are possessed, as if an "entity" has taken them over, they are no longer there, and they have no idea, of the situation they are in. They are now in what I call a 'dumb or an idiot zone'. It is **almost** impossible to get someone out of it.

Here are some more gems from Carl Gustav Jung:

1. The growth of the mind is the widening of the range of consciousness, each step forward is a very hard work.

2. "Don't hold on to someone who's leaving, otherwise you won't meet the one who's coming."

3. "Until you make the unconscious conscious, it will direct your life and you will call it fate."

4. "Everything that irritates us about others can lead us to an understanding of ourselves."

5. "The meeting of two personalities is like the contact

of two chemical substances: if there is any reaction, both are transformed."

6. "I am not what happened to me, I am what I choose to become."

7. "Knowing your own darkness is the best method for dealing with the darkness of other people."

8. "If you are a gifted person, it doesn't mean that you gained something. It means you have something to give back."

9. "Mistakes are, after all, the foundations of truth, and if a man does not know what a thing is, it is at least an increase in knowledge if he knows what it is not."

10. "Your visions will become clear only when you can look into your own heart. Who looks outside, dreams; who looks inside, awakes."

11. "Loneliness does not come from having no people around, but from being unable to communicate the things that seem important to oneself, or from holding certain views which others find inadmissible."

12. "Depression is like a woman in black. If she turns up, don't shoo her away. Invite her in, offer her a seat, treat her like a guest and listen to what she wants to say."

13. "A man who has not passed through the inferno of his passions has never overcome them."

14. "Your perception will become clear only when you can look into your soul."

15. "What you resist, persists."

16. "A dream is a small hidden door in the deepest and most intimate sanctum of the soul, which opens up to that primeval cosmic night that was the soul, long before there was the conscious ego. This whole creation is essentially subjective, and the dream is the theater where the dreamer is at once scene, actor, prompter, stage manager, author, audience, and critic."

17. "We may think that we fully control ourselves. However, a friend can easily reveal something about us that we have absolutely no idea about."

18. "Everything about other people that doesn't satisfy us helps us to better understand ourselves."

19. "Emotion is the chief source of all becoming-conscious. There can be no transforming of darkness into light and of apathy into movement without emotion."

20. "I find that all my thoughts circle around God like the planets around the sun and are as irresistibly attracted by Him. I would feel it to be the grossest sin if I were to oppose any resistance to this force."

21. "No nation keeps its word. A nation is a big, blind worm, following what? Fate perhaps. A nation has no honor, it has no word to keep."

***

"The over development of the maternal instinct is identical with that well-known image of the mother which was glorified in all ages and all tongues. This is the motherlove which is one of the most moving and unforgettable memories of our lives, the mysterious root of all growth and change; the love that means homecoming, shelter, and the long silence from which everything begins and in which everything ends. Intimately known and yet strange like Nature, lovingly tender and yet cruel like fate, joyous and untiring giver of life-mater dolorosa and mute implacable portal that closes upon the dead. Mother is motherlove, my experience and my secret. Why risk saying too much, too much that is false and inadequate and beside the point, about that human being who was our mother, the accidental carrier of that great experience which includes herself and myself and all mankind, and indeed the whole of created nature, the experience of life whose children we are? The attempt to say these things has always been made, and probably always will be; but a sensitive person cannot in all fairness load that enormous burden of meaning, responsibility, duty, heaven and hell, on to the shoulders of one frail and fallible human being-so deserving of love, indulgence, understanding, and forgiveness-who was our mother. He knows the mother carries for us that inborn image of the mater nature and mater spiritualis, of the totality of life of which we are a small and helpless part." (see my book; 'Painless, Effortless and Natural Birthing Method').

"The woman who fights against her father still has the possibility of leading an instinctive, feminine existence, because she rejects only what is alien to her. But when she fights against the mother she may, at the risk of injury to her instincts, attain to greater consciousness, because in repudiating the mother she repudiates all that is obscure, instinctive, ambiguous, and unconscious in her own nature." - Psychological Aspects of the Mother Archetype" (1939). In CW 9, Part I: The Archetypes and the Collective Unconscious. P. 186

"Even for a moment we should not succumb to the illusion that an archetype can be totally explained and disposed of. Even the best attempts at explanation are only more or less successful translations into another metaphorical language. The most we can do is dream the myth onwards and give it a modern dress. And whatever explanation or interpretation does to it, we do to our own souls also, with corresponding results for our own well-being. The archetype, let us never forget this, is a psychic organ present in all of us. A bad explanation means a correspondingly bad attitude toward this 'organ', which may thus be injured. But the ultimate sufferer is the bad interpreter himself."- Father Archetype.... The Psychology of the Child Archetype (Das göttliche Kind 1941), 1963 translation. II, 1: The Archetype as a Link with the Past; also in Collected Works, Vol. 9, Part I, p. 160

"No one can flatter himself that he is immune to the spirit of his own epoch, or even that he possesses a full understanding of it. Irrespective of our conscious convictions, each one of us, without exception, being a particle of the general population, is somewhere attached to, colored by, or even possessed by the spirit which goes through the masses. Freedom stretches only as far as the limits of our consciousness. We are so captivated by and entangled in our subjective consciousness we have forgotten the age-old fact that God speaks chiefly through dreams and visions.

The unconscious is not just evil by nature, it is also the source of the highest good: not only dark but also light, not only bestial, semi-human, and demonic but superhuman, spiritual, and, in the classical sense of the word, divine." - The Practice of Psychotherapy, p. 364 (1953)

"We can never legitimately cut loose from our archetypal foundations unless we are prepared to pay the price of a neurosis, any more than we can rid ourselves of our body and its organs without committing suicide." - J.B. Priestley, Times Literary Supplement, London (August 6, 1954)

"There are as many nights as days, and the one is just as long as the other in the year's course. Even a happy life cannot be without a measure of darkness, and the word 'happy' would lose its meaning if it were not balanced by sadness." - "The Art of Living", interview with journalist Gordon Young first published in 1960.

"The idea of an all-powerful divine Being is present everywhere, unconsciously if not consciously, because it is an archetype. There is in the psyche some superior power, and if it is not consciously a god, it is the 'belly' at least, in St. Paul's words. I therefore consider it wiser to acknowledge the idea of God consciously, for, if we do not, something else is made God, usually something quite inappropriate and stupid such as only an 'enlightened' intellect could hatch forth." - C. G. Jung. 2014. Collected Works of C.G. Jung, Volume 7: Two Essays in Analytical Psychology. Princeton University Press. p. 71

Carl Gustav Jung is my favorite European psychologist.

The great doctor of the soul and definitely one of the most inspired psychologists of the twentieth century. He had great insight into what is currently playing out, both individually and collectively, in our modern-day world. Jung writes; "If, for a moment, we look at mankind as one individual, we see it is like a man carried away by subconscious powers." We are a species carried away, "possessed" by, and acting out, the subconscious. Jung elaborates, "Possession, though old-fashioned, has by no means become obsolete; only the name has changed. Formerly they spoke of 'evil spirits, 'now we call them 'neurosis' or 'unconscious complexes.'

Possession, according to Jung is "a primordial psychic phenomenon" that "denotes a peculiar state of mind characterized by the fact certain psychic contents, the so-called complexes, take over the control of the total personality in place of the ego, to such a degree that the free will of the ego is suspended."

Though the possessed might imagine they have free will, their freedom is an illusion. They are unwittingly being used as an instrument for some "other" energy or force to incarnate and express itself through them. Having programs is not necessarily pathological as everyone has them. What is pathological, however, is thinking we don't have complexes, which is the precondition that makes us most vulnerable to possession. Jung explains: "Everyone knows nowadays that people 'have complexes.' What is not so well known is that complexes can have us."

The more complexes we have, the more we are possessed. We don't need to get rid of our complexes, rather, we need to become consciously aware of them. It is of great importance what we do with our primordial programs.

These programs are the psychic agencies which determine our psychological view of the world. These imprints are the living elemental units of the psyche, acting like the focal points of psychic life, in which the energy charge of the various archetypes of the collective subconscious are concentrated. An emotionally charged complex attracts and assimilates into itself everything that has any resonance, both inner and outer, into itself. Complexes, when split off from consciousness, swallow and possess the whole personality.

Jung writes; "since the world began, mankind has been possessed." Possession is synonymous with bondage. Jung on state of possession; "the same age-old experience: something objectively psychic and strange to us, not under our control, fixedly opposed to the sovereignty of our will."

Possession means being displaced by something stronger, being taken over and "owned" by something other than ourselves. Jung states; "Wherever we are still attached, we are still possessed; and when we are possessed, there is one stronger than us who possesses us."

At any moment any one of us can become "possessed" by the subconscious in a way such that a more powerful energy than our conscious Ego moves and animates us. Jung; "…it easily happens to any one of us that we do not act through our own volition. Then I cannot say I do, but it is done through me; something takes possession of me, the very action can take possession of me."

When we have fallen into our subconscious and compulsively enact a subconscious program, we become manipulated by more powerful forces than ourselves. In Jung's words, "a person then becomes the devil's marionette. This could happen only because he believed he had abolished the demons by declaring them to be superstition. He overlooked the fact that they were, at bottom, the products of certain factors in the human psyche. In dismissing the demons as being mere illusion without realizing their psychological reality, we unwittingly become possessed by them. The demons are ultimately split-off, rejected, and disowned parts of the psyche that are experienced as alien and other than who we imagine ourselves to be."

The demons, psychologically, are very real, in that they alter our experience of ourselves. Jung says: "As a rule there is a marked unconsciousness of any complexes, and this naturally guarantees them all the more freedom of action. In such cases their powers of assimilation become especially pronounced, since unconsciousness helps the complex to assimilate even the ego, the result being a momentary and subconscious alteration of personality known as identification with the complex. In the Middle Ages it went by another name; it was called possession. We, as "modern civilized" people, to the extent we are acting out our subconscious, are possessed just as people in the Middle Ages were."

Jung writes, "...in all cases identification with the unconscious brings a weakening of consciousness, and herein lies the danger. You do not 'make' an identification, you do not 'identify yourself,' but you experience your identity with the archetype in an unconscious way and so are possessed by it." Anything we are unconsciously identical with we are possessed by, and compelled to act out in our life without understanding why. Jung, "...man himself has taken over their role without knowing it and does the devilish work of destruction with far more effective tools than the spirits did. In the olden days men were brutal, now they are dehumanized and possessed to a degree that even the blackest Middle Ages did not know."

Jung states; "...an unknown 'something' has taken possession of a smaller or greater portion of the psyche and asserts its hateful and harmful existence undeterred by all our insight, reason, and energy, thereby proclaiming the power of the unconscious over the conscious mind, the sovereign power of possession."

When we are possessed we are not free, we are not masters in our own house.

Psychic 'independent' programs (imprints) are parts of the psyche which have split-off due to shock, trauma, or breach of our boundaries, and have developed an autonomous life and independent will of their own. Autonomous programs act upon us, they feel like our most intimate self, eventually need to be owned, but paradoxically don't belong to us. The apparent autonomy of the archetypes and complexes is what gives rise to the idea of supernatural beings. Endowed with an other-worldly energy, autonomous programs are what our ancestors used to call "demons." Autonomous complexes are a psychological name for the demons in the archetypal process of addiction that animate us to compulsively act out our addictive behavior. A demon or autonomous program, to quote Jung, "behaves like an animated foreign body in the sphere of consciousness. The complex can usually be suppressed, with an effort of will, but not argued out of existence, and at the first suitable opportunity it reappears in all its original strength."

Due to their lack of association with the conscious Ego, these independent structures are typically not open to being influenced, educated, nor corrected by "reality." Jung states: "If left un-reflected upon, these demons or autonomous complexes wreak havoc for everyone within their sphere of influence…any autonomous complex (program) not subject to the conscious will exerts a possessive effect on consciousness proportional to its strength and limits the latter's freedom."

This inner, psychological condition can manifest both within our psyche and out in the world at the same time.

Demons (daemons) or self-governing programs have a possessive and obsessive effect on consciousness. The word "obsession" originally meant to be under the influence of an evil "possession." Obsession refers to certain ideas that have taken possession of the person. We can become possessed by unshakable ideas of the way things should be or who we think we are. Jung writes: "The idea is like an independent being that wants a body so much that it even incarnates in the body; one begins to play, to perform the idea, and then people say one is completely mad. The idea has taken possession of one 'till it is as if one were out of one's mind.' Reflect for a minute what ideas have done during human past."

These independent programs are like "splinter psyches" that can become overly imbued with psychic energy, and then will propagate themselves within the psyche, consuming the healthy aspects.

An autonomous complex can't stand to be seen. A demon or self-governing complex will hide and do everything in its power to resist being illumined, for once it is seen, its autonomy and omnipotence are taken away; it just becomes another part of the memory. Anchored, connected and related to consciousness, the demon or autonomous program can then no longer revert back into the subconscious. It is no longer able to possess us from behind and beneath our conscious awareness.

It is very important for us to re-introduce the words "demon" and "possession" back into our vocabulary, minus the fear we will be seen as being primitive, crazy or even possessed ourselves if we use such words. India has over 2,500 spiritual words that English language does not have. We need to expand our psycho-spiritual fluency to enable us to better navigate our inner and outer landscapes. Being "possessed by demons"–taken over by subconscious, psychic forces, is something that happens to all of us, and it is very important to properly name our experience. Finding the name empowers us to deal with these parts of ourselves that are emerging from behind the curtain.

The daemonic is an archetypal energy which can take over a person, group or a nation. Archetypes are living, dynamic 'entities', psychological programs or informational fields of influence that can manifest in any form.

The word daemonic is related to "the devil," which in turn is related to the word diabolic, whose inner meaning is to divide, separate, and dis-integrate. Being divisive, the diabolic splits us into multiple fragmented and compartmentalized pieces. This way it diminishes our power and has full control. Jung writes: "Possession by the unconscious means being torn apart into many people and things, a disiunctio. That is why, according to Origen (an early Christian theologian), the aim of the Christian is to become an inwardly united human being."

Becoming a true follower of Christ, who is a symbol of the wholly integrated Self, is to transform the diabolical nature of the disiunctio into a sacred coniunctio, where all the parts of the psyche (conscious, subconscious and SuperConscious) are connected and the opposites unite.

The antonym of diabolic is the word symbolic, which, in addition to being the language of dreams, means to unite, bring together and integrate. The daemonic contains both the symbolic and diabolic encoded within it, which is to say that hidden within the daemonic is the creative seeds of its own transformation. Both constructive and destructive forces are fully present in the daemonic simultaneously, and either energy can potentially manifest, depending upon how our consciousness interacts with it.

Jung: "...the daemon of the inner voice is at once our greatest danger and an indispensable help." Hidden in the subconscious Archetype is our inner voice, our guiding spirit, our angel, and our genius. Jung refers to the daemonic as the "not yet realized creative," which is to say it is creativity not yet "made real" or actualized by the Ego. Developing a healthy and strong Ego is urgently important in entering into relationship with and creatively expressing the daemonic energies within us.

Jung states: "Generally, the daemonic is that moment when an unconscious content of seemingly overwhelming power appears on the threshold of consciousness. It can cross this threshold and seize hold of the personality. Then it is possession." Before an archetype can be consciously integrated, it will always manifest itself physically. Further Jung says; "...it forces the subject into its own form. This intoxication is most direct and dangerous form of possession, unless it is reflected upon, and therefore illuminated and transformed by the light of consciousness, it inevitably leads to self-destruction.... Insanity is possession by an unconscious content that, as such, is not assimilated to consciousness, nor can it be assimilated since the very existence of such conditions is denied."

One of the main ways that daemons become empowered within us is when we are unconscious of our 'shadow'. Jung says: "Anyone who is unaware of his shadow is too wonderful, too good, he has a wrong idea of himself, and to that extent such a person is possessed."

An archetype has a life of its own; the life that is proper and peculiar to the archetype shows its autonomy by the fact that it can swallow one's own life. It is so strong that one can be swallowed up into it and be nothing but that archetype. Of course, one does not know it." The formless, invisible archetype has formed itself and made itself visible through the person, group or nation which it seizes.

An essential quality of being possessed by the subconscious is that we don't know we are possessed, for if we knew, we wouldn't be possessed. To quote Jung: "When you are just at one with a thing you are completely identical– you cannot comprehend it, you cannot discriminate, you cannot recognize it."

Jung: "suppose I am identical with an archetype; I don't know it and the archetype of course won't tell me, because I am already possessed and inundated by the archetype... archetype uses man, simply as an instrument, as a tool of a most transitory kind." Even though an archetype expresses itself through individuals, an archetype is an impersonal energy. Archetypes enlist us for their purposes, taking possession of us like a piece of property, and drop us when we are no longer of use. But the man is, of course, in an awful situation. He is possessed, and he cannot defend himself, for he doesn't even know he is possessed, and that is a wonderful opportunity for the subconscious. Without noticing it, the conscious personality is pushed about like a figure on a chess-board by an invisible player. It is this player who decides the game of fate, not the conscious mind and its plans. It is as if an invisible coup has taken place within the psyche. Falling into self-deception, the conscious mind is under the illusion it is deciding, that it is in control, while it is actually being led and manipulated like a puppet.

Jung states: **"The devil is the aping shadow of God. Archetypes have the most disagreeable quality of appearing in your own guise."**

Describing the experience of being taken over by the subconscious, Jung states; "whenever a powerful content emerges from the unconscious, which we cannot yet grasp with our consciousness, there is a danger that the whole ego-consciousness will be pulled down into the unconscious and dissolved…Consciousness is completely emptied, because its contents are attracted by the unconscious as by a magnet. This process leads to a complete loss of the ego, so that the person in question becomes a mere automaton. Such a person is actually no longer there."

Jung writes on the process of falling under the control of an activated archetype when he states, "…an archetype is mobilized within him which affects him like a narcotic. That is typical; when you get into a situation where an archetype becomes constellated, you will undergo this peculiar hypnotic effect; you fall asleep rather suddenly. It has a peculiar fascination which makes you unconscious."

When we are possessed by an archetype, we are a paradoxically touching upon subhuman and superhuman qualities at the same time.

Jung continues, "…anyone possessed by an archetype cannot help having all the symptoms of an inflation. For the archetype is nothing human; no archetype is properly human. The archetype itself is an exaggeration, and it reaches beyond the confines of humanity…Anybody possessed develops inhuman qualities…we see the characteristic effect of the archetype: it seizes hold of the psyche with a kind of primeval force and compels it to transgress the bounds of humanity. It causes exaggeration, a puffed-up attitude (inflation), loss of free will, delusion, and enthusiasm in good and evil alike....when a person has an unconscious content–say a certain archetype is constellated–then his conscious, not realizing what the matter is, will be filled with the emanation or radiation of that activated archetype. And then he behaves unconsciously as if he were that archetype, but he expresses the identity in terms of his ego personality... For he unconsciously plays a role and tries to represent something which he has taken to be his own self."

Jung writes; "...people who constellate an archetype have such a hypnotic effect." People who are gripped by an archetype have a gripping effect on others; when we are under the fascination of an archetype, we unwittingly have a fascinating influence on others. Jung makes the point that "identification with an archetypal figure lend almost superhuman force to the ordinary man."

In other words, when someone is possessed by an archetype, they are literally the channel through which that archetype is materializing in the field which is to say they command great energetic influence on their surroundings. Jung says, "But the power of the archetype is not controlled by us; we ourselves are at its mercy to an unsuspected degree...because everyone is in some degree 'possessed' by his specifically human preformation, he is held fast and fascinated by it and exercises the same influence on others without being conscious of what he is doing. The danger is just this unconscious identification with the archetype." To the extent we are identified with and therefore possessed by the archetype, is the extent to which we are not conscious of the corresponding influence we have on others' subconscious. This is a dangerous situation because it is unconsciously being enacted in such a way that guarantees we will abuse our unresolved power issues to the extent that we stay unconscious.

Explaining the hypnotic power of the archetype, Jung

writes, "It gets you below the belt and not in your mind, your brain just counts for nothing, your sympathetic system is gripped. It is a power that fascinates people from within, it is the collective unconscious which is activated, it is an archetype which is common to them all that has come to life." When an archetype is assembled, rational logic and facts have no effect. The deep emotion which is characteristic of an activated archetype ensures that, to quote Jung; "…the possibility of reason having any effect ceases and its place is taken by slogans and chimerical wish-fantasies. That is to say, a sort of collective possession results which rapidly develops into a psychic epidemic."

Being subconsciously identified with an archetype is extremely dangerous; it is at the root of both individual and collective psychoses.

Jung writes: "Nobody can realize an archetype without having been identified with it first….you cannot realize them without having been thoroughly caught by them."

In the process of integration, we have to learn to experience our archetypal demon from the outside as well as from the inside. Experiencing the archetype from the outside means to experience it objectively, as other than ourselves, which is to separate ourselves from it, for an archetype, in Jung's words; "…can be truly understood only if experienced as an autonomous 'entity'."

Mythologically, the figure of the "would-be-hero," which is all of us in potential, is always inhabited by a demon. The demon is the source of all creativity. It takes genuine courage to do battle with these internal forces and wrest from them the mythic "treasure hard to attain," which is none other than our soul-filled selves, a SuperEgo.

When we become possessed by the subconscious, we become subconsciously taken over by our animal instincts in such a way we regress, devolve and fall into our lower nature. Jung writes; "Only the animal man can be possessed…It is easier to talk or to argue with a dog or a cow than with someone possessed by such a figure. For nothing that one says permeates, it is impossible to pierce the wall they put up, it is a wall of unconscious beliefs, and people behind the wall cannot be reached. They are totally inaccessible. There is no access because the human being is degraded to the state of an animal, and the thing that seems to function is not a divine being, it is a ghost." I have seen people in this "idiot zone" many times, and it is a sad sight. It is amazing how when I was in it I was totally unable to recognize the situation I was in.

Once these archetypal contents become activated in the unconscious, Jung expands, it is like "they have taken possession of certain individuals, irresistibly draw them together by mutual attraction and knit them into smaller or larger groups which may easily swell into an avalanche."

When we become taken over by the subconscious, to quote Jung, "…the unconscious in large measure ousts and supplants the function of the conscious mind. The unconscious usurps the reality function and substitutes its own reality. Unconscious thoughts…manifest themselves in senseless, unshakable judgments upheld in the face of reality."

Demons work through our psyche, "managing our perceptions" in a way such that we aren't able to see their influence. Subconscious programs manipulate our consciousness we become blind to our own underlying reality. We fall under hypnotic spell when we become entranced by our own version of reality so to think the world "objectively" exists as we perceive it, separate from our own mind. In other words, we fall under the power of the demons when we become fixated in our non-negotiable viewpoint and imagine that what we are seeing objectively exists, in solid form, outside of ourselves, in a way that applies to everyone. We then draw to ourselves all the evidence we need to prove to ourselves the seeming truth of our self-evident viewpoint, confirming our delusion that we are separate from and not participating in helping to create the very situation we find ourselves in. We only break the spell of the demons when we realize that every moment of our experience is inseparable from our own consciousness.

Just like figures in a dream, the demons are ultimately our own energy, not separate from our own mind. Just like a dream, the way we observe the world literally evokes the very world we are observing.

Jung writes: **"The psychological rule says when an inner situation is not made conscious, it happens outside, as fate."**

Jung says, "The world powers that rule over all mankind, for good or ill, are unconscious psychic factors…We are steeped in a world that was created by our own psyche." This brings to mind various quotes in the Bible about "powers and principalities" that rule over humanity, which is the metaphysically equivalent expression of our psychological situation. The Gospel of Luke, for example, has the devil say that the kingdoms of the world are under his control (4:5-6). The Gospel of John speaks of the devil as "the ruler of the world." (14:30, 16:11). The First Letter of John says that "the whole world lies under the power of the evil one." (5:19). Paul speaks of Satan as "the god of this world." (Gal. 1:4; Cor. 4:4). Whether we call it a demon or an unconscious psychic program, the force that rules over us is created by and an expression of our own psyche.

In this work I have extensively quoted Carl Gustav Jung to illustrate the great importance for any aspiring Spirit Traveler to understand the functioning of his psyche.

Double-arrow is a beginning of the freedom.

Lucifer-Bringer of light! Are you kidding me!!! Mass murderer and Satanist Richard Ramirez murdered 30 people in a most gruesome way. (eg; He murdered a man in his bedroom, then by the body raped man's wife and mother, then he raped eight-year-old son and then murdered them all.) At the court hearings he stated he was inspired by heavy metal group AC/DC. This is just one example out of thousands.

Research by US Today from 1985 about heavy metal music shows 50% of the songs are about murder, 32.5% about Satanism, and 7.4% about suicide.

In USA there are about 2.5 million Satanists; over 200,000 children disappear every year never to be seen again. Not to worry, it is only a coincidence.

***

Fritjof Capra: "I see science and mysticism as the complementary manifestations of the human mind. Neither is comprehended by the other, nor can either of them be of use to the other, but both of them are necessary, supplementing one another for a fuller understanding. Science does not need mysticism and mysticism does not need science, but man needs both."

It is said philosophers collect explanations for which they have no facts while psychologists collect facts for which they have no explanations. The same goes for religion and science.

There are two major poles of a human personality, those of objectivity and subjectivity. These poles also grow two main nervous systems, the autonomic nervous system and the central nervous system, respectively. The two headquarters of the autonomic and central nervous system are the cerebellum and the cerebrum, two great masses of cortex found in the head. The two great brains in our heads are themselves paired in construction. That is both the cerebellum and cerebrum are made up of two hemispheres joined together. This arrangement already suggests to us there are two major systems, which are physiologically the central nervous system and autonomic nervous system.

Subjective and objective existences are themselves

polarized internally, so there is polarity within subjectivity and polarity in objectivity. On top of that autonomic nervous system is itself physically divided into two well defined subsystems, the parasympathetic (passive) and sympathetic (active). Autonomic nervous system itself, which cerebellum is only the headquarters, is clearly divided at the physical level into two hemispheres. Parasympathetic system is involved in the receptivity and sympathetic system is heavily involved in states of anger, arousal, aggression and activity.

The laws of magic, the laws of subjectivity, are the precise reverse of the laws of science, the laws of logic. Question that needs to be asked is; are we each two creatures, double, or doppelgänger? And if this is true is the other than a friend or an enemy? The way it is at the moment, society in general strives to make it an enemy. We could actually go a little further and ask a question; are we actually three creatures; subconscious entity- subconscious mind; conscious entity- Ego- ourselves, and the Superego - SuperConscious mind.

The legends, fairytales and religious myth are far from being a kind of psychological junk pile, they actually offer the only hope of making some sense of important features of our psychological makeup and the nature of our present society. Strongly developed Ego consciousness is a barrier, but at the same time it is a power. The barrier can be mastered and the power can be retained. Highly developed capacity for relative knowledge is not to be scorned.

The dream state is so important something more should be said concerning its nature. Some of the states entered, while body sleeps, are far more truly waking states than any which are possible while in the physical body. This universe has no more real existence than a dream, but it is held together by enormous power of all beings within it. The whole field of a dream, together with its problems is destroyed by simple process of waking up. This is so because the dream is yours only. However, this is not the case with the universe which is being dreamt by infinite number of sentient beings. This leads us to very important point. Whenever we recognize any state of consciousness as being a dream at that moment we have discovered that it is unreal, in other words it is devoid of self-existence.

A man suffers while in the midst of ordinary dreams simply for a reason that at the time of dreaming he believes the state to be real. Not only in a manner when he wakes to the higher consciousness he destroys his universe, but in a sense of realizing that it never has been real.

Dream of jokes. If you wake up laughing your whole day will be very pleasant. Practice laughter Yoga in your dreams.

***

Niels Bohr, the Nobel Prize reports, for example, that he developed his model of the atom in a dream. Von Stradonitz attributed his interpretation of the ring structure of the benzene molecule to a dream as did Otto Loevi whose experience with frogs nerves contributed to his eventual Nobel Prize. There are many such examples of great things coming out of the dreams.

In schizophrenia and other forms of psychosis the afflicted person sees people, animals and objects which are not actually or objectively there. One patient might see the devil sitting at the foot of his bed. Another that the kitchen is full of snakes. There are other deviant behaviors; such people may cut pieces of themselves with knives or razor blades. They may viciously attack friends or strangers. Recently a man cut off the head or passenger sitting in front of him in a bus in Canada. Or they cannot bear the sight of presence of real animals. They cannot sleep, or they cannot eat, they spend hours writing nonsense, they might bang their heads against the wall continuously, they might attempt a suicide and so on, and on.

Author Stan Gooch narrates his experiences:"... having

for some reason woken abruptly on one such occasion, I open my eyes to see a large snake coiled on the bed. I reached for it but in the act of my reaching out the snake disappeared. Much more often my hallucinations are human figures. I'm now fairly used to them but once or twice the figure persisted long enough for me to believe that I am, this time, fully awake and that the apparitions is really there. To a tall angel dressed in a flowing white coat I recently shouted; "what do you want?" The figure faded. More recently I was confronted by shining a replica of myself. I waited briefly, but the figure persisted. I shouted 'yes' with great excitement but then after all the figure vanished."

Writer Franks deliberately put about a completely fictitious story that particular place was haunted by a particular ghost, describing the appearance of the alleged ghost in detail. After a while the reports began to flood in a people claiming to have actually seen the said resident. Still more impressive was the second experiment when a young woman was told under hypnosis she would be in a particular place at a particular time and see a ghost which the hypnotist described in detail. When taken to that locality and questioned, the woman in fact duly saw the ghost.

Organisms are a bridge between paranormal- mental universe and the objective so-called material universe. As human beings we have a foot in both camps. Our physical body obeys the laws of material universe and consciousness sometimes does not. Science is quite unable to tolerate the idea that the relationship and interactions of paranormal events may not always be casual. Science insists that supernatural events, like material events, can be broken down into ever simpler stages, until we discover the basic building blocks of the paranormal. But sometimes this is just not the case. Paranormal breaks otherwise unbreakable laws of the physical universe; it goes back into time and forward into time not yet come.

Physical matter can only move forward. It can only

change onwards and is the complete prisoner or its own present. Thus it can only be what the forces acting upon it, at any particular moment, permit. Human beings and all other organisms are not entirely the prisoners of the present; they're not entirely the prisoners of the physical universe. They can exit momentarily and pass into some other 'dimensions'. Subjective world (just like objective) is beset with quite real dangers. So-called evil spirits may take over and refuse to go away. What takes over is an aspect of one's own mind, and definitely not some independent entity. Figures of ghosts are just hallucinations of the same, no different in principle than hallucinations of mentally ill people or persons under the influence of drugs. They are made up and projected for us by our own subconscious minds. At best it is one-way traffic of ghosts from past to the present. One-way traffic is the hallmark of physical universe.

The subconscious mind then is a reality; it has considerable powers of self-government and decision. It frequently overrides, contradicts or more subtly circumvents the orders or normal consciousness. However the conscious mind also has powers; it is also sometimes able to override and contradict the wishes of the subconscious.

***

Sigismund Schlomo Freud, 'father of psychiatry' was a sickoid who fainted almost every time someone disagreed with his theories. He was heavy cocaine addict and a womanizer. For years he had sex with his wife's sister, and other women. His nebulosus are still affecting humanity.

Carl Jung - "I still recall vividly how Freud said to me; "My dear Jung, promise me never to abandon the sexual theory. That is the most essential thing of all. You see, we must make a dogma of it, an unshakable bulwark." He said that to me with great emotion... (Memories, Dreams, Reflections, p.150)

In some astonishment I asked: "Working against what?"

To which he replied; "against the black tide of mud", and here he hesitated for a moment, then added "of all occultism" meaning anything spiritual or paranormal." Jung has been discussing religion and faith with Freud, and has stated that it did not seem to him to be reducible to repressed or sublimated sexuality, or to the sexuality of any kind. This deeply distressed Freud.

Jung wrote about a paranormal account that happened in Freud's study were Jung and Freud were talking together. Jung had specifically asked Freud for his views on recognition of parapsychology in general. Freud lapsed into the rejection of these matters, in the shallowest of terms. Jung was angered by this snub and said he he felt curious sensation as if his stomach was made out of iron glowing red hot. Instantly there was a loud bang from the bookcase, so loud that it frightened both men. Young remarked that that was an example of phenomena he had been referring to and added that there would be now another bang. Just as he said this the second loud bang went off in the bookcase. Freud was visibly shaken.

Now this is considered impossible from a physical-materialistic point of view, but if you think of existence in energetic terms, this is quite possible.

We will never know if there were actual bangs in the study. Two men heard them but that doesn't mean sounds were there. They could have been subliminally induced in their minds. The only way to know would be to have had a sound recording device on at that time.

Neurotic behavior is characterized by defensive intent; that is to defend some part of the personality against attack or hurt but also characterized by self-defeating consequences of the solution. The 'solution' is in fact the illness. For example, in agoraphobia the person concerned is afraid of going outdoors. The obvious solution to them is to stay indoors. But this solution only means they are going to suffer from the illness permanently. The true solution would involve finding out what the outside world represents to the sufferer on subconscious level.

There is amazing phenomenon known as multiple personality where a deep-seated mental problem is a converted into another person. The solution is; I don't have this depraved desires and this sexual problems, she or he has them. I'm not like that all. This is usually the result of the extreme abuse and trauma in the early life of a child.

Within one human brain the nervous system of the mind constructs one or more additional, coherent, functional personalities who periodically take over consciousness and the entire body, and act out unacknowledged and unwanted desires and thoughts. The integrity, depth and differences of this fully functional personalities is utterly staggering. Such alternative personalities will take over from normal consciousness for extended periods sometimes for hours, weeks or even months. During this period the normal conscious personality disappears completely, it simply is not there. The later reestablished normal personality has memory gaps in the respective events and the alternative time it used up by the visitor in particular. Sufferer will typically have no knowledge at of the existence of the alternative personality. The new takeover personalities have different beliefs, views, ideals, temperaments, ambitions, tastes, habits, experiences, and memories from those of the normal owner of the body in question and from each other. Such alternate personality would even have different diseases than their original conscious personality. Not only do they have different thoughts, views and emotions, they even exhibit different handwriting and can show different brain wave patterns, and even produce different performances on psychological tests, word association and vocabulary tests.

The subconscious mind sees and the records everything in our lives on its own account, quite independently of consciousness.

Here is an account of subconscious influencing the conscious perception: "I saw rainbow colors everywhere, and the trees studded with bright jewels, golden light surrounding objects, with my eyes wide open, this experience brought also sense of great joy, a feeling of warmth, love of all and everything, a oneness with objects animate and inanimate, the love of stone, a speck of dust on a sunbeam, a twig, the stars moon and the sun. With eyes closed there would be fantastic colors, always bright clear colors, many, many archways, beautiful golden archways studded with precious stones of many hues. The light was very bright, of intensity that one could read by, as it were, and sometime this light would also fill a dark room where I sat. I did not realize then that the light was within me, not in the room. What a superb experience it was. It lasted for many weeks. I thought I was in the fairyland, and no one knew about it, it was my very own magic land."

It should be clear to anyone that a person should prepare himself or herself for the onslaught of a subconscious mind in whatever form it may come. And if for some reason you believe it is not controlling YOU, you better think again.

Until we have met the monsters in ourselves, we keep trying to slay them in the outer world. And we find we cannot. For all the darkness in the world stems from the darkness in the heart. Personal "monsters" are in subconscious mind which must be entered consciously, and all the transmutation work can be done there.

When a student of Tibetan teacher Chogyam Trungpa was discussing reincarnation and asked his teacher what is it we bring with us when we reincarnate into the next life, Trungpa answered; "our neuroses".

CHAPTER TWELVE

DREAMSCAPE

The first known textual description of lucid dreaming dates to before 1000 BCE from the Upanishads, the Hindu oral tradition of spiritual lessons, philosophy and proverbs. The Vigyan Bhairav Tantra is another ancient Hindu tract that describes how best to direct consciousness within the dream and vision states of sleep. In the early centuries, Indian influence spread to the mountainous region of Tibet, where the animistic tradition of Bonpo maintains that lucid dreaming has been used in their meditations for over 12,000 years.

The textual legacy that has survived the cultural fusion of this shamanic practice with Buddhism is the Tibetan Book of the Dead, conservatively dated to the 8th century. In the West, the concept of lucid dreams is almost as old. In general, dreams had a privileged position in the foundations of Greek philosophy; Socrates, Plato and Aristotle all addressed their inquiries into the nature of reality and our nightly journeys. Lucid dreams were first clearly described by Aristotle (350BC), in his 'Treatise on Dreams' Aristotle writes, "When one is asleep, there is something in consciousness which tells us that what presents itself is but a dream."

Lucid dreaming may have played an integral part of the history of Islam. Mohammed's Laylat al-Miraj is an account of a nighttime vision that provided him with spiritual initiation. The 12th century Spanish Sufi Ib El-Arabi suggested that controlling thought in dreams is an essential ability for aspiring mystics. In the seventeenth century, lucid dreams began to surface again, this time couched within the European culture of reason. Many dreamers shelved old superstitions and began to look inward again (or at least talk about such explorations openly). Pierre Gassendi and Thomas Reid are two Enlightenment era philosophers who discussed having waking-life levels of scrutiny and cognition within their dreams. Interestingly, Rene Descartes, who is most famously regarded as being dismissive of subjective reality, actually wrote passionately about his lucid dreams in a private journal known today as the 'Olympica'.

Three hundred years later, Sufi mystic Shamsoddin Lahiji recorded an inspiring night vision of the heavens that also may have been a lucid dream experience.

A few centuries later, in 415AD, the first lucid dream report was recorded, from one of St Augustine's patients.

Astral is just a word, meaning belonging to the stars; starry, an epithet descriptive of a supposed supersensible 'substance' which pervades all space and enter into all bodies; odic; biogenic.

Nirvana is a human state in which bliss is being free from the physical body. Instead of looking outward, to change a direction Astral Travelers turn their gaze inward, and at that which is not yet present.

In the astral world, everything is changeable at the command of the mind.

There are no limitations, no forced routine, in heaven. Advanced astral beings can order their environment and actions just as they please. It is freedom eternal. If you want to go to the farthest star, traveling through the ether faster than light, you are allowed to do so. You can be a star, a human being, an angel, anything you want to be, all at will.

Astral light (Clear Light illuminates all dream objects from within, this is why those "objects" cast no shadows), the Buddhists call Svabhavat, and some higher metaphysical schools even state that this astral light is a self-existent 'matter', which has never been created, but always was, without beginning or end, past or future.

Desire-stuff may be described as a type of force-matter, in incessant motion, responsive to the slightest emotion. The dream world is also said to be the abode of the dead for some time after death.

***

Radio and TV signals fill the room we are in right now, and if our eyes and ears were built a little differently, we would actually be able to see and hear them, And some do (see; Solomon Veniaminovich Shereshevsky) just the way we can see sunbeams streaming through the window onto the furniture and hear the cat purring on our lap. If we could "see" the radio and TV signals all around us, we would be overwhelmed by the many songs, the personalities, and dramas, news programs, and action movies all competing for our attention.

Radio and TV signals vary in vibration or frequency, so that each signal remains distinct even though they're all jumbled together in the same space. That way, the electronic circuits within a TV or radio can tune-in to a single signal, allowing us to hear only one program sent by only one station. The signals are separated from each other by frequency, so they can't overwhelm us.

The mental space we're in is also filled with countless realms of existence beyond the physical world, all teeming with life, and again, if our eyes and ears could see and hear those nonphysical realms, the room would be incomprehensibly crowded, and we would be completely overwhelmed by the sights and sounds of the many 'entities' here among us.

Likewise, the many realms of existence all inhabit the same space, but each realm remains distinct by its vibration. In this case it is not a radio or TV frequency, but rather the vibration of consciousness that makes each realm of existence unique and discrete, so that the inhabitants and activities of that realm aren't disturbed by the many other 'beings' inhabiting other realms.

For the Astral Traveler, the power of expectations (both

conscious and subconscious) can be a major hindrance. Not least because of the direct emotional implications of mingling with the spirit world. One example is from the blogger Erin Pavlina who described her first astral projection experience as terrifying:

During sleep paralysis, Erin sensed three other 'entities' in her bedroom, trying to coax her out of body.

She struggled to breathe. To scream. To free herself from the terrifying paralysis. She felt sure it was all real, including the malicious entities. The more she fought it, the more terrified she became, until she eventually woke up.

She later had a nervous breakdown.

Erin believed her spirit was in a literal tug-of-war against the presences in her room (who, incidentally, she could also hear talking about her).

How messed up would you feel if you genuinely believed every vivid nightmare you've ever had actually happened?

Because of her spiritual belief system, Erin was convinced these visions were real. Sleep paralysis can be scary enough, even when you know it's all in your head. Imagine the intensity of the fear if you truly believed these were evil beings from a spirit world.

To feel safe in your lucid dream explorations, I suggest you consciously recognize that any entities you perceive be accepted as dream figures. This calm recognition will help reduce your fear and lead to better lucid dream outcomes (this is so in YOUR dream but not quite so in mutual, group dream or collective dream world.)

The most vital step is when you enter into a state of vibration. This state may take longer if you are new to this. When you do begin to feel the vibrations, your dream body has begun to 'leave' your physical body. Just acknowledge this and feel the vibrations. Focus on the vibrations as they travel throughout your body. Using your will-power, control them with your mind. As you feel them, try to control the frequency of the waves as well as stopping and starting them. Once you master changing the frequency, you can induce them when needed.

Heaven and hell are really just the astral planes, separated by vibrational frequencies. You can say earth is also a level of "hell" because it's so low vibrational, along with the lower astral realms, and the higher astral planes are "heaven" because they vibrate at a very fine rate and are quite gorgeous.

***

Theravada Buddhist cosmology describes thirty-one planes of existence in which rebirth takes place; but why complicate things.

Just as there are seven colors in the rainbow and seven tones in a musical scale, each with a different vibratory rate, there are seven planes of existence on the spectrum of creation, according to some. Let me make it clear, this is just an arbitrary description. The slowest speed of vibration occurs on the physical plane; the highest, on the plane of pure consciousness.

Physical plane: The densest of the seven planes; where we presently reside.

Dream plane: The second plane of creation. It is energy plane. It is where our consciousness is focused between lifetimes and when we're finished with the physical plane.

It is Karma World, the second lowest of the seven worlds; it contains emotions, desires, and passions. Immediately after physical death disintegrated parts of a man enters this karmic world where they function for timeless durations varying on the state of development. Like attracts like.

Causal plane: The third plane of creation. Its medium is concrete intellectual energy.

Akashic plane: The central, neutral plane of creation that

interconnects the other six. The distilled knowledge of the universe is recorded there. This is the record of everything that happens in the universe as it occurs. All matter and energy have a sort of built-in digital recording device, storing its entire history in a tridimensional photographic code. These records are actually windows into the past. The records show events exactly as they were experienced, so the information in them is not necessarily clarified, understood, and assimilated until consciousness takes responsibility for doing so. Once assimilated they are stored on the akashic plane.

Mental plane: The fifth plane of creation. Its medium is abstract intellectual energy, emphasizing three-faceted truth.

Unconditional Love plane: The sixth plane of creation. Its medium is abstract emotional energy, emphasizing love.

SuperConscious plane: The highest plane of creation. Its medium is pure or abstract kinetic energy.

Each of the planes can further be broken down into three sub-planes; lower, the middle, the upper.

Demons, evil spirits, ghosts, malevolent monsters, all reside in the lower Dream World. We should ask ourselves; where am I living right now? Just look around the world and be honest.

Astral Plane is actually composed of many different planes, and the lower astral plane is a repository of the collective evil and fears of humanity. Unfortunately, to be able to access the higher levels of the astral realm, this lower astral plane has to be crossed, and it is during this crossing that the dangers can arise. In fact, if an astral body is shining so brightly, even if they are in the higher levels of the astral realm, lower level, or lower vibrational 'entities', may still follow, as they are attracted by the bright glow of the astral body. Solution is not in escape or rejection but in love and transmutation.

What these 'monsters' seek and desire is the energy and

light of your astral body. They are drawn to it like moths to a flame. Lower vibrational entities are attracted to fear, doubt, sadness, hatred, and other negative vibrations. In order to not attract the attention of these malevolent 'beings', you have to raise your vibrations to a higher level, that of love, courage, joy, compassion. Once your frequency is higher, it will be very difficult for lower vibration 'entities to see you, let alone reach you'. But we are talking about a dream world, where so called entities are not real, where seeing is not really seeing, where distance does not really exist. Words cannot really explain the dream world.

Being at higher vibrational level will attune you to the other higher vibrational beings that you can interact with. Once you increase your power you might seek these lower 'entities', transmute them and integrate them into your being.

The primary step to protect yourself from the lower vibrational entities is to avoid them entirely. This is easy to say, for subconscious knows you have entered it.

If you place different kinds of lights in a room such as kerosene oil light, mustard oil light, petrol, candle light, electric light; these various lights interpenetrate in the room. Just like that, the planes interpenetrate. Each plane has its own 'matter' of an appropriate degree of destiny, which interpenetrates the matter of the plane next below it.

When you pass from one plane to another, you do not move in space. You simply change your focus of consciousness. You can have different vision through the telescope or microscope by using lenses of different degrees of potency or power. Different bodies within yourself correspond to different planes and which can function in different planes.

In the physical plane one gets knowledge of objects through the five organs of perception; ear, skin, eye, tongue, nose. In the mental plane or astral world we do not hear, see and feel by separate and finite organs. We get a Divine Eye, an extraordinary new power or faculty. We can hear, see, feel and know everything of an object instantaneously, through this new mental eye. We get an accurate and perfect knowledge of all 'objects'. We are not deceived or misled by any external appearance. There is no misunderstanding.

There is neither day nor night for a Spirit Traveler, or an inhabitant of the mental plane, or 'heaven'. He is neither sleeping nor waking. When he enters 'heaven', he experiences intense happiness. This is his waking state.

But what are all these celestial realms based on? Fifth-element of course. Fifth element is an infinite force that has no interest whatsoever in us, however it responds to a powerful intent, the true power. It does not respond for the most part to ordinary thoughts and prayer, or the response is feeble. Every thought, every word, every image, every feeling, every emotion, every action stirs itself inside the fifth element which is like infinite, bubbling super-colorful, transparent molasses; 'clay' God is creating everything from, enlarging and diminishing at every single point, forever morphing. Even if we pronounce a single letter like letter "A" it manifests itself as energy movement within Akash. Consciousness perceives it, brings it into existence, and then files it in the memory bank.

"All matter comes from a primary substance, the luminiferous (light-producing) - ether," - Nikola Tesla.

Not light as we normally understand it. Not light from some source. Not even tridimensional light. Try to imagine a tridimensional super-colorful "mass" that is not a gas, a liquid or any kind of solid. Not perceiving it through a sense of vision, but being one with it. Vibrating, oscillating, disappearing and appearing. Where (everywhere) it disappears it does not leave any space. Where (everywhere) it appears, immediately it is changing. It appears with infinite number of components, yet it is one whole. It is beyond any description by any words. Astral lights, lights of SuperConscious mind. Quantum theory refers to it as 'virtual particles' coming in and out of existence. Hogwash; nothing can describe it! It is beyond comprehension by Ego-mind.

Just as Akash is the infinite omnipresent 'material' of this universe, so is this prana the infinite omnipresent manifesting power of this universe. The Akasha is everywhere. In it we live and move and have our being. All is but one 'substance'. Prana is the universal principle of energy or force. It is the sum total of all energy manifested in the universe, all the forces in nature and powers which are hidden in men and which lie everywhere around us. All forces, all powers and prana spring from the fountain or common source, known as Atman in Hindu terminology. Heat, light, electricity and magnetism are manifestations of prana. It may be in either a 'static' or a dynamic state. It is found in all forms from the highest to the lowest.

Whatever moves or has life is but an expression or manifestation of prana. It is prana that shines in your eyes. It is through the power of prana that the ear hears, the eye sees, the skin feels, the tongue tastes, the nose smells and the brain and the intellect perform their functions. Prana is force, magnetism and electricity. Prana is the link between the astral and physical body.

"Prana is said to be of the color of blood, red gem or coral." Well, it is not! Imagine small live corals in infinite number of translucent colors, tridimensional mass that includes you the "observer", vibrating, shimmering, forever changing almost geometrical patterns, becoming and unbecoming, everywhere, with no space in-between, a mass of energy that is infinitely many but at the same time one. For myself. I called them 'neon angels.'

Thinking does not help here, instead try your best to visualize what is being said.

Desatir:- "Mezdam (God) separated people from the rest of the animals and gave them a soul which is free and independent of all substance; without body, without matter, which cannot be broken down into its parts, which does not take space and with whose help man can reach the domain of Angels. With his knowledge he is going to unite his soul with elemental body and he will leave his inferior body, he will arrive into the world of Angels and he will be able to comprehend Me."

Ancient commentary; "Nothing can happen without being paid for. All the joy and happiness, all the unhappiness and pain, are the consequences of our previous actions. If a man has high intelligence and knowledge and still does evil, when his material body falls apart, he will not get his second eleMENTAL body, nor will his soul access to higher domains, but his evil predispositions will torment him with some forms of fire, cold, snakes, dragons, demons, etc., and this way will give him a deserving punishment.

(This is identical to the teachings of Desert Christian fathers in North Africa; "Without mortifying our body (real meditation) there is no access to the world of angels.")

This transcendental knowledge, besides Desatir, can also be found in Pertuestan (Castle of Light) and Avesta, so that every soul of every man can find the pleasure of learning about it. Pertuestan is one more book of secrets of the infinite God. "Often, daily, you get out of your body and you come close to me"

Commentary: "Siamek's body, through many meditations and mortifications (conscious shutting off of all senses), worshiping God, has become like the jacket for him. But when he wished to visit with angels and Yezdan, he often went out of his body, and he went to the place of his wishes, then return to his body upon God's wish."

The sole purpose of human existence seems to be just to kindle a light in the darkness of pure and simple being.

Called or uncalled, God is present. - Desiderius Erasmus

***

According to spiritual teachings the astral plane can be visited consciously through astral projection, meditation, near death experience, lucid dreaming, OBE, or other means. Individuals trained in the use of the astral vehicle (dream body) can separate their consciousness in the astral vehicle from the physical body at will. Dream world, the world of your subconscious mind is your own. But collective Dreamscape of all humans is obviously not just your own. Your own subconscious landscape is hard to navigate. Navigating the collective dreams is much harder. On top of that you add your personal and collective human heritage Archetypes and you can begin to understand the immensity of challenges for Spirit Travelers. Many Spirit Masters (like Sri Aurobindo) attempted to bring down the Divine Light into this material level, but collective darkness was just too powerful.

In his book Autobiography of a Yogi, Paramhansa Yogananda provides details about the astral planes learned from his guru. Yogananda claims nearly all individuals enter the astral planes after death. There they work out the seeds of past karma through astral incarnations, or (if their karma requires) they return to earthly incarnations for further refinement. Once an individual has attained the meditative state in an earthy or astral incarnation, the soul may progress upward to the "illumined astral plane". After this transitional stage, the soul may then move upward to the more subtle causal spheres where many more incarnations allow them to further refine before final unification.

Traditional esoteric theory tells us that the astral dimension contains seven major levels, or planes, each housing many lesser sub-planes, internal realms, and kingdoms. Many descriptions for this structure ;Hindu, Buddhist, spiritualist, New Age, etc., even the multidimensional theory of modern physics, often appear to conflict, mainly because of cultural and religious beliefs. This is similar to human level. Let me make it clear; no two human beings have same level of consciousness. Add to this all the living beings on this planet, all of which influence each other. On top of that each human has over 600 trillion living beings living in him or on him, each with their own chemistry, energy and consciousness influencing us.

***

Exploring and mapping the Dream World is like trying to explore a whole planet on foot, without maps or instruments.

Walking is very awkward in a dream world and especially walking up and down the stairs. Using the eyes is a great way to move; just focus dream eyes anywhere you want to be, intend and let the eyes pull you there. It's instantaneous and saves so much energy. Your dream body knows exactly how to do that or you have to do is intend and focus your dream eyes. Very effective way of moving the dream body is to fly glide or soar.

It takes years of exercises to perfect the energy body and the dream body and make it fully functional. The behavior of a dream body must be under full conscious control. The Intent needs to be practiced over and over again.

Through the usage it make us stronger. There is no other way. When in a dream world move around as much is possible. Again, do not be obsessed with details.

One of the greatest exercises that can be performed in a dream state is to dream of seeing the energy inside the images. Once a dream body is made fully functional and complete, this ability will transfer into the everyday world and the dreamer will now see the energy in the items of the waking world.

Good analogy would be the movies. Real-world items contain energy within themselves, the very opposite of the dream world of projections.

Ordinary dreams do not generate energy. In a mutual dreams or group dreams dreamer can come to the point where he can tell apart energy generating items or simple phantom projections.

Intent within a dream world can be somewhat

strengthened by voicing it with words filled with emotion. Eventually you will not have to waste your words and emotions. You will simply Will it silently. Ordinary dream images are projections of your subconscious mind, these images are existent in your mind only. You are a director, actor and stage. But are you? You do not have the slightest clue how dream is produced, so why do you take ownership of its creation?

Using the eyes to move can carry us over incredible distances in a second, but the Dreamer can even move over the distance not accessible to the dream eyes, by using a mind to focus the intent, let's say, to the end of the galaxy. Think about it for a second, there is no real space there, real distance. There it's only a dream space and a dream distance; so called short distances, or long distances are easily navigated.

Of course there is possibility of going beyond all this dreaming, to meditate, to sit and meditate inside the dream. A dream to shut down the dream. All the dreaming senses are shut down, dream thoughts are shut down, as well as dream emotions. Dream Yogi goes beyond, to the pure consciousness, where there are no objects of any kind.

At first the dreamer has a sense that everything experienced in a dream world is just a dream which will be over and you will wake up; but this is just a case in ordinary dreams. In a group dream, mutual dream, the game is completely changed, completely different, and the new rules of engagement have to be learned.

As was stated elsewhere, the subconscious mind is about million times more powerful than a conscious mind; so when a dreamer ventures further into a dream world he/she needs to be in a permanent state of 'tensed' and sustained alertness, otherwise the dreamer might be in real danger of being swallowed up by the subconscious mind. If venturing deeper into the Conscious Dreaming a dreamer needs to start regarding dreaming as something extremely dangerous.

Not only can our five sense abilities be increased, another 40 senses, which are presently in the subconscious world, can get activated to a degree. In our everyday world senses become four (or more) dimensional and everything in it glimmers with an inner light; its own energy. Our world consists of many inner layers of shimmering colors.

Imagine what tetrachromats, pentachromats, sixtachromats, and septachromats can see; imagine all other senses could open to that degree.

Additional dimensions are not out there somewhere; they are right in front of our noses. So why don't we perceive them? It is actually a blessing we do not, for if he did we could not handle it in a state we are in, and we would go mad.

In a dream world even maleness and femaleness is only a preconception, something that has no inherent reality. You know dream body is totally arbitrary. We in a dream world do not see with our eyes, hear with our ears, touch with our hands, smell with our noses, or taste with our mouth. It is all a dream; it is our consciousness that experiences all this.

Astral planes are complex, multi-layered, energetically generated multi-dimensional environments with variable perception-based aspects. It is easy to get lost in them. Remembering our physical body, our home base, when travelling the dream world is of utmost importance. That connection has to be firmly established and constantly built on until we finally exit physical world for good.

The way the dream planes and their contents are perceived, experienced, and remembered can be extremely variable, depending greatly on the projector's level of energetic activity at the time of projection, and on the state of their belief system, their level of consciousness at the time of projection, and the state of their base level of consciousness.

All this affects how the physical brain works, and how much of what is perceived during a projection the brain is capable of storing as a recognizable memory. After all, the only thing left after a projection is the memory of it, which will be perceived, interpreted, and recalled by the base level of consciousness.

In the astral dimension, reasoning power, the energetic qualities of travelers' projected Dream Body strongly affect their perception, but even more so their state or level of consciousness. This is true not only during the experience, but also afterward. It affects the memory and how it will be stored in the physical brain at the base level of consciousness, and thus, how an experience will be recalled after the fact.

***

All experiences, including astral, arise in Consciousness, which is both the foundation and 'substance' of creation. Divested of all limitations fabricated by the mind, Consciousness is formless, eternal and unbounded. For these reasons, it is considered absolute and divine in nature; it is the Holy Spirit itself.

When we speak of Consciousness, we're not referring to something 'out there', in space. It's the foundation of our own awareness, which shines behind the mind, making it possible to read and understand these words, right now. From this perspective Consciousness is the recognition of our own essential nature.

Because Consciousness is purely spiritual in nature, it's completely hidden from view forever. We cannot know it objectively because it's the subjective reality behind all experience. As such, its character is mysterious and paradoxical. Some call it the impersonal and non-dual reality underlying manifest creation. Others refer to it in personal terms as the Creator and Supreme Divine Being. Both views are correct, and at the same time. Consciousness transcends all conceptual limitations.

Just as sunlight separates into different bands of color,

Consciousness separates into different planes of experience. Each plane corresponds to a particular type of body, or platform of conscious experience. Each plane and its corresponding body are actually two sides of the same coin. For example, the physical body and the physical plane are two aspects of the same experience and cannot be separated one from another. The same holds for dream body and dream world.

After death, at least for the short while, our conscious experience doesn't cease. It simply recedes from the physical plane to the subtle, dream, or astral plane, and the corresponding astral body. The dream body is essentially a bundle of psychic impressions (conscious and subconscious), which accumulate during Earth life. From this perspective, the astral plane is like a reflection, or an echo of the Earth experience. Although the dream body survives death of the physical body, it is not eternal and has its own definite life span of about five and a half years; but this is true only in case it was made fully functional prior to death. Even this time period is up for discussion, for advanced dreamer can alter both time and space.

Beyond the astral plane is the spiritual plane, and the corresponding spiritual body or soul, which also has to be made fully functional. The spiritual body is the most fundamental unit of creation and as such, it is both immortal and eternal. It's a manifest form of Divine Consciousness, plus the spiritual ancestral essence which has accumulated over many cycles of Earth life.

From the foregoing, the descending order of existence can be illustrated in this way: Divine Consciousness - spiritual plane - dream plane - physical plane.

These different planes are not locations in time or space. They are states of consciousness, or levels of subjective experience within us. Whether we realize it or not, as human beings, we live and function on all three levels simultaneously.

The lower dream world is a repository of our densest thoughts and creations. This is where we find fragments of ourselves that were split off in anger, rage, terror and grief. This is the "hell" referred to in religious writings. Every time we disown a part of ourselves in anger or guilt that fragment is cast into the lower astral realm. As I said; like attracts like, so there are tons of it introduced to our mind through liminal and subliminal means during our lives. If universe is of the mental nature, and it is; think for a minute where do all the mental parts go after death and disintegration of the Ego?

Anything we focus on intensely becomes a Thought Form and takes on a life of its own. That is because we are creators and what we put on the canvas of our minds becomes real within the realm in which it was created. Watch your thoughts and emotions like a hawk once you are able to enter Subconscious World.

The more we focus on a particular thought or idea, the more real it becomes. As it becomes more and more real, it becomes a powerful force to be reckoned with. This force can take on a shape and appearance, and can move and interact with other thought forms. Some negative astral 'entities' are fragments of minds that have been disowned and hurled into the depths of the subconscious, netherworlds or hell; other names for the lower astral plane. The primary fragments of these souls may be human beings living in this outer 3-D world, without the knowledge that parts of themselves remain trapped in this world of mind and REAL imagination.

Upper etheric realms are beautiful and full of light and magic. Many aspirants on the path has confused the etheric realms with the 'celestial heavens'. The so called celestial planes vibrate at a much higher and more refined level and can only be reached once a soul has mastered the fourth dimensional aspects of self. In the etheric realms, thought becomes manifest instantly. Here is the realm where you can have anything your heart desires, if that is your wish. This world is guided by faeries, elves, gnomes, devas, angels, archangels, holy men, and master teachers. You are never to forget you are just perceiving higher energetic vibrations and your mind is adding the images. At this point you are also just a dream image. Time and space still exist in the etheric realms, but can be distorted and compressed. Many earth-bound souls supposedly remember being in the etheric realms before coming into embodiment. Magic of our Dream World is limited only by our imagination.

The mental realms are where we go when we visualize, meditate and project ourselves psychically. All the psychic and spiritual gifts utilize the mental planes as a means of creating reality. This is the scratch pad of the conscious mind. This is the realm we use to create our physical reality. Every time we take an action, it is preceded by a thought (not in an earthquake and other extreme situations. Also not before you have learned to think.).

***

At death the self that is identified with the subtle body completely detaches itself from the parts of the physical body such as the hands, eyes, etc. Person is not able to preserve the physical body through the life-force at the time of departure. Just as he/she detaches himself from the body and the organs, and enters deep sleep, even so, he detaches himself from this body during death and attaches himself to his dream body. As frequently as man moves from the dreaming to the waking, from the waking to the dream and thence to deep sleep, so frequently does he transmigrate from one body to another. He has transmigrated from many such bodies in the past and will continue to do so in the future. He gets his future birth according to his past work, knowledge and so forth. He goes from one body to another, only for the unfoldment of the vital force. It is by this-life force, that he fulfils his objective, the enjoyment of the fruits of his work.

When the man is about to die, the various organs withdraw

themselves into their original sources and help no more the function of the body. In death there is a complete withdrawal of the energy of organs into the heart or the heart-lotus or Akasha of the heart. But in the state of dream the energy is not absolutely withdrawn. Here lies the difference between sleep and death.

Then the dying man hears not, sees not, smells not, speaks not and becomes senseless. He loses his consciousness. He never remembers he is Mr. So-and-so. He loses his understanding, memory and waking consciousness. The external world becomes void for him. Consciousness implodes.

The passage of the self from the body varies according to the number of good actions done by the man and the knowledge gained by him. If he has a good store of virtuous deeds and spiritual knowledge that would take him to the Light, the self leaves the body through the eye. It leaves through the head if he is entitled to the world of Source of Creation. It leaves through other passages according to its past work and knowledge. Of course; an asshole will exit thorough the anus. Sages used analogy to describe how each sole exits at death. So let's dispose of analogy; soul departs through inner direction and not the outer.

A man attains whatever he thinks, feels and intends at the moment of death. Therefore, in order to have freedom of action at the time of death, those aspirants who desire liberation should be very alert and knowledgeable in the practice of Dream Yoga, and the acquisition of merits during their lifetime.

When the soul passes from one body to another, through the Law of Attraction, it is enveloped by the subtle parts of the elements which are the seeds of the new body.

***

The Path of Light is the path by which the Dream Yogis

go SuperConscious. This path takes the Dream Voyager to Heavenly Realms. Having reached the path of the 'gods' he comes to the world of incomprehensible beauty. But there is still one more step, pure consciousness itself.

It cannot come by a stray practice in a day or two, in a week or a month. It is a lifelong endeavor and struggle, even many lifetimes. United with a subconscious mind the Ego Intends to travel up to the SuperConscious mind.

The Path of 'Darkness' or the Path of Ancestors leads to rebirth. Path is seeded with super-powerful heritage Archetypes which have to be overcome by the aspirant. There are "entities', 'smoke' that obscures the vision, and dark-colored objects throughout the path. The dark path is that of forefathers who do good or charitable acts acquiring great merit. The aspirant as such is carried on the shoulders of his ancestors.

Soul of the wicked meets a hideous hag, the embodiment of his evil thoughts, evil words and evil actions.

Here I would like to recount a story that illustrates the nature of the existence: The holiest man that ever lived passed away and arrived to Heaven. God greeted him and appointed angels to show him around and gave him a choice where he wants to abide. The heaven was fantastic, everything was perfect. But the sage wanted to see the hell also. Upon a visit Holy Man come before a God, who then asked him where he wanted to live. The sage said; "Please God reincarnate me to the deepest realm of hell, this is where my help is needed most."

***

Birth and Death are the most common phenomenon in nature and yet the least understood.

Death is only a change of form. Death is only separation of the dream body from the physical body. Birth follows death just as waking follows sleep. You will again resume the work that was left off by you in your previous life. Therefore, do not be afraid of death.

The Sun (light) of pure consciousness is shining in the chambers of your heart. This spiritual Sun of suns is self-luminous. It is the Self of all beings that transcends thought and mind. If you realize this Self, you will no more return to this; the world of death.

The knowledge of the Self destroys all fear of death. Death is like sleep. Birth is like waking up from sleep in the morning. Just as you put on new clothes, so also you CAN put on a new body after death. Death is a natural incident in its course. It is necessary for our evolution. When the physical body becomes unfit for further activities and use, Consciousness takes it away and supplies a new body.

There is no pain at the time of death; pain belongs to this world.

***

Everything is uncertain here, but only death of the body is certain. Seek the immortal soul or the Imperishable Self which hides in the chambers of your heart. Spiritual wealth is real inexhaustible wealth. Divine knowledge is real knowledge. Find out the way to conquer Death. Do good actions. Entertain sublime, divine thoughts and build your character. Have one, pure, holy desire, the desire for liberation from the wheel of suffering, birth and death.

Your character is built by your thoughts. As you think, so shall you become. If you think nobly, you will be born with a noble character. If you think badly, you will be born with a bad character. This is the immutable law of nature. (Emotions are inherited over the Eons). Desire determines which sort of objects you will have in your next life. If you desire wealth very much, you will get it in your next life. If you desire power you will get it in your next life. But money and power cannot give you eternal bliss and immortality.

You must be very careful in your choice.

Consciousness is neither born nor does it die. Like a person passing from one room to another the soul passes from one plane of existence to another. In the period between death and rebirth the individual works out his Karma in subtler spheres.

***

I am Infinite, imperishable, self-luminous, self-existent. I am beginningless, endless, decayless, birthless, deathless. Never was I born. I am ever free, perfect, and independent; I alone am; I pervade the entire universe; I am all-permeating and inter-penetrating; I am Supreme Peace and Freedom Absolute.

Spirit Voyager lives forever; he has attained life everlasting. Cravings torture him not; sins stain him not; birth and death touch him not; he is free from all cravings and longings; he ever rests in his own Being. He sees the one Infinite Self in all, and all in the Infinite Self which is his Being; he remains forever as the Infinite Self of Consciousness and Love.

Heaven and hell are certain degrees of consciousness, neither one are not entirely 'outside'. Existence on this Earth can certainly be hellish (wars, rapes, murders, diseases, Hiroshima & Nagasaki, agent Orange, etc.).

Death is not only a necessity for those who die, but it is also necessary for the evolution of those who are left behind. Death helps devolve responsibilities on new shoulders. They accept the challenge of life and grow in experience. In fact, individual soul could never grow without death. The evolutionary process is a long one. It requires various types of experiences of poverty and riches, of purity and pollution, of ignorance and education, of every country, climate, culture, race and religion. It requires experiences of both sexes as well. In a single body all this is not possible to assimilate. Therefore by virtue of necessity we die and are born again under different circumstances for a different set of experience.

Those who diligently practice double-arrow are aware that our ego is composed of many different I. If aspirant fails to unite them before the death, when life-force retreats and Ego cannot follow, body chemistry stops, all different I disintegrate and rejoin the fifth- element.

***

So-called normal people believe they can think and make decisions. Nothing can be further from the truth. Conscious mind is only the executor of the decision that has been made by the subconscious mind milliseconds or even up to fourteen seconds before. Learning to meditate gives you more awareness of your subconscious brain activity. Advanced meditators eventually succeed achieving the unity of the conscious and subconscious mind and become able to make their own decisions. They achieve freedom. This is not an easy task considering subconscious is over million times more powerful than conscious mind.

Meditation helps you to become aware of your internal bodily processes. People who are easily hypnotized, which are about 30%, are also less aware of the internal processes that are going on in the body and the mind. They have less conscious access to the subconscious intentions.

Hypnotisability and mindfulness are the opposite ends of a spectrum of self-awareness. People who meditate are less easily hypnotized, and people who achieved unity of subconscious and conscious minds cannot be hypnotized under any conditions.

Whenever we have a thought, our life- force moves in the direction of the thought. Thoughts are like leaders that cause the body to move along certain pathways, usually pre-programmed once.

Ordinary 'thinking' involves about 60,000 thoughts floating through your mind every day. Great deal of it is total nonsense. This thoughts are not even yours; you have borrowed them from someone, or something else. Take a look inside your memory bank; when was the last time you thought an original thought, your own thought? Chaotic thinking uses an enormous amount of your life-force and generally does not accomplish anything.

At this level of mind development, it is much better to stay away from spiritual development. Mind cannot handle what is coming at you; some of it is of enormous power. The events will simply suck you in. The danger is real and it should not be taken lightly.

Higher level thinking is Contemplation when a person concentrates on one subject and examines it from every angle. Puts it on paper (like this book), consciously thinks about it, examines every possibility, including worst-case scenario, and then sleeps on it. Next day examines it again, and again, until the answer comes. At this level you can choose a direction, and can hold it, instead being dragged all over the place.

Even higher is Concentration. This is where a person concentrates his mind on one object; be it physical, emotional, or mental. When concentration becomes pinpointed, like a laser, it can punch though into a present moment. This ability is very important, because your very sanity might depend on it, some day.

Fourth level of the use of the mind is Meditation; an effortless concentration on nothingness. Everything else that comes under the heading of meditation, now days, is just an attempt to meditate. This open effortless concentration needs to be applied persistently before the door to the subconscious will open. Opening the door too early is utmost folly.

Fifth way is that of Nikola Tesla. When the door to the subconscious opens, a person can see his thoughts, direct them and project them into the outer space. Thoughts become visual images. The trick is to have this super-powerful subconscious machine under conscious control. At this level you are becoming friends with your subconscious. However, keen vigilance at all times is highly recommended, because of the enormous power of subconscious.

Sixth way: And then, there are THOUGHTS of the SuperConscious mind, a mind that is also ours; better said, we belong to it. A "place" where everything is understood instantly.

Seventh; the Creators Intent.

Ouspensky: "Try, for instance, to compare the speed of mental processes with moving functions. Try to observe yourself when you have to perform many quick simultaneous movements, ...or when having an instinctive movement. You will see at once you cannot observe all your movements, nor can you fit a thought inside a reflex movement. There are many similar observations which can be made, particularly on the emotional center which is still faster. Everyone of us really has many observations on the different speeds of our functions, but only very rarely dowe know the value of our observations and experiences. Only when we know the principle, do we begin to understand our own previous observations. The difference in the speed of centres is a very strange figure which has a cosmic meaning, that is, it enters into many cosmic processes or, it is better to say it divides many cosmic processes one from another. This figure is 30,000. This means that the moving and instinctive centres are 30,000 times faster than the intellectual, thinking, centre. And the emotional centre, when it works with its proper speed, is 30, 000 times faster than the moving and instinctive centres. It is difficult to believe in such an enormous difference in the speeds of functions in the same organism. It actually means that different centres have a quite different time. The instinctive and moving centres have 30,000 times longer time than the intellectual (thinking, reasoning) centre, and the emotional centre has 30,000 timeslonger time than the moving and instinctive centres."

This might be true only for the average person, but much higher thinking speeds are possible. As I said elsewhere, I have my doubts as to this being accurate (see; '33 Pillars of Life'), for speed of our thinking center is not constant but can be increased to almost N-th level.

CHAPTER THIRTEEN

SKYGATES OF THE MIND

We approach first gate of dreaming the moment we change our primary direction from outer to inner. From that point on it just becomes a matter of dedication. At this time we clearly understand that our physical body needs to fall asleep while our mind stays awake and conscious.

Just becoming lucid in a dream at random is not huge accomplishment. We need to make the crossing easy and regular.

There are seven gates (pillars, portals, doors) of dreaming. The first Dreamgate is a threshold you must cross by becoming aware of particular senssation before falling asleep; a sensation which is like a pleasant heaviness that doesn't let you open your eyes. Symphatetic, active nervous system is shutting down.

Here is how to get familliar with this feeling. When you go to sleep, focus your eyes on a point on the ceiling, point eyes about 30 degrees backwards, keep staring without blinking with a strong intent to stay awake. Within a minute your eyelids will feel so heavy you cannot keep your eyes open. This is how your entire body might feel.

This is also excellent way to fall asleep if you have a problem with it. You must still focus on now imaginary point on the ceiling. In another minute you will fall asleep if your concentration is focused.

As the body is falling asleep and being tranquilized it might feel like it is getting very heavy or light. Soon it will dissapear.

If your consciousness slows down this process it might feel like you are falling down the light tunnel in a counter-clockwise direction. You are 'exiting' waking world. Your body has its own consciousness and energy, as do all your organs and cells. Body will function just fine, like it does every night when you are sleeping.

You might start to feel your body vibrating, As the active nervous system is shutting down that vibration will simingly increase in power and at one point this is all that is perceived. Do not panic, enjoy instead. Hook your awareness to this vibration, it will carry you across the gap.

Intending to observe yourself falling asleep takes you into a darkness that feels heavy, yet pleasant. As though you are wrapped up in a heavy kilt. Remain in this blackness, you have reached the threshold of the First Gate. Now you have learned to watch yourself fall asleep. To cross this gate you need to surface from the blackness into a dream. And engaging your intent to do so, you're likely to see images floating just beyond your grasp at the edges of darkness. The objective is to step completely into the dream.

Look around you right now, the dream looks exactly like what you are perceiving at this very moment except somehow more real. In a later, much later, date you'll find out that a dream world looks many times more real than this waking world.

We reach the **first gate** the instant we become conscious we are falling asleep and are suspended in the 'mist' and heaviness. If our intent and our energy is strong we can remain conscious during entire falling asleep process.

At the moment of falling asleep ordinary person falls into a gap, into an abyss, of unconsciousness and darkness. Hour and a half later greately reduced consciousness raises up and Ego starts dreaming, but the dream lasts only for about ten minutes.

Now, it is a totally different story with a Yogic Dreamer. He/she carries the consciousness, the awareness over that gap, over that abyss, into a dream world. It is this awareness, this double-arrowed attention, and an Intent, that enables the Spirit Traveller to jump over the gap between a waking and dream world. It is this expanding consciousness and the Will power that builds a bridge over this gap. Now, instead of having ten minutes of unconscious dreaming, a Dream Worrior has an hour and forty minutes of fully conscious dreaming. Stupendous things can be accomplished then. But first you have to be able to get there and sustain the higher level of consciousness.

Let me explain this in another way. There is no gap between waking and dreaming world. There is only difference of frequency; lucid dreaming frequencies occuring not just in delta and theta ranges, but also higher-than-REM frequencies in the gamma band, peaking at around 40 Hz. Our waking consciousness is not sufficient to bridge the 'gap'. We must raise our energy and everyday consciousness to a higher level by practicing self-awareness, self- consciousnes, split-attention, double-arrow, witnessing consciousness, every millisecond of our life. Transcendental Rebirthing, proper Meditation, Dark Room Retreats and other methods greately speed up this process. Then one day it happens; you have walked through the first gate of the mind!

You have stabilized the first level when you can hold a dream without shifting. other words you can flow with the same dream for as long as you intend. Use your imagination and purpose to establish dreaming in every cell of your body, so you feel dreaming energy throughout the your entire being. You have to deeply feel it, every cell of your body has to feel this energy, this vibration.

Lucid Dreamers get the excess energy by redeploying it in a more intelligent manner. The energy that we normally lose through one-directional senses, constant chatter of useless thoughts, and myriads of negative emotions daily, wasting sexual energy, can be conserved. We all have a predetermined quantity of basic energy; that quantity is all the energy we have, and we use all of it for perceiving and dealing with our everyday world. All that energy is already used and occupied and there is not a single bit of it left for us; for any extraordinary perception, such as conscious dreaming; which puts us in quite a predicament. We must become a misers of energy, and must save it wherever we can and prevent a constant loss.

Conscious Dreamers intelligently redeploy their life-force, by cutting down anything they consider unimportant in their lives. They must create a different habits that will conserve energy on a daily basis. They must modify awareness of everything by using double-arrow, this way they can get enough energy to reach and sustain the dream body.

To go through the first gate of dreaming we need to try and try again, absolutely every night to the point of exhaustion. When the gate finally opens, as we become even a bit more proficient, now something that was dormant all this time, suddenly becomes functional.

The faint images appear; if there is enough awareness and energy these images become clearer. At this point we should examine the elements in one's dreams.

The mind and all its rational defenses cannot cope with powerful persistence and determination. Sooner or later the door will open. To progress further we must redeploy our existing life-force by any means possible. **Second gate** of dreaming is reached when you 'wake up' from one dream and enter into another dream. You intend another dream from a dream you are presently in. Now this is already a higher control so this is exercising the awareness and intent at bit higher level. You just intend to dream that you wake up in another dream. This is similar to using the eyes to move instead of the legs. Just look at the any distant point, focus, intend, and you travel there instantly. Your dream eyes pull you to a new location instantaneously.

It should be obvious that ability to enter from one dream to another could be endless. Once that ability is achieved it definitely should not be indulged in.

The ultimate goal of these exercises is to establish more and more control over your dream attention; the double-arrow attention. True goal of higher lucid dreaming practices is to perfect a dream body. Consciousness must be exercised to the point when it is perfectly capable of surfacing, waking up to this world, at any given time.

Getting past the second gate of dreaming is a very serious affair; it requires the most disciplined effort, great energy and higher consciousness.

At Dream Gate Two you experience more control within the dream, your lucidity takes greater proportion. To cross this SkyGate you dream you woken up from the dream, or use one dream to propel yourself into another dream. Simply isolate a small component within your dream, focus on it, and use this concentration to be a springboard, to propel you into another dream.

One of the most important things while travelling the dreamscape is to reconcile the fearful reactions to anything that is being perceived. Spirit Voyager needs to be able to create a powerful emotion of Love, it is the only thing that can instantaneously transmute morbidity, ugliness and evil into beauty. If fear is not conquered these "entities" from a subconscious world can use the energy of fear to follow us into our daily world, with catastrophic results. When facing fearful images or feelings inside a dream, a dreamer must project power and love. Love needs higher consciousnes; SuperConsciousness needs unconditional Love. Without it they are both defficient.

Subconscious 'entities' are similar to the entities on the movie screen or on your computer monitor, but being produced by a biological, live, 'computer'- your mind. They will promise the world and all knowledge. If you fall under their influence you will lose your awareness, you lose your consciousness, you will become a puppet on a string, and the game is over. The subconscious 'beings' are fully capable of imprisoning us, by catering to our deepest desires. By creating your desired projections they also create phantoms to try and please the dreamers (angels) or frighten them (demons). Subconscious has a power to project seemingly live cosmic movie; it is the ultimate deception.

The moment our consciousness grows the subconscious recognizes it and makes a bid to acquire it. It will use any means to do so.

Dreamer must reject anything that is offered by subconscious 'entities'. It is very tempting, for they can tell you things you could not poosibly know. Remember; subconscious mind has an acces to another 40 senses that are presently out of our reach. To ignore this, the consequence could be a fate worse than death. Your very sanity could be at stake. While travelling deep on this path the dreamer must be vigilant, for subconscious world can distract you at any time.

The subconscious mind will offer anything and everything in exchange for your soul. The lure of the subconscious mind is very powerful, just look at the millions of cases of people in the mental hospitals where mind and consciousness has been swallowed. Temptation of the Jesus by the devil is a good analogy.

Matthew 4:1-11- "Then Jesus was led by the Spirit into the wilderness to be tempted by the devil." (I hope you understand metaphors, parables, similitude, alegories, myth, symbols, cyphres and hidden writing.)

When the temptation from the subconscious is totally and utterly rejected a dreamer has passed the test and can proceed to the next level, next gate.

Even lies have an intention and are based on words and thinking; but the real intent is not based on words and thinking; it is energetic, silent Will.

"Silence is the language God speaks and everything else is a bad translation."- Thomas Keating.

Subconscious mind can use powerful trickery to lure you, unless your consciousness is highly developed and the real power is very strong. It will set up a trap in such a way you want even suspect it.

If you think I am over-exaggerating do take a look at examples cited in my eBook 'SuperConscious Meditation', and remember millions of people in the mental hospitals all over the world.

We need to learn to eliminate fear from our dreams and from our life in order to safeguard our unity and our sanity. This is only possible with total trust in a SuperConscious. When facing subconscious 'entities', the best approach is to totally deny their actual existence. At the same time, do not forget anything is possible in a dream world. Like with everything else in existence, the dream coin has three sides to it.

Upon crossing this first and second sky gate the dreamer has reached the next level. **Third gate** of dreaming is reached and crossed when a dreamer learns to isolate energy in his dream. This is where a Dreamer can perceive the energy within dream images.

How to recognize if the dream images are just an empty shell or an image that is imbued with consciousness and energy. Just wave your hand as if it's a magic wand, fully intending to see the energetic charge of the image, hold the intent. If it is not merely a dreamed, hallucinated, image you will be able to see its vibratory charge

Here he/she might also be perceiving 'entities' or hearing voices. The problem with these subconscious voices is that they are telling you things you already know or should have known. At this point the degree of detachment and awareness is of outmost importance. If you take this subconscious entities and voices for real, the price is very high; your freedom, your energy, your sanity, and your life as you know it, is at stake.

There are two phases to each of the gates of dreaming. The first is to arrive at the gate and the second is to cross it. The second part is to move around the space you're in. At this level of dreaming you begin to slowly and deliberately merge dreaming reality with the reality of the waking world. Here it is easy to get lost in a detail, and lose the sight of wider picture. Dream Voyager needs to view everything with great care and curiosity, and must resist, the nearly irresistible temptation, to plunge into detail.

Spirit Travelers begin solidifying dream body by fulfilling the exercises to make dream multifunctional. When a dream body begins to be functional; this newfound freedom can be dangerous because the dreamer can easily get lost in irrelevant details and keep spending the energy on something unimportant. The amount of energy needed to consciously direct the dream body is staggering.

The most interesting aspects of the dreaming bodies is that they are natural fact of human perception. Dream body experiences have been reported as astral projections and other out-of-body experiences throughout the recorded history. The most skilled practitioners contend that we all use our dreaming bodies regularly, but we just don't remember doing so. At this level you slowly begin to merge dreaming whith your daily world, like in case of Nikola Tesla. He was able to project his thougts right into the space in front of his eyes and see what he intended to, just as you see the pages of this book. At this stage the energy body is ready to act; exercising a more defined and awake energy body. This will increase the dreaming energy. You also need to redeploy existing energy. Real purpose of the dream body is to enhance perception, in other words you capitalize on its higher vibratory rate to achieve deeper and more significant energy alignments. By doing so you stretch your energy awareness through the entire energy body.

Fourth Gate of Dreaming is deliberately placing a dreaming body at specific locations. Say you are sleeping on your bed and you wake up inside your dreaming body which is sitting on your patio deck. This means that your cohesion has shifted and now your focal point is the spot known as patio. As a Dreamer you develop a dreaming body to the point that such shifts are not only commonplace but also controllable. This practice then gives you far more radical shifts to different locations. Dreaming levels, or dream gates, reflect pronounced shifts in cohesion. Accordingly they reflect degrees of handling the real power. The critical component of passing any Dream Gate is Intent. However there are no specific steps other than to intend what you are going after. You intend something simply by intending it. Intent definitely requires imagination, purpose, and discipline. Only then can Intent be experienced and controlled as an energy; which is something other than reasoning power. It has nothing to do with thoughts.

SkyGate Five of dreaming is reached when you find yourself in a dream, looking at someone else who is asleep. And that someone else turns out to be you.

Here you can already dream of being inside somebody else's dream. Of course this presupposes that two or more can enter and hold a conscious dream.

Those type of dreams cannot be haphazard and out of control they must be conscious and intended. The mutual dreams can be done but cannot be fully explained or comprehended by logical ego-mind. Upon exiting mutal dream the paticipants are able to confirm the meeting in a same way they would describe a meeting in waking reality .Two accounts would be exactly the same. Group dreamers would have to vizualise the exact, and in minutest detail, the same location.

This is very high level of dreaming. By now you have performed countless excercises to solifify the dream body and made it much more functional. Now Dream body has such power, such force behind it, it may be perceived by others as though it were a complete entity independent of your physical body, on the astral level of course (but not solely). This dream body seems solid, as solidity stems from the memory of how an event is described.

At **SkyGate Six** you can project complete energy body (dream body) to a physical location with a sense of physicality, other words you are dreaming another physical body and projecting your dream body to a particular location. It would almost seem as if you teleported.

Higher Conscious Dreaming liberates perception, enlarging the scope of what can be perceived, and activates the senses, which have been sublimated all our lives and the lives of our ancestors.

If you sit in a meditative state and enter your dream world and then have enough conscious power and intend to sit in identical position in a dream; this identical position and identical dream location, liberates enormous energy. Identical position and identical location (your bedroom for example) of your physical body and a dream body then make one unit. This Twin Meditation liberates huge energy and ability to concentrate greatly increases. It enables a Dream Voyager to do a dream exercise of 'falling asleep' a second time, of shutting all the dream senses, including thinking and any emotion exactly the same as it was done to the physical body. This is the Dawn of Clear Light.

One of the techniques to enhance the meditation inside a dream is to bring the tip of the tongue up and press it hard against the roof of the mouth (dream tounge, dream mouth).

SkyGate Seven. Akash , eather, fifth element... By now you have joined the energy of the physical body with the energy of the dream body and you have arrived at the pure awareness unfettered by any form or definition. You arrived at the specific dreaming position of the focal point known as Total Freedom. The dream body principle characteristic is it has awareness beyond the physical body. For example; if you're centred in your dreaming body on the opposite side of the room from your physical body, you perceive the room, including your physical body from the perspective of your dreaming body. Second, this consciousness has a form of some kind, has a body due to our habits of perception. 99% of the time it is shaped like a physical body but it can change its form according to the limits of your imagination. Besides dream body traveling, this point of awareness, point of consciousness, without the form can also leave your dream body and travel in a similar manner. The third characteristic is that the dreaming body carries emotions (E-motion- energy in motion).

Dream body, as it becomes more and more functional, often brings experiences to life even more vividly than does the physical body. You may also enhance all of your five physical senses and also activate other senses that are presently mostly on a subconscious level.

Here you can perceive Fifth Element directly.

Akasha is also known as ether, Chaos, Spirit-Matter, First Logos, Root Matter, Orgone, etc.

There are four physical elements (earth, air, water and fire) that describe the material universe. But ether, the fifth element, describes the Spirit that exists beyond matter. It is the 'space' out of which all material objects spring forth.

Eather is a subtle sea of energies that stores everything that has ever occurred throughout all of Creation, and out of which everything becomes. As part of your field of energy, ether is also stored in your DNA spirals (better said your DNA spirals are based on akasha, ether). This 'cellular memory' contains records of every experience you have had in all of your lifetimes on earth, following your genetic heritage, every thought, action and emotion. These are the akashic records of your own past, present and future.

The term ether (also written as 'aether') was adopted from ancient Greek philosophy and science into Victorian physics (see Luminiferous aether) it corresponds to akasha, the fifth element (quintessence) of Hindu metaphysics.

The Ether, Chaos, Spirit-Matter, infinite Whirlpools, energy vortices, Torus, is quantum world populated with a multitude of entities known and unknown.

Ether exists as an emanation of SuperConscious Mind. The truth is the entire universe (4 elements) is made from one basic "substance".

Scientists know energy is vibration, but science fails to fully understand that there can be vibration only if there is something that can vibrate. There can be no wave unless you have an ocean. Therefore, there can be no energy waves, and thus no material universe, unless you have an ocean of something that can vibrate. This "ocean" is tridimensional and infinite, live, forever moving, appearing and disappearing at every point, yet being whole. Infinite number of vibrations, appearing as infinite number of super-luminous colors with almost geometrical tridimensional patterns, at the 'edge' of Creation and Uncreation, EVERYWHERE.

This word 'spirit' in English has been terribly abused, especially in the last one-hundred years. Nowadays, no one can give an accurate or consistent definition to the word 'spirit'. We use it for things ranging from the feeling of a certain music or art, to descriptions of ghosts and phantoms, to discussions of God, and even alcohol (spirits). So, our definition of 'spirit' is very imprecise, and not founded in the ancient, accurate, specific knowledge regarding how to awaken Consciousness. Latin, spiritus 'soul, courage, vigor, breath,' related to spirare 'to breathe'. The Hebrew word 'ruach' can mean "breath-wind-spirit" and refers to our inner Spirit, the consciousness.

"And (earth) was without form, and void; and darkness (was) upon the face of the deep. And the Ruach Elohim moved upon the face of the waters." - Genesis 1:2. This statement is wrong. There was no darkness upon the face of the Deep; there was (is) tridimensional, moving, live Light in infinite number of colors. This "water" does not have a face, does not have a surface, for it is all-pervading.

Real spirituality begins when connection is established. So, spiritual growth can be defined in that way. First, by accessing and acquiring that connection, so we no longer believe in God or theorize about our inner Self, but we Know it. We can experience it, we can taste it, we can touch it, we can talk to it, we can get information from it, and we can be One with it. We know what it is from experience. That is the beginning of real spiritual growth.

Tesla sensed the universe was "composed of a symphony of alternating currents with the harmonies played on an infinite range of octaves."

Vivekananda (Tesla's friend), who did so much to reveal the soul of India to the West, says: "According to the philosophers of India, the whole universe is composed of two materials, one of which they call akasha. It is the omnipresent all penetrating existence. Everything that has form, everything that is the result of the compounds, is evolved out of this akasha. It is the akasha that becomes the air that becomes the liquids, that becomes the solids; akasha becomes the sun, the earth, the moon, the stars, the comets; akasha becomes the body, the animal body, the planets, every form we see, everything that can be sensed, and everything that exists. It itself cannot be perceived (Yes it can, and a person can be one with it.); it is so subtle that it is beyond all ordinary perception; it can only be seen when it has become gross, has taken form (Not true; our SuperConscious mind can perceive it in its most basic form). At the beginning of creation there is only this akasha; at the end of the cycle the solids, the liquids, and the gases all melt into the akasha again, and the next creation similarly proceeds out of this akasha.

It is our SuperConscious mind that can perceive this level of existence. To accomplish seeing that which is invisible it adds to it infinite number of colors in infinite number of vibrations and variations.

Three thousand years ago.....Zoroaster:......" Life is not a privilege of this planet only, there exist huge number of planets with life in this infinite cosmic space. Life is a form of Cosmic energy and will manifest wherever favorable conditions occur."

"Sub-quantum kinetics proposes the existence of a primordial transmuting ether composed of subtle "etheron" particles. These continually react with one another in prescribed manners and also diffuse through space." Well, these 'particles' are forever changing, so they have no solid existence. They do not react with one another, because there is no space between them, allowing for individuality. They definitely are not prescribed. They do not diffuse through the space, they are the only space there is.

***

By gazing and using Tratak in this waking world a person can also reach the dreaming attention. The switch from a waking consciousness to being conscious in dreams is sometimes felt as a jolt of energy that transports you from one point to another. However when it is slowed down, the perception is of gradually slowly falling down the pale light tunnel in a counter clockwise direction, arriving to the 'other side'.

As time goes by, a Yogic Dreamer begins to recognize some form of energy in his dreams. As dreaming progresses, dream images seemingly become more and more real. It is very important at that time to remember and keep the idea in the mind you're dreaming a dream.

Subconscious mind is immense and our only weapons are double- arrow attention, double- arrow consciousness, empathy, and concentrated logical thinking. Most of the time the dreamer speaks in the term of what he sees, but must be kept in mind that all other senses should be developed equally.

CHAPTER FOURTEEN

CLEAR LIGHT

Experiencing death is very similar to entering a dream, difference being our senses can no longer access everyday world, the waking world, and our body energy, the life force will retreat from conscious Ego level at death of the body. There is one peculiar thing about this. Nails and hair still grow. At this moment, not a single cell out of 65 trillion has died. So called Death is not the end. Hundreds of genes remain active, continuing to synthesize molecules and perform many other tasks, up to four days after death. This is why our ancestors knew not to burry a person before four days because that person can still come back to life. Life-force connection did not completely separate yet.

Now we enter the world or of subconscious with no way of waking up.

Or everyday consciousness is like a little ball inside a huge subconscious ball, which is inside the infinite SuperConscious ball.

The object is to die consciously. When a person is aware, conscious, during the dissolution process liberation can be attained and a person can ascend. Normal process of sleep occur as consciousness withdraws from the senses and the mind loses itself in a dream world. In ordinary sleep consciousness is lost until the dreams arise. When dreams arise the sense of self is reconstituted through dualistic relationship with the images of the dream until the next deep sleep. Alternating periods of unconsciousness and dream make up a normal night sleep. For the absolutely pure awareness, which is the bases of our being, there is no sleep. It is always awake, it is always witnessing. When we develop the ability to be present, conscious, in that awareness we find that sleep is luminous. This light is Clear Light. It is our true nature, a base of everything that exists.

Dream Yoga develops lucidity in relationship to the dream images. But in Sleep Yoga there are no images. Sleep Yoga is imageless. This is the practice of direct recognition of awareness by awareness, like illuminating itself. It is not the light shining on anything, for there are no images of any kind. When Clear Light experience become stable even the images will not distract the dreamer. In an ultimate Clear Light experience there is neither subject nor object. If there is any identification whatsoever with the objects then there is no entry into the Clear Light. Actually, nothing enters the Clear Light; nothing can ever do that. The Clear Light is the base of the existence recognizing itself. Using dualistic language to describe the non-dual experience always results in a paradox. It is impossible to describe it by any words and by any means. The only way to know the Clear Light is to know it directly, to become one with it.

Emotional activities are primary cause of dreams known as Lucid dreams; the secondary causes our actions based on likes and dislikes.

Clear Light is defined in most spiritual textbooks is the unity of emptiness and clarity. It is the pure, empty awareness that is at the base of every human being and everything that exists in this infinite universe. You are the Clear Light, it is not an object of your experience or some kind of mental state. But even here we have a choice. We can create a Spirit Body, Crystal Body, the ultimate body.

Strong intent is the foundation of the dreaming practices. Develop a devotion to make an intent one pointed and powerful enough to pierce the clouds of unconsciousness that cover up the luminosity of the Clear Light. In normal dreams, as the external support of identity is lost, you also lose yourself, but in Yogic Dreaming, or Clear Light Dreaming, you're learning to exist without any support. When all sensory experience ceases it is very quiet, all the senses are shut and there is barely any contact with the external world.

The mind must have something to hold on to. If it does not have the light, it would grab something else. Before we have the experience of the Clear Light, pure consciousness, it is difficult to imagine how we can remain aware with neither a subject nor the objects. Awareness normally requires an object which is what is meant by consciousness being supported by a form or attribute. Sleep Yoga is not only a practice for sleep. It is a practice of remaining in a non-dual awareness continually throughout the four states of waking, sleeping, meditation, and death. One of the main obstacles to realizing the Clear Light of sleep is ordinary dream state. The Clear Light is meditative clear light, or consciousness clear light, thoughts are obscuration of clear light in the early stages of practice. Both in a dream and waking state there are many moments of life in which the natural clear light can be found, in fact it can be found at any moment. The Clear Light of death is obscured by afterlife visions. Clear Light of dreams is obscured by dream images, Clear Light of the waking state is obscured by images of existence.

CHAPTER FIFTEEN

SPIRIT VOYAGERS

"Keep walking, though there's no place to get to."- Rumi

Inner space is just as infinite as outer space.

Quantum laws tend to contradict common sense. At that level, one thing can be two different things simultaneously, and be at two different places at the same time. Two particles can be entangled and, when one changes its state, the other will also do so immediately, even if they are at opposite ends of the universe, seemingly acting faster than the speed of light.

Particles can also tunnel through solid objects, which should normally be impenetrable barrier. And now scientists have proven that, what is happening to a particle now, isn't governed by what has happened to it in the past, but by what state it is in the future, effectively meaning that, at a subatomic level, time can go backwards.

To bamboozle you further, this should all be going on right now in the subatomic particles which make up your body.

To illustrate how fast knowledge is changing, let's take a quick look at astronomy. At the turn of nineteenth century we believed there was only one galaxy, our own Milky Way. Now scientists estimate there are over 500 quadrillion galaxies in the universe, each with 100-200 billion stars. What will we believe in hundred years?!

Time itself is not moving. Only are our minds move. Our mind has a super-narrow slit we call present, and mind always goes into past and projects into is the future. But where is the present moment, and where does it disappear? The whole idea is absurd! How can the present move suddenly into nonexistence? It just can't? How can existence become nonexistence? How can the future which is at this very moment supposedly non-existential come into existence? Existence always remains existence and nonexistence will always remain nonexistence. Only our mind moves, it creates divisions of time.

The mind has a basic law: it can move to the opposites very easily, but it cannot remain in the middle. Balance is the most difficult thing for the mind, the extremes are always easy. Going to one or the other extreme is a big problem because in extreme you have chosen a half and the other half has been denied. The truth is the whole.

In the mind a person cannot find any center: thoughts change, feelings change, emotions come and go; it is a constant flux. You always remain ill at ease, and you can never be All. But there is also another layer of existence, the deepest. The first is the outer, objective, material world; science and its world. The second is the thought and emotional world. Then there is a third world, that of a spirit, and that is the world of consciousness, of a witness. The one who looks at the thoughts, and the emotions; the one that looks at everything. Does not matter what is happening, the onlooker remains the same; Witness is the only center.

***

Everything consciously experienced can be transcended: anything suppressed can never be transcended, can never be overcome.

Our reasoning power needs to develop, but often develops at the cost of the heart.

The center of our body is the naval, hara, the being center. Our heart is in feeling center and the head is in knowing center. Knowing is the furthest from being. Feeling is nearer. If you miss the feeling center, it is very difficult to create a bridge between reason and being. Heart means capacity to feel what others feel, head means capacity to know, and being means the capacity to be One. Japanese samurai, when facing each other, were on a verge of death. They would be thrown back to hara. Two superb warriors fighting with the sword, any moment the death is possible. In that type of fight mind goes into a zone where there are no thoughts. Thinking is way too slow. The second that thought would come the warrior would be cut down. They had to fight without thinking because thinking needs time.

It is same in us, in ordinary life when there is no danger, you think first then you are. In extreme danger, the whole process is reversed; you are first, only later you think. In conflict, in fight, in duel, and wars, man has always been seeking dangers.

The very structure of the mind is movement, movement in time; the structure of the higher consciousness is no movement, the silence.

A person can see its body structure from within, you actually see the bones, blood veins, you can hear your heart like a huge drum. It is even possible to see and feel your own spine center core. If that happens suddenly you will feel the explosion of the light within you.

Even if you get everything you wish, you become rich, powerful, you have everything you heart desires, you will still have a constant nagging sense that something is missing within you. The reason is that this something that is missing, is not related in any way to anything outward.

One basic thing is to be understood: the heart and the head centers are to be developed, not the naval center (hara, two inches below belly button); the naval center is just to be discovered there's nothing to develop there. Many enlightened persons are centered in the naval (hara, tantien). To the reason, to the brain, to thinking center, heart always looks childish, but to the heart brain seams useless, empty, superficial. Create a bridge between your head and your heart, and then all doors will become open.

***

Desire is nothing but your experience in search of another repetition again. Desire means just an old experience you want to repeat and again and nothing else. When it arises, do not place it on a person in question or on an object in question, remain centered, remain aware, and remain conscious. Remember that you are the source of that desire, so do not allow all of your attention to flow toward the objects. Return half of your attention. When you feel hate do not go to the object. Observe; what is the point from where the hate is coming?

The object of your hate is not the source; source is always within you. The other person or other thing is just a trigger. The source is hidden in your past. Someone (or something) is giving you a chance at this moment to be aware of your anger. Thank him/her immediately. Close your eyes, look within, look at the source, find the point where this anger is coming from. Be aware and you will find the source of that anger, or hate. Then learn how to harvest the energy of that, and every other emotion.

Our entire lives are just the preparation to be aware in death. Everything you do should be done with alertness, with awareness, with attention, with consciousness. The more awareness we have the more awareness we will attract. Surround yourself with those who have gone higher than you, be near them, be in their presence as often as possible, and your consciousness will grow higher and higher. Do not follow your teacher, walk side by side. If she/he cannot show you, and teach you, how to be like her, run as far as possible from her.

The common tendency of the mind is always to associate with inferiors; you feel superior there, and you feel you are somebody.

"If you do not change direction, you may end up where you are heading."- Lao Tzu

In a provocative new paper in Behavioral and Brain Sciences, a team led by Dr. Ezequiel Morsella at San

Francisco State University came to a startling conclusion: "Consciousness is no more than a passive machine running one simple algorithm, to serve up what's already been decided, and take credit for the decision."

Rather than a stage conductor, it's just a tiny part of what happens in the brain that makes us "aware." All the real work goes on under the hood, in our subconscious minds. The Passive Frame Theory goes like this: nearly all the decisions and thoughts that need to be made throughout the day are performed by many parts of the unconscious brain, well below our level of awareness.

When the time comes to physically act on a decision, various unconscious processes deliver their opinions to a central "hub," like voters congregating at town hall. The hub listens in on the conversation, but doesn't participate; all it does is provide a venue for differing opinions to integrate and decide on a final outcome. Once the subconscious makes a final decision on how to physically act (or react), the hub, consciousness, executes that work and then congratulates itself for figuring out a tough problem. Similar to the screenwriter, consciousness doesn't debate or solve conflict in our heads; consciousness needs to be "on" in order to relay the final outcome, so it is essential, but it doesn't participate in decision-making.

When you speak, you're only consciously aware of a few words at a time, and that is only so you can direct the muscles around your mouth and tongue to form those words. What you're saying is prescribed behind the curtain; your conscious mind is simply following a script.

***

There is no doubt that mental patients, alcoholics, and drug addicts see visions, some good some bad. But these visions do not have any objective existence. The problem also arises when a person totally aligns himself with the subconscious Self; such allegiance can only result in a loss of touch with objective reality. The one-sided allegiance to the Ego leads to the destruction of subjective reality, and therefore the loss of universal reality. The Ego controls without concern, and the Self is concerned without control. The first state is emotionless the second state is hysterical. The Self is an experience, unique personal subjective experience. But not always, there are ways for that to be objective, shared experience, like in cases of mutual hypnosis and group dreams.

The laws of magic, the subjective world, are exact reverse opposites of the laws of science, the laws of logic. This is the reason why the Self or those who fall under its influence cannot produce anything objective. They steal from the Ego creations and reverse things; like upside down cross, upside down pentagram, reverse swastika, etc.

The magical spell cannot cause anything to happen, just like ordinary prayer cannot. What these practices can do is to put you into frame of the mind where you can be in touch with magical aspects of your own being, at least potentially. Magic cannot be caused just like electricity cannot be made, it can only be gathered. The dynamo of the generator gathers electricity it does not make or manufacture electricity. Similarly a good magician gathers magic.

Whatever you gain through any spiritual methods, let it remain a secret. Do not brag about it, do not talk about it. Use it only for teaching purposes. Keep it inside you, let it remain pure. Only then will it be used for inner transformation.

When your energy moves to the Third Eye, you will come to know the light without the source; it is not coming from any source and yet it is there. Pure consciousness is another side of the world of objects. Senses are just in the middle. From the senses doors swing both ways; you can move toward the objects, or you can move to your own center. "Distance" is about the same.

Travel this world with awareness, learn from it and further develop yourself. Take your evolution into your own hands.

Travel the dream world with awareness. Develop your Dream Body to the point where it is as useful as your 'physical' body. Then comes the time to become familiar with your Spirit Body, which is immortal.

We are all potential shamans and healers, for as we metabolize the darkness and assimilate our own demons, we add light to and "lighten-up" the collective shadow for everyone. We are all Shamans-in-training.

Spirit Travelers develop and expand the limits of normal perception. Great Spirit is a watcher of witness consciousness itself. The dream world is not rational, not logical; in a dream world we can only intend and act. Dreamers are capable of dreaming without sleeping. During the day they conduct their activities like everyone else, they engage in a normal expected everyday behavior. During the night, they become dreamers. They systematically dream dreams that break the boundaries of what is considered being a reality. They are able to dream while being fully 'awake', fully conscious.

In a mutual dream world it is possible to communicate without words, telepathically, directly from one mind to another. Homing device, the calling device in mutual dreams, or group dreams, are the feelings that one has for another and the image that a person, a caller can create in his/her mind.

Oneironauts must learn to separate two tracks, the track of everyday affairs and the track of dreams; since each one of those had a very different state of awareness. The priority is to check the reality of the dreams first to see if a person is dreaming or awake; it is necessary to confirm with no doubt whatsoever that a person is awake. One way over confirming if you are in a dream state is to rely on a feeling of a dream body. If you trying to feel something bodily like a pinch or scratch and it does not come back, then you're dreaming.

In a dream world time normally passes same is in a waking world but in many instances it can be radically different.

Freedom is a total absence of the concern about yourself. To fix things in memory, it is good to experience the experience twice. Dreamers know something greater exists than what our senses can perceive. Dreamers are not involved in measuring time. They use it and stretch it, or compress it just by intent. To reach a degree of knowledge the dreamers have to work twice as hard as normal people. The dreamers have to make sense of everyday world as well as a dream world to accomplish things. Spirit Travelers have to be highly skilled and sophisticated mentally as well as physically. When in a conscious dream world we have access to direct knowledge; advanced dreamers are perfectly able to align themselves with it because they are able to give up what defines them either as a man or a woman, among other things. The difference between advanced Lucid Dreamer and an ordinary person is the Yogic Dreamer enters into a state of conscious dreaming at will.

The dream world is also populated by monsters, demons, flying dragons, and all kinds of ugly things you can imagine. But of course, they are just an impersonal energy driven by our fears and the programs installed into our mind; this makes that impersonal energy into hellish creatures.

Conscious dreamer's mythology belongs to a subconscious world. The dream world is brought into being by concentrated desire of those who are participating in it; similar to our everyday world which is being held together by every living thing within it.

Freedom for a dreamer can be attained only by dreaming without hope and by being willing to lose it all, even the dream itself. Dreamer dreams without the hope, struggles with no goal in mind, for a reality is there is no such a thing as the ultimate goal. Advanced dreamer is able to perceive energy in a dream world and then transfer the ability to our everyday world. In so called waking reality we perceive surfaces but never underlying energy.

Intent, the true will power is the principle underneath everything.

Before birth a human being is not split in two. There is no imposed quality, but upon the birth the two parts are separated by mankind's intent, teachings and experiences. One part turns outward and becomes the physical body and the other turns inward that becomes a subconscious dream world. At death the Ego disintegrates and the body returns to earth to be absorbed by it; and the light part, the dreamer, the subconscious, becomes free, but unfortunately since the dream body was never perfected it experiences freedom for only an instant before it's discarded into the universe. If you die without erasing our false dualism of body and mind, you die an ordinary death. Before death that duality needs to be transcended. All other life attainments are meaningless in comparison. This is the only attainment that makes sense.

CHAPTER SIXTEEN

RECAPITULATION

The recapitulation technique makes a space for something new to be introduced into our being. The recapitulation technique consist of writing a list of all the important people you have met from the present to the very beginning. Take the first person on it and recollect everything you can about that person; every single detail. It is better to recapitulate from the present going back to the past because the memories of the present or fresh. What practitioners do is to recollect and breathe. Inhale slowly and deliberately fanning the head up and down in a barely noticeable swing and exhale in the same fashion. Start with your mom and dad first and try to remember everything about them.

The problem with the recapitulation is it stirs up all the garbage of our lives and brings it to the surface.

Temptation to rationalize things and think it out must be resisted; reasoning can only get you so far. Intent to recall must be exercised. Awareness of what fear can do on any level must also be understood.

The reason average people lack willpower in their dreams is that they never remember their lives, which are filled to capacity with heavily loaded emotions, memories, hopes, and fears. The more the memories, loaded with heavy emotions, come to light, to the awareness, the less dreams become chaotic and scary. Remembering and dreaming go hand-in-hand, as we recollect our lives especially early lives, dreaming will become clearer. This remembering sets energy free. It is presently imprisoned within us. Recapitulation frees the energy that is still running programs, imprinted long time ago, that are not necessary anymore.

(Transcendendal Rebirting is very effective method to uncover past events trapped behind the curtain.) Recollection technique becomes very effective if is combined with a natural, rhythmic breathing. Long exhalation are performed as the head moves gently and slowly down and long inhalation are taken as the head moves up. These recollections can be organized by reconstructing the events by family, sexual relationships, jobs, spouse, friends, etc. Object being to remember the things that are behind the curtains and the programs that have been established in very early years of life. On the exhalation try to eject energy deposited in you.

During the memory being recapitulated on the inhalation pull back the energy people themselves left behind. This remembering creates instantaneous tridimensional virtual live pictures in a subconscious mind. When we review past actions and feelings, the memory oscillates between the present site we are at, and the site that was occupied when event being remembered took place. It's a very effective technique that can recover some of the energy trapped in a past programs.

The Recapitulation, Recollection, Remembering, in this context, is the act of calling back the energy we have already spent during our lives and past actions. To recapitulate means recalling all important people we have met, all the places we have seen, and all the feelings, and emotions we have had, in our entire lives, starting from the present back to the earliest memories. But it would take another lifetime to do so. So we chose what to recall. Only events that had a high energetic and emotional charge are chosen. We sweep the memories, clean them one by one, with the sweeping breath.

Inhale through the nose as you hook onto the memory by gently raising the head and closed eyes up, 'look' into the center of the head and then exhale slowly, lowering the head and eyes, concentrating on hara which is two inches below the belly button. In China it is called Lower Tantien, loosely translated as 'elixir field', 'field of cinnabar', 'sea of qi', or simply 'energy center'. It is second chakra. Hara also means 'sea of energy', being the center of the etheric or chi body.

This point can store unlimited energy. This is our 'second brain' connected to our brain by a vagus nerve. Inhaling allows for energy that was lost to be pulled back; while exhaling permits us to transmute undesirable energy that has accumulated in us. It is of utmost importance recapitulation is done consciously, other words in a double-arrow mode. If your awareness slips repeat the motion.

Interacting with our fellow humans led to many negative emotions and feelings. Normally, the energy spent on living is gone forever from us. If we use the recapitulation technique, we have a chance to get to those negative energies and recover some of them. When doing this technique try your absolute best to feel the emotions that were involved in a particular memory or even a feeling. It is important to re-experience the event, feelings and emotions in as much detail as possible and grab them with your breath thereby releasing ones trapped energy within those memories. FEEL the way your body felt at that moment, what emotions were you experiencing, what were you thinking?

You should begin by making a list of all important people you have met, starting from a present and going back to your earliest memories. Set the scene, breathing with head movement up and down and keep on breathing until there is no feelings, and there is no emotions, 'till the scenery is flat. This is how you know that you have accomplished the technique properly. While doing this technique you should be aware of the feelings and emotions you have created, and energy that was trust into you by others.

Because sexual energy is the only energy that ordinary person is aware of and experienced it directly, we must start recapitulation by focusing our consciousness on our past sexual activity. This is where bulk of our energy is confined. This is why these memories need to be freed first.

Recapitulation is remembering, or more precisely, reliving. It is the bodily recovering all past experiences. Recapitulation is a natural act. It is the last act the living being does just before disintegration of their individuality, which is death. It happens to everyone just before the moment of death; the time of last remembering. Time is altered. Life memories are played backwards. When it is finished there is a burst of total awareness. It lasts only several seconds before death itself arrives. That awareness is normally swallowed up by the fifth-element. Dying person in the moment of death, thanks to recapitulation, becomes pure consciousness, pure awareness. Everyone is going to die and everyone will recollect. The effects of recapitulation or remembering are too far-reaching to be ignored. Remembering is more like a sense memory having to do with feelings. In ordinary remembering it is the Ego that is remembering by means of thinking process. To this imagination is added. In the recapitulation it is the body remembering, and it does so by liberating the feelings stored in it. It is very important that with every memory a person remembers the feelings and emotions of that particular memory. So recapitulation is the relieving your experiences.

But why bother with past? These events are recorded in our mind-body system and they're still active as if it's happening now.

Typical examples would be houses in which I have lived, love relationship, family relationship, friend relationships, work relationships, school relationships, etc.

Sit in a meditative position. Spinal column must be straight, but not stiff or rigid, eyes closed. Facing forward with the lungs empty. Movements and breathing should be slow and synchronized. You are back to the starting point. Central element in exhalation and it purpose is to separate or detach, refine and transmute during recapitulation, and re-experience moments in which energy filaments from other people become attached to our own energy. Exhalation liberates the body of foreign energy and liberates and transmutes the promises that can no longer, or should no longer, be honored. Let me be clear, this exhalation most be coupled with double-arrow awareness and Intent. There is no other reality other than the one which you feel. Reality is a feeling.

So recapitulation is not remembering something that happened and is no longer existing; it rather represents an encounter with something that continues to operate in us right down to the present moment, profoundly affecting each instant of our present life. Recapitulation is a very important technique that can open the doorway to freedom. For those who recapitulate their lives certain memories open. When we understand the importance of what transpired we can be very perplexed as how in the world we could forget such a huge impact.

Do the recapitulation barefoot. Recapitulate so that the body is not constrained in any way by tight clothing, belt, bra etc. Remove glasses or contact lenses. Recapitulation is a magical act in which Intent and the breath play indispensable rules. Breathing gathers energy and makes us circulate it. What we experience in wakefulness in terms of energy we can practice in dreams, and whatever power we experience in dreams should be used while we are awake. What really counts is being aware regardless of whether one is awake or asleep. Ancient sages claimed it is feasible for one's personal awareness to link up knowingly with all-encompassing awareness of Tao, the Existence, then when the death comes one's individual awareness is not dispersed as in ordinary dying but expands and unites with a greater whole.

Take the first person on your list and work your memory to recall everything experienced with that person from the moment you met to the last time you have interacted. If you prefer you can work backwards from the last time you have dealings with that person to your first encounter.

Recapitulation is an exercise to recall, review, release, and recharge your energy. All of your experiences have been stored inside your energy fields. In recapitulation the important thing is to experience the events in as much detail as possible, not so much thinking about them but experiencing them on an energy level, on a feeling and emotional level. This is not an ease method, it needs a lot of practice.

Now as you breathe in intend your breath to pull in the energy of the event, person, or feeling you're working with. Feel yourself connected with your subject of attention and use your breath to bring that energy into your body. The dreamer needs to enter fully the energy of a recapitulation. As you tap your memories, as you access them, work with all the items surrounding the event, to the people involved, and to your feelings and emotions. Let your body do the work. Pay a double -arrow attention to how the body feels and how it felt when you're recalling particular memory. Allow yourself to relive the occurrence without indulging, always being in a self-remembering, self-conscious mode. When accessing the particular energy of particular feeling and emotion let the purified energy from the hara discharge throughout your body. Later, when you are fully experienced in work of life review, recollection, remembering, it can be done anywhere and at any time. A word of caution, if done without double-arrow, it is just another daydream, costing you more energy. When an individual is close to death human awareness is a subject to a huge force which can only collect individual's awareness. The recapitulation technique evens the flow of energy making it fluid and nonreactive, transparent. Now you are like pure Crystal Human. Since this external force encounters no resistance there is nothing for it to act on. Individual awareness thereby remains intact as it passes through the force.

During the recapitulation we should review all the promises we have made in our lifetime, especially the ones made in haste or ignorance or faulty judgment. For unless we deliberately retrieve our intent, our decisions, from them, we will never become free in the present moment. Anything we do is really an expression of our inner state. Your inner state is reflected in the way you move, talk, eat or do anything else.

In Recollection, tense, gross, draining, enslaving energy is scrubbed, cleansed by breath and double-arrow and deposited into hara, center of our being.

But why are we recapitulating? Why are we remembering, recalling, reviewing our lives? What is the purpose of it? First, this is not ordinary remembering but bodily remembering significant energy impacts in your life. You are making a carbon copy of your life experiences. At the time of death when all your senses are shutting off for the last time, body chemistry stops, huge amount of energy becomes available for few seconds. Dying person faces a mirror of SuperConsciousness. In a normal circumstance Ego disintegrates and this unstoppable force sucks out the memories. This is what Existence is after. Advanced Spirit Traveler substitutes a carbon copy of his life memories and offers them to the Existence. Original memories are preserved and Ego remains intact free to dance a cosmic dance, to the tune the Existence plays.

Recapitulation method can also be done in the dream world, remembering both dream events and waking events.

CHAPTER SEVENTEEN

SUN YOGA

Nikola Tesla: "My idea is that the development of life must lead to forms of existence that will be possible without nourishment and which will not be shackled by consequent limitations. Why should a living being not be able to obtain all the energy it needs for the performance of its life functions directly from the environment, instead of through consumption of food, and transforming, by a complicated process, the energy of chemical combinations into life-sustaining energy?"

Sun gazing (also known as sun-eating) is a strict practice of gradually introducing sunlight into your eyes at the lowest ultraviolet-index times of day–sunrise and sunset. Those who teach the practice say there are several rules to the practice. First, it must be done within 44 minutes after sunrise or before sunset to avoid damaging the eyes. Second, you must be barefoot, in contact with the actual earth–sand, dirt or mud; and finally, you must begin with only 10 seconds the first day, increasing by 10 second intervals each day you practice. Following these rules make the practice safe, says sources.

When you see the sun sitting on the horizon, it is not there really. It's actually below the edge of the horizon, but our atmosphere acts like a lens and bends the sun's image just above the horizon, allowing us to see it.

This effect lengthens the amount of daylight for several minutes or more each day; we end up seeing the sun for a few minutes in the morning before it has risen and for a few extra minutes in the evening after it actually already has set. Sun's disk is already about one diameter below the horizon when sunset is observed. Sun rises three minutes earlier than it would if the Earth had no atmosphere, and sets three minutes later.

Hira Ratan Manek was originally from India and is commonly referred to as HRM.

HRM has allegedly subsisted, and lived off the sun's energy since June 18th, 1995. That is right, he has not eaten solid food in 12 years. He has been studied by various researchers, such as the Thomas Jefferson University, and the University of Pennsylvania. Not only have they found his claims to be true, but medical evidence suggests this man is healthier than a normal person of his age.

In Brazil, Australia, Germany, over 3,000 people are subsisting on light. This is a rebirth of a science that was practiced long time ago. Originally this was a spiritual practice in the ancient times and now it is slowly becoming a scientific practice.

Hira Ratan Manek submitted himself to NASA for scientific testing to confirm that he does indeed possess the almost 'superhuman' ability of not eating, gained through his dedication. Funded by NASA, a team of medical doctors at the University of Pennsylvania observed Hira 24 hours a day, 7 days a week for 100 days. NASA confirmed that he could indeed survive largely on light with occasionally a small amount of buttermilk or water during this time.

Since food gets its energy from the sun, it is said to be readily available to sun-eaters without the trouble of digestion. Though hunger is said to eventually cease, it is fine to continue eating regularly during initial stages, until appetite disappears naturally.

After nine months of sun-gazing, reaching a maximum of 44 minutes, it is advised that you give up sun-gazing and redirect your attention now to the Earth. Shri Manek's method: ....is to be practiced standing BAREFOOT on BARE EARTH. No wearing shoes, and no standing on concrete, stone or even on grass in a meadow or lawn (The grass absorbs the solar energy). One has to stand either on sand or on gravel/mud/ earth. Bare feet have to be in contact with the bare earth.

Here I would like to know was any scientific investigation done on this?

Science discovered bacteria that survives on nothing but electricity, rather than food, they eat and excrete pure electrons. These bacteria yet again prove the almost miraculous tenacity of life. As you may recall from high school biology, almost every living organism consumes sugar to survive. When it gets right down to it, everything you eat is ultimately converted or digested into single molecules of glucose. Without going into the complexities of respiration and metabolism, these sugars have excess electrons, and the oxygen you breathe in really wants those electrons. By ferrying electrons from sugar to oxygen - a flow of electrons, energy is created, which is then used to carry out various vital tasks around your body (triggering other electrons, beating of heart, etc.) These special bacteria, however, don't need sugars; instead, they cut out the middleman and feed directly on electrons. Well, we are supposed to be a superior creation.

When we cultivate the garden, it absorbs the energy from the sun and makes things grow. The sun gives its energy to the Earth and causes things to flourish. If you allow sun's light to enter your body, your energy will flourish. It does not matter what you (on a good side of the coin) do as long as you are self-conscious and harvest energy with your actions and transform it into a personal power. The human body has an extra energy system that comes into play when we are under extreme stress. Stress happens any time you do anything to excess.

To practice Moving Sun Yoga find a wide open area where you have a clear view of the sunrise. You are standing facing the sun. Your gaze is relaxed, you're in a double-arrow attention. Arms hanging down, palms facing toward the sun. You are using Transcendental Rebirthing breath, fill in the lower lungs by pushing your tummy out with diaphragm, then fill middle and then all the way up to the clavicles. Slow, long full breath. At the very beginning of the sunrise begin to trot slowly in the place and gradually increase your speed of movement and breath as the sun rises. Keep increasing the speed of trot and increase both speed and volume of breath. By the time the sun is completely risen above the horizon your arms should be extended horizontally in front of you and open toward the sun. By this point your legs should be moving at maximum possible speed with your knees rising as high as possible. Use emotions to increase your movement. This exercise should be done until there is a feeling of internal energy, or complete exhaustion, a burning sensation, ecstasy, or some other climatic experience. Here include the maximum time allowed for Sun Yoga. You can do this method safely up to twenty minutes. A person should be barefoot; and sometime the earth energy can be felt rising up through the legs up the spine all the way up to the head after all our planet from an energetic point of view is just a huge ball of energy. Hands are by now open wide to the left and to the right, palms toward the sun.

***

Sunyogi Umasankar is teaching Sun Yoga for past ten years. Now his followers number an estimated 10,000 people throughout India. During his three month period of concentrating on the sun, Umasankar-ji had developed a great interest in how trees and plants can receive energy directly from sunlight. His discoveries now made him believe he had found a way of absorbing the sun's energy directly into his body, charging his body's cells with kinetic energy and therefore removing the need to eat food. So, as an experiment, Umasankar-ji stopped eating breakfast and continued concentrating on the sun. Six months later, he stopped eating his dinner, then six months after that, he stopped eating food at all. From the 17th August until the 7th December 1996, Umasankar-ji stopped eating and sleeping altogether. His body weight remained the same, and he continued his daily routine working in the ashram in a perfect state of health. Shortly after this period of his life, he began his journey through India teaching his discoveries to people he met along the way. During his travels, he has become a source of great interest to a number of scientific and medical research centers where he had his claims tested, examined and verified–at least up to the level of sophistication that modern scientific instruments are capable of reaching.

***

A solar flare is a burst of light, radiation and intelligent energy which erupts from the sun's magnetic atmosphere. Solar flares affect all layers of the solar atmosphere, when the plasma is heated into millions of kelvins, the flares produce radiation across the electromagnetic spectrum at all wavelengths. These light frequencies range from radio waves to gamma rays although most of the energy is spread over frequencies outside the visible spectrum to the naked eye.

Listening to some of these sun gurus it is obvious they are under the powerful influence of the subconscious mind. If technique is physical, science should be able to measure its benefits and detriments.

If you watch some of the videos on sun yoga, you might notice followers not claiming to be food free and gurus going back to eating food supposedly not to upset the followers when they offer it. The amazing part is that science did not examine this in more detail to reach undeniable conclusion. Assertion of not needing food has staggering implications for this planet. You would think enormous attention would be payed to it.

New timeline marks the early initiation that ends the rule of the King of Tyranny archetype and its continual abuse of power through technological mind control upon the earth. The awakening is illuminating return as the Spiritual Sun behind the Sun, returning benevolence merged with true power. However, the end of the rule of the material tyrant must be internally and spiritually chosen by the individual.

For many on the earth this archetype has become a bad addiction of victim/victimizer polarity that may be hard to break free of. The ending of control requires the spiritual responsibility to end all victim related patterns. Humanity must wake up from its bad dream and find the courage to imagine new consciousness possibilities as we free ourselves from the past grips of tyranny.

The main Solar Body (our visible Sun) is undergoing an evolution in that its magnetic pole is reversing which is further altering its Solar Ray transmissions to Earth.

Uma Sankar Sunyogi taught Sun Yoga to over two million people. He suggests moving the eyes upwards and 30 degree backwards, concentrating on the middle of your head, where Pineal gland is located. (but than with this technique gazing at the sun is not necessary) If done properly sun yoga can give many benefits. If done improperly, great damage, like with everything else in our life.

Can we safely look at the sun other than at sunrise and sunset? The trick is to look in brief snatches at the physical sun through the corner of your eyes (peripheral vision) maintaining a constant awareness/knowledge of the suns position throughout the day and have that carry over into your dreams as a lucidity trigger.

Passive method uses meditative approach, either standing up or even better sitting down, using meditative posture. Use peripheral vision (defocus the eyes) to gaze at the sun. You can do this safely at the beginning of the sunrise for 20 minutes, even the first time, gradually increasing the time by one minute every day to reach maximum of 44 minutes. Put attention between and behind your eyes, in the centre of the head, and when you concentrate there, you might feel sun's vitality entering and glowing inside your head.

Healing powers of the sun and the spiritual practices of Sun Gazing and Surya (Sun) Yoga is known for thousands of years. During the day, it is safe to gaze at Sun through the UV shielded glasses. Be careful, never overdo things.

You will notice rapid movements and colors around sun's corona. This doesn't have anything to do with movement on the sun's surface nor corona. It is how our eyes see and focus through saccades at subconscious level.

All things have an inner and outer life, and that includes the sun. We may say there is the outer sun of the material universe, and there is also the metaphysical sun of the psychic universe. They operate simultaneously, being the same thing. It is amazing; dream sun is just as bright as waking world sun. The sun truly awakens us in the deepest sense. As the germinating seed struggles upward toward the sun and out into its life-giving rays, so all higher forms of life reach out for the sun, which acts as a metaphysical magnet, drawing them upward and outward toward ever-expanding consciousness. The Chandogya Upanishad discusses it in this way: "Even as a great extending highway runs between two villages, this one and that yonder, even so the rays of the sun go to both these worlds, this one and that yonder. They start from the yonder sun and enter into the nadis (energy channels in our body). They start from the nadis and enter into the yonder sun. When a man departs from this body, then he goes upwards by these very rays, or he goes up with the thought of Om. As his mind is failing, he goes to the sun. That, verily, is the gateway of the world, an entering in for the knowers, a shutting out for the non-knowers."

The solar rays do not just strike the surface of our body, but actually penetrate into the physical nerves (nadis). The nadis are also the 'channels in the astral body' that correspond to the physical nerves. Just as the electrical impulses flow through the physical nerves, the subtle life force, or prana, flows through the subtle nadis and keeps us alive and functioning. The prana, then, is a vehicle for the solar energies that produce evolution.

***

Giri Bala employs a certain yoga techniques which enable

her to live without eating. Her close neighbor in Nawabganj near Ichapur made it a point to watch her closely; never did he find evidence she was taking either food or drink. His interest finally mounted so high he approached the Maharaja of Burdwan and asked him to investigate. Astounded at the story, he invited her to his palace. She agreed to a test and lived for two months locked up in a small section of his home. Later she returned for a palace visit of twenty days; and then for a third test of fifteen days. The Maharaja himself said that these three rigorous scrutiny had convinced him beyond doubt of her non-eating state.

Giri:"From the age of twelve years four months down to my present age of sixty-eight period of over fifty-six years I have not eaten food or taken liquids. "But you do eat something!"- My tone held a note of remonstrance.

"Of course!"- She smiled in swift understanding.

"Your nourishment derives from the finer energies of the air and sunlight, and from the cosmic power which recharges your body through the medulla oblongata." As I left the river bank, my wet cloth around me, in the broad glare of day my master materialized himself before me!

"Dear little one" he said in a voice of loving compassion, "I am the guru sent here by God to fulfill your urgent prayer. He was deeply touched by its very unusual nature! From today you shall live by the astral light, your bodily atoms fed from the infinite current."

"He initiated me into a kria technique which frees the body from dependence on the gross food of mortals. The technique includes the use of a certain mantra and a breathing exercise more difficult than the average person could perform. No medicine or magic is involved; nothing beyond the kria."

We had recorded for posterity many photographs of the only woman in the world who has lived without food or drink for over fifty years. From 1923 until her death in 1962,

Therese Neumann professed to have consumed no food other than The Holy Eucharist, nor to have drunk any water from 1926 until her death.

***

The most powerful sun yoga is Dream Sun Yoga. Gazing with your dream eyes at the dream sun.

For a dreamer the real division is between the physical body which houses the mind, and the dream body which houses our energy. As long as positive or negative forces are in balance they cancel each other out, and that means that their ultimate charge is zero. It also means that person cannot get upset when somebody criticizes them nor can they be pleased when somebody praises them.

So called Third Eye human state is the one in which mind is free from the body.

The Third Eye gazes inwardly and is immovable; and so is infinity looking back at you.

The true sun you are supposed to gazing at/contemplating is the Etheric Sun of the Dreaming. Followed by the Astral "Sun behind the Sun," not the Physical/Material sun.

Our physical body must remain absolutely still, suspended as if it were in a deep sleep. The difficulty lies in convincing our physical body to cooperate, to entirely give up its control. So we must let our body feel as if it is sound asleep by deliberately removing your awareness from it. When the body is asleep, and the mind is awake and if there are no thoughts and no emotions; the dream body wakes up and takes over. At that point the body is asleep; the dream body comes into being and is fully conscious; it knows it is in a dream world.

Intending in a dream world is not done by our thoughts; intending is done by your intent which is the layer beyond our thoughts and emotions.

The dream body is in communication with universe and life-force, and in a dream world the energy can be perceived in things just by intending it.

On the one hand we are as real as we can be; an on the other hand we are only empty appearances. Spirit Voyagers learn how to focus their attention with infinitely more force and precision than an ordinary person.

For Spirit Voyager there is no room for defeat. Soul Travelers have only one path open to them; that is to succeed in whatever they intend.

In a dream world we need to learn to scan things using the quick glances. If you stare the things those things suck you in; suck your attention. If you decide to make your hands a starting point, scan the surroundings of the dream world quickly, and then always come back to the starting point, your hands. This will now greatly increase your consciousness and the power of your intent.

Ego is made up of words, it is a description. Psychosis has to do with falling structure of reality, and the Ego of an insane person is really one with the internal uncontrolled process of the restructuring the Ego. While psychotics are immersed in madness not of their own choosing, Spirit Travelers are involved in transmuting the Ego harmoniously. We are the ones who did all the work forming the Ego, so we possess the ability of 'erasing' it and creating another one in its place, one created by us intentionally. Our true identity is a field of energy, and not the Ego made of thoughts and memories. In a recapitulation we are dealing with a body memory which is marked much nearer to the feeling than to the reasoning power. Spirit Warriors make the awareness of inevitable death their corner stone of knowledge and struggle.

One absolutely sure event of life is death itself. Using death as an advisor is a form of non-doing. When you're facing big problems, when you feel a worn-out by life just remember your death. Compare your present problem and the situation and measure it against the fact of your inevitable death. When you place anything alongside death and examine it carefully everyday problems pale in comparison. We are all alive and death reaches for each one of us. That's the only thing that matters; the rest is just a small stuff.

Ego usually wants to brag, to reveal what you're actually doing. Thoughts are what makes up the basic nature of the Ego; thoughts are the substance the Ego is made of.

We can convert a simple walk into walk of awareness. We can turn consciousness into meditative consciousness just by using double- arrow attention.

Advanced Lucid Dreaming requires a special form of attention. Generally it is a capacity of awareness to give the order to the reality encountered beyond the ordinary description of the world. In a dream world we cannot stare at the particular image without transforming it into an image of something else. In ordinary reality we should strive to use peripheral vision to achieve inner silence and to perceive reality as a whole rather than as a fragmented and contradictory. In a dream world what is required is ability to focus. To sustain the vision, instead of using the peripheral vision, we use quick focused glances. Doing on one side of awareness becomes a non-doing on the other side. We can create points of contact between the two sides, of the dream world and everyday world and gradually integrate both sides of awareness into a single unit. Eventually the practice of conscious dreaming develops a dream body to the point it becomes very functional; to the point it's not only functional in a dream world but is useful in our everyday affairs.

***

In Dreaming you use your intent, your willpower to move you, instead of walking. Focus on where want to move to, will it, and let your eyes move you. As in any space you need to be able to orientate yourself. In a dream space also, and you should be able to control dream time. A Dreamer needs to begin by choosing a selected place during a day or at night. The next step is to choose exact time, exact hour in which you are asleep and dreaming. Making the time coincide with the time of the external events of the everyday world. When you can make the time and space coincide with that of the everyday affairs, you're ready to begin to influence your daily life using your dreaming body. When you're capable of controlling the time and place of your dreaming, you can verify directly whether your dreaming is taking place during the same time as your everyday world by having an encounter with your 'physical' body asleep in bed. Then simply look at yourself. More often than not this is just another dream.

To be in a mutual or shared dream experience requires that both persons should be able to control time and the place of the dreaming.

Worldview is not some kind of truth. It is a technique learned in early formative years. It is learnt from other humans. In the case of twin sisters in India who at birth were thrown into the forest and brought up by wolves, even though they had a human body, their worldview was that of wolves. Any worldview is a coherent and organized set of assumptions about reality that really doesn't have nothing to do with what reality actually is. Whatever type of the world view we are participating in, our memories, even our primordial memories, shape that view.

All objects, be it physical, mental or emotional are just different forms of energy; and all that exists is from a single source, from the fifth element. So the entire universe is made of energy; first in a form, later the form is made up by our ability of creation. Fully functional Spirit Travelers learn to perceive the world of energy.

Our source of finer energy is our breath. If our breath is shallow, our energy is definitely not optimal. Food is a source of a gross energy in our body. Poor diet distorts your energy field. Many of our moods could be the results of it eating dead processed foods. We need to think of all four elements, air, water, earth and fire (sunshine) as the food. But we are immersed in the fifth element. As we breathe the air and get the energy from water, sun and earth, Spirit Voyager 'breathes' Akash- the fifth element.

A sense of humor and ability to laugh at yourself is essential for the Spirit Traveler. This ability counteracts the sheer power of the spirit world. One of the keys for well-being of the Spirit Traveler is to look for fun in the world and have fun with everything. Always try to do your best without concern for the outcome of any activity. Expectations are detrimental, a very powerful obstacle on a spiritual path. Use a double -arrow attention when you notice criticizing someone, judging them. You should immediately examine yourself for this exact same faults. To develop this sense of observation, just imagine yourself observing yourself from about 2-3 feet in the back of yourself. Always act without any expectations of any reward especially when it comes to the supernatural abilities.

CHAPTER EIGHTEEN

DARKLIGHT MEDITATION

"Darkness within darkness. The gateway to all understanding."- Lao Tzu

Darkness has a bad rap. Most of us look at the color black and see nothing useful or pleasant about its essence. We are programed to think of evil, fear, hatred, and loneliness as we peer down a dark alley or sit in an unlit room. But we have in our skin and within our nervous system a melanin molecule that is absolutely black. It never releases any light it has swallowed, so there is no way to know what transpires inside.

Moreover, fear of darkness belongs to the lower nature, to the lower self, and in approaching the higher Self fear must be put aside, before we can enter into SuperConscious presence.

The darkness is a primal force aiding us in our personal and spiritual development. If we embrace it for a longer period, we experience an ever deeper healing, a reconnection with ourselves, the universe and higher powers. Retreating into darkness, be it in caves, or closed chambers, is a custom found in all traditional cultures, particularly in Japan, India and Tibet. Pythagoras even built an underground chamber beneath his house where he spent a lot of time in the dark. According to the pre-Buddhist Bön religion in Tibet, Darkness Retreats represent the "golden road to meditation". Using the night as a tool for sensory deprivation and de-conditioning is a self-discovery; procedure known across all cultures and religions. Darkness Retreats are the primordial way to enlightenment. Spending a certain amount of time in complete darkness helps to shut off the mind's biggest distraction–our sense of vision. Since we aren't used to living in the darkness, our range of possible activities and preoccupations also decreases. As a natural consequence expanded states of consciousness occur; that is if you are using a double-arrow technique.

Everybody knows about Himalaya caves, but even North African Christian Desert Fathers for first three centuries of NE still knew the technique. They entered the tombs at grave yards and stayed overnight 'fighting evil spirits'.

After a few days in the dark, your physiology goes into night mode. Deep relaxation and many stress releases are felt. Aside from a heightened sense of touch and hearing, we naturally engage in an internal 'dialogue' with our subconscious mind.

***

Belief is one thing but reality is entirely different thing. Eleven members of the Kogi, a remote indigenous tribe along Colombia's Caribbean coast were killed after a lightning bolt hit a roofed hut where they were gathered. Obviously their supposed perception of 26-Dimensions did not help them when Mother Aluna struck. Sometime we have a tendency to aggrandize native peoples.

Also fifteen members of the Wiwa tribe that live high in the coastal Sierra Nevada range were injured with burns, six of them seriously.

The electrical storm took place around midnight as the tribe was performing a traditional ceremony accompanied by tribe elders known as "Mamos".

The lightning strike reduced the area to ashes.

Among the injured were men, women and children, who were taken to hospital and clinics for treatment in the nearby city of Santa Marta.

From birth the Kogi attune their priests, called Mamos (which means sun in Kogi). As said; elected male children are taken from birth and put in a dark cave for the first nine years of their lives to begin this training. In the cave, elder

Mamos and the child's mother care for, feed, train, and teach the child to attune to "Aluna" before the boy enters the outside world. Through deep concentration, symbolic offerings, and divination, the Mamos believe they support the balance of harmony and creativity in the world.

The Kogi do not see us as "sleeping" as many of the Hindu and Oriental religions perceive us. The Kogi see us as "dead". We are not alive, but only shadows of the energy we could be. We do not have enough life -force energy and consciousness to be classified by them as real people.

But let's not be sentimental here; they lived in paradise, close to equator. There were no seasons. Mother Nature provided almost everything. Now compare Eskimo people and northern Europeans. Think for a minute what was happening to northern people during the onset of Ice Age. Part of the northern hemisphere was covered in ice and snow 2 kilometers high for 25,000 years. In past two million years there were twenty Ice Ages and twenty global warmings. In nearly ideal conditions of the jungle you do not have to struggle as much, you do not have to be inventive, or you are but on a different level. Too bad humans are so hell-bent on destroying other human accomplishments.

***

Jacob named the place Peniel (which means 'face of God'), for he said, "I have seen God face to face, yet my life has been spared."

Total isolation from external light causes the pineal gland to flood the brain with the neurotransmitter melatonin (average 2 to 5 mg/day), manifesting initially as the need for sleep and rest. The eyes recuperate from the over-stimulation of the visual world, releasing the grip of mental concerns, plans, agendas, and letting the energies settle. Melatonin is essential for maintaining the hibernation state, which facilitates the emergence of higher consciousness. The highest concentration of melatonin is around midnight.

After about three days, when melatonin concentration reaches sufficient levels, the body then produces superconductor pinoline, whereby a greater fluidity of thought and healing of body occurs. Pinoline induces cell replication (mitosis) and intercalates with DNA molecules. The 'pinoline stage' is normally activated only in womb, in lucid dreaming, or in near-death-experiences. Within this state it is possible to program the brain to the Unity of Self, heightening awareness of the pathways with which we filter reality. At this stage, the nervous system becomes aware of itself. Sense perception system is now on a high alert and double-arrow becomes much easier.

The body has approximately sixty trillion cells. Each of these cells can be seen as a computer with unlimited power and potential. Each cell can become superconductor, able to receive information.

Pineal gland starts to produce the neuro-hormone 5-MeO-DMT. This psychoactive tryptamine is highly luminescent and also extremely phosphorescent due to the amount of phosphene it transmits onto the visual cortex. DMT switches on over 40% more of the cerebral cortex and awakens the nervous system to become aware of itself; 'beingness' results. Hence, the possibility of programming the nervous system's bio-computer, and activating healing.

One begins to 'see' in 3-dimensional images.

Through total light isolation your consciousness can be expanded to the wider wave frequencies and transduce the core hologram of reality.

Many exercises can be practiced during this period; from physical to compacting energy, consciousness and awareness into the nervous system, working with the Silent Self and making the Dream Body more functional.

When DMT (dubbed God-molecule) reaches higher level one's experience can become very visual. DMT is the visual body neurotransmitter. It enables the energy body and Spirit Traveler's journey into inner-space, beyond third dimensional realms of time and space. After extended time one could begin to see in infrared, and ultraviolet, or even seeing heat patterns. The images sometime exteriorize and one is walking in a Virtual Reality.

When you reach the 'DMT state', you are in a very high alertness, and you begin to function more consciously using double-arrow attention.

During a Dark Retreat, we should do some meditations with open eyes and others with closed eyes. We should constantly keep the Witness Consciousness, double-arrow, and asking the questions like "Who am I?" Here it is even more important not to dramatize or let ourselves be taken over by imagery. It is of utmost importance not to fear anything. In this way, we develop the capacity of witnessing any thought, sensation or emotion that may appear. The attention is on the darkness as the expression of the absolute. Remember there is no darkness anywhere in the universe; this is just a matter of perception.

Darkroom retreats have been used by a variety of spiritual traditions throughout the centuries as a higher-level practice. The aspirant enters a room specially prepared to admit absolutely no light and spends a number of days, or weeks, under this sensory deprivation in order to bring about a profound shift of consciousness. I would recommend seven days for the first time, assuming Mind Traveler has at least some TR or meditation experiences behind him.

Research has shown that in prolonged darkness a biochemical reaction in the brain is causing extraordinary molecules like DMT to be synthesized, which trigger altered states of perception, allowing for accelerated evolution of the mind. Dark Room Retreat is definitely not recommended for those whose mental stability is in any way compromised.

Visions are just visions though, and as fascinating or beautiful they can be, do not give much importance to them, try to ignore them, do not interact with anything and just focus on the object of your meditation. Sometimes the visions of the bed and other furniture are so real you could forgot that you couldn't truly see them and then bump badly into a wall or real furniture. Always navigate a dark room by touching and traveling along outside walls. Move in slow motion. At other times you might actually see the furniture.

***

Make sure you chose a provider that has a flush toilet, shower and a sink. Also food should be given through a small opening in a wall that has sealed door on the outside and inside. Preferably there should be a large (5gal) water bottles in a room with a pump or a tap. There should be a latch on the inside of main door as an added assurance, for you can dream that someone entered the dark room.

"The darkness actualizes successively higher states of consciousness, correlating with the synthesis and accumulation of psychedelic chemicals in the brain, providing you are in a double-arrow mode.

I highly recommend Mantak Chia book: 'Darkness Technology'-Darkness Techniques for Enlightenment.

Edited testimonial by Kali Aney:

"The thought of doing a 40 days Dark Retreat came quite unexpectedly to me during meditation, but I was feeling the need of doing a long retreat for quite some time. Having never done either a solitary, or a long, or a retreat in darkness, I knew it was going to be a challenge.

By doing a Dark Retreat, I was hoping to finally face myself fully. Stopping to escape through distractions, I would learn to sit, watch and accept my mind and my emotions for prolonged period of time, and hopefully get some insights in the process.

The first day was quite challenging, I finally realize the full extent of the experience: I was going to be in the dark, with nothing to distract me, alone, for 40 days. My mind freaked out a little bit, but I checked myself and started designing my program of practice: meditation from wake up time till breakfast at 9, then long meditation, hatha yoga, and another meditation until lunch at 3. Little rest after lunch then meditation until sunset (I could hear the crickets starting to sing), hatha yoga and exercises, shower, meditation and bed where I would continue to meditate until I fell asleep. I have been following my schedule pretty well, and overall I did about 7 to 10 hours of formal practice per day, the rest being spent watching my mind or meditating while lying down.

Week one:

Day 1 till 3 I slept quite a lot and had a lot of very lucid dreams, then I started to adjust to the darkness and slept much less. The visions started on day 5 with a lot of geometrical shapes, then the vision of a beautiful bright white moon in a castle in the sky appeared, and very pictorial visions never stopped again until the end of my retreat, only growing stronger and brighter as time passed. The visions were quite varied, from cartoon-like technicolor movies to 360 immersion into beautiful purple or turquoise landscape with characters moving around, interacting with me, from flying boats filled with kittens wearing hats to huge stone like faces staring at me.

I got scared a few times by very dark floating shadows, or characters coming from horror movies, not so much from their presence (although my first reaction was fear, I decided very firmly from the beginning of the retreat that I would NOT be scared by my own mind), but from sudden movements. It's already a bit unsettling to be doing your yoga, trying not to watch the tortured woman from the Martyr movie crawling towards you, but I really jumped in shock when she actually suddenly extended her arm to touch me.

I realized how important it is to guard the sense doors and to be very aware of what you are letting in. As the Tibetan Buddhists say, whatever is still in your mind at the moment of your death will face you during the Bardo, so a dark retreat is also the opportunity to face these images and fears in a more conscious state than after death, and integrate or release them.

So the first week has been mainly about mental purifications, accepting and letting go of fears and attachment towards disturbing images.

Week two:

As I am meditating for extended periods of time I am getting more and more insights into my mind and myself, and some beautiful experiences, like experiencing the true meaning of the mantra 'Om Mani Padme Hum',

I sometimes close my eyes and put my hands in front of them to convince myself that I am looking inside myself and not outside. It's very fascinating to see my mind recreating the outlines of my hand, but still keeping them transparent, and to be able to look at the visions through them. From this week on my whole body looks transparent and usually glistening with light, which can become quite tiring at night as the bright lights shooting right in my eyes sometimes prevents me from sleeping, as if having cars coming towards me with headlights on full beam while trying to get some rest.

Week three:

My body is shaking more and more from inside in meditation, and I really feel an inner tremor growing as I go deeper inside. Sometimes it feels like my whole body is vibrating, and a few times it got to the point of giving me the impression that the whole room was shaking with me. I do not see the darkness anymore as everything is so colorful and bright most of the time. The only moment when I can see the darkness are when I wake up in the morning and when I go in some deep meditation on the crown chakra where only black and glistening diamond white light remains.

It's interesting to witness the different colors and textures of the images projected according to my state of mind. For example, after eating I always get visions of caves made of clay or stone, filling the whole space around me, full of people looking like medieval peasants or wooden figurines, transferring a feeling of heaviness and constraint. When I am restless and my mind keeps thinking about what I could do outside, I get fast moving landscapes with very bright lights. When I'm extremely happy, amazing blue sky, turquoise, pink and purple glistening light with very thin particles, quite still, filled with tree like silhouettes or canopy. In extremely peaceful and blissful states the quality of the light become even more subtle and beautiful, the space becoming huge, sometimes looking like the inside of a gigantic and beautiful cathedral. If I'm upset though, everything shrinks, the wall becomes closer and closer and more dense, I get lines of characters surrounding me, shouting at each other and at me, upsetting scenes or landscapes spinning faster and faster, exhausting me. All these different images allows me to watch closely my states of mind and realize how truly important it is to be careful of the kind of thoughts and feelings I am allowing to settle inside myself.

I start again to lucid dream quite a lot. Usually I am dreaming of being in the dark room but filled with light and I am desperately trying to cover the gaps letting the light in, or upset at someone for opening the windows before the end of the retreat, and then realizing it is not possible and that I am dreaming. I guess it was the war between my subconscious and conscious mind, one being happy to be there and wanting to continue while the other was trying to get out.

I get from time to time weird smells, some like incense and other that I cannot define. This is when I started to hear voices as well, which really scared me. Visions are ok, I can tell myself, "this is just the Darmakaya of my own mind", and ignore them. Visions still look external, but voices are more challenging, as I really hear them happening inside my head, and it made the whole visions thing more real, more like being in contact with another world, the astral world. Luckily they didn't happen too much though, but when I started to hear some ethereal chanting, lasting for several hours, or a crazy loud laugh inside my head, or a voice telling me "Let it go...", I had goosebumps all over me.

I'm also starting to see beautiful clouds exploding into multicolor fireworks happening randomly during meditations, with green, purple, fushia, blue and violet light. Hatha Yoga is starting to become very entertaining as I see each asana or kriya producing different colors and quality of light in my visions. For example pranayama produce a very light and pristine atmosphere while nauli kriya creates a lot of green light during sublimation and red during the actual practice. Then if I hold my breath long enough amazingly realistic visions appears, which I used as my personal 3D TV when I was becoming bored or restless. With bhujangasana or the bound lotus on the other hand the light becomes bright clear blue or pink/violet, with a lot of diamonds particles in it.

Week four:

A lot of very interesting meditations, fascinating worlds of purple colors with castles in the sky, flying boats, full of characters and animals, filled with life, amazing halo of white light around my head feeling very hot, like being kissed by the sun, when meditating on Sahasrara chakra, etc. I am more and more feeling like being in a dream, witnessing worlds arising and falling in my mind eye.

Week five:

I am getting a bit tired of the visions and start to feel excited about getting back to life and having a more balanced practice. I'm not really thinking about coming out though and keep working on building discipline and determination to witness whatever is happening.

Week six:

I still get a lot of deep and silent meditations, and get some of the most important releases and understanding of the retreat in the last few days, when I think that all my concentration is lost, and that it is almost pointless to sit. That makes me realize how each meditation sessions, no matter how "bad" or useless it might seem to the mind, is actually moving things in the depth and preparing you for the next unexpected "good" one. I am learning more and more not to look for experiences or particular states, to just sit, accept and love myself and my struggles, to just be present and let time do the work.

I also feel more and more how truly everything in the world is the projection of my own mind, how life is a just a dream which can be enjoyed as such.

I get a very strong intuition that I am not the doer that everything is happening in consciousness as in a full immersion 360° movie that everything moves in the mind but that the one who is experiencing in me is forever silent and immobile. With pristine purple and blue light glistening with diamonds surrounding me, I see that my mind is as boundless as the sky and is the matter permeating everything.

I came out of the Dark Retreat. I made a short last meditation and thanked the Universe for this beautiful experience and stepped out in the world. The air was fresh and crispy, the birds singing, I could hear the small waves of Lake Atitlan rushing to the banks, everything looked so wonderful and sharp. I sat down quickly as my balance was very shaky and my eyes kept jumping from focusing to refocusing, part of the astral visions still superimposed on the world. I waited for maybe another half an hour, taking in deeply everything that was happening, feeling at once very quiet and aloof while extremely happy and grateful for the gift of this wonderful world."

***

Another testimonial from Hindu perspective: "I start to exercise as well to stay a bit fit and to compensate for the long hours of still meditations and working out before showering makes the showers a bit less threatening. Praise to the jewel in the lotus" (the lotus being the heart). I literally see myself being somehow inside my own heart, which became huge and is shining with an incredibly bright blinding white light, exactly like a diamond. I very often during this week see light shining extremely bright from my body, huge beams of white light shooting out of my heart or my head, bright red light coming from the navel, glistening gold or purple light filling the whole room, etc.

It's incredibly beautiful and fascinating to witness this saying of Rumi becoming true in front of my eyes: "Don't you know yet? It is your light that lights the worlds!"

A lot of mental purifications and letting go happened this week also, reminding me of this quote: "Nothing ever goes away until it has taught us what we need to know." -Pema Chödrön

I also get a lot during this week a huge lion face right in front of me whenever I close my eyes, like 1 cm away, it's looking a bit like a mask where I can look through the lion eyes into other universes. It's a bit unsettling to see this feline face almost attached to mine whenever I close my eyes, but I get used to it and after a few days it eventually disappears.

"Everything in the universe is within you. Ask all from yourself."–Rumi

Restlessness has been the most challenging part for me. I was used to ten days silent retreats, and 40 days of darkness and solitude is really something else. I passed through so many phases, from never wanting to leave the retreat to being desperate when thinking how many days were left. I felt so much energy and need of acting in the world sometimes that it was hard to just witness and detach from it. See the stories as unreal and impermanent and use the repetition of a mantra (Japa Yoga) if you cannot stop your mind from wandering. I even used japa yoga aloud from time to time, either with a mantra or through chanting some bhajan, when my mind was becoming too insane."

I would strongly recommend that you do not let your meditations in a dark room slip toward lower (dark, south) energy centers like hara and sexual center. You can recognize this quickly by noticing images going dark-red and dark-brown, shadowy or black, and then becoming sexual. Keep your mind concentrated in the center of your head (pineal) or if you are so inclined on your heart.

Meditation is nothing magical; it is the natural process of doing away with attachment to the flesh and transferring your consciousness to the spiritual side of your nature. We meditate not only for the peace and joy and happiness it is supposed to bring, but also to free ourselves from the limitations of material existence. Everything in the material world is a copy of its counterpart in the astral world (and the other way around?); but the material manifestation is a gross one, limited and distorted by the law of relativity. The dream world is often synonymously referred to as the astral plane because it replicates the physical world.

***

When reading spiritual and religious books you need to separate "wheat from the chaff." Once more; learn about allegories, metaphors, similitudes, parables, myth, ciphering, codes and other forms of secret writing.

Printed in 1600s The Book of Lambspring; A noble ancient philosopher, concerning Philosophical Stone… "With the help of God I will show you this Art and will not hide or veil the truth from you." (At the time it was written you can be sure he was hiding it.) Writer promptly admits it: "If you were to show it to the outer world we should be derided by men women and children, therefore be modest and secret and you will be left in peace and security."….." Be warned and understand truly the two fishes are swimming in our sea. The sea is the body, the two fishes the soul and the spirit. Two fishes in our sea are without any flesh and bones. Let them be cooked in their own water, then there will also become a vast sea, the vastness of which no man can describe. Moreover the sages say that two fishes are only one, not two; there are two, and nevertheless they are one, body spirit and soul...... Cook these three together. Conceal your knowledge to your own advantage. Hear without terror that in the forest are hidden a deer and an unicorn. If we applied the parable to our art, we shall call the forest the body. The unicorn will be the Spirit at all times the deer desires no other name"...etc. You get the gist. There are thousands of similar treatises written allegorically, metaphorically.

The Dark Retreat has its significant correspondences in Alchemical work:

Alchemists "work" began with 'Nigredo', or blackness. This first phase in alchemy means putrefaction or decomposition, shutting down of sympathetic nervous system. As a first step in the pathway to the 'philosopher's stone', all alchemical ingredients (your characteristics) had to be cleansed and 'cooked' extensively to form a uniform black matter. This is a death and return to formless chaos, leading on to the white phase and finally to 'Rubedo', the red phase of Spiritual freedom. 'Albedo' is literally referred to as ablution, or the washing away of impurities by aqua vitae (the 'Water' of Life).

The journey into Darkness is not just a first stage, but it is the essence of the spiritual alchemical work, because without it, the individual will remain only at the superficial level of mere rational thinking and social existence, dominated by dogmas and useless rituals. There is an important alchemical adagio:

Visita Interiora Terrae Rectificando Occultum Lapidem (Visit the interior of the 'earth' (material body); rectify what you find there, and you will discover the hidden stone.) To describe the "descent into Darkness," summed up in the word "vitriol," alchemy has preserved some very ancient symbols.

The individual (actually only his/her personality) descending into its original nature will suffer a great loss. He must abandon all his old moral, social and religious values. Thus, he will open himself to a different order, more in tune with the Harmony of the Whole.

This is what happens in a Dark Retreat.

St. Dionysius referred to it as divine darkness, the 'nigredo' of the Alchemists.

"Why has God been symbolized everywhere as light? Not because God is light, but because man is afraid of darkness. This is human fear, we like light and we are afraid of darkness, so we cannot conceive God as darkness, as blackness. This is human conception.

If you can love darkness you will become unafraid of death. If you can enter into darkness, and you can enter only when there is no fear, you will achieve total relaxation. If you can become one with darkness, you are dissolved, it is a surrender. Now there is no fear, because if you have become one with darkness, you have become one with death. You cannot die now. You have become deathless. Your physical body will die, but not you.

First a deep friendship with darkness is needed. (while keeping in mind there is no such thing as darkness anywhere in existence. As I said elsewhere, darkness on any level is just a matter of perception.)

First uncover your subconscious fears and try to live and love darkness. It is very blissful. Once you know, and once you are in contact with it, you are in contact with a very deep cosmic phenomenon.

Darkness envelops you, accepts you, not as a distinct person; it simply accepts you without any definitions.

Some Tibetan monks recommend a 49-day Dark Retreat. This period was recommended only to the advanced practitioners because such a retreat requires great stability in the fully conscious state.

"When you go into the dark and this becomes total,

the darkness soon turns into light."- Mantak Chia

Psychonauts entering the cave initiate a phase of groping in the dark, and at first speculate on its variety of dangers. It is not darkness to be feared, but what we bring in. Profound darkness, in and of itself, creates a primordial biochemical shift in the human organism that literally is light revealing. It awakens the immediacy of luminous awareness, where physical vision is superseded by multidimensional mystic vision that is 'now', yet eternal and opens to all past and future generations.

The cave itself is symbolic as a liminal threshold where we can enter the womb of the earth. But that dark retreat has a dramatic alchemical effect that is literal, 'material' and life changing.

***

From the time of our conception until our birth, in only nine months we go through three billion years of evolution– from protozoa to a human being. This evolution-creation process moves at lightning speed. Therefore, the average speed of growth is 10 million biological years per each 24 hours! Introduction of toxic chemicals and external drugs into this super sensitive system during the prenatal period greatly damages the intended process.

One single cell recreates itself over and over again with one purpose: to create this body of ours, a temple of the Holy Spirit, a home of the unbounded consciousness. Perfect intelligence builds our body from one cell into a beautiful form of about 70 trillion cells and guides the body's functions throughout life. It does not desert us when we are born. It keeps us going despite the enormous abuses we heap on ourselves. Give this inner intelligence a chance and it will set things right.

At sixteen days after the conception our heart begins to pulse. So were we dead before that? Of course not! All the cells building the body were alive and intelligent, including the sperm and an egg that fused and formed the original cell.

If we put two cells under the microscope at a certain distance, we will notice they pulse at different time and frequency. If we keep bringing these cells closer, at the certain point they will start to pulse in unison. The gap has been bridged. From the time our hart begins to pulse all the cells of the body join. When the level of the heart beat is experienced in a meditation, it sounds like a humongous cosmic drum, vibrating the entire existence.

It is said when two people fall into Love their hearts begin to pulse in unison. The separation, the space in between, has been bridged. The two have become one.

On the Way of Devotion, where love rules, there is no will to power; and where power rules, there is no love. The one is the shadow of the other.

It is to be understood that there is love (Ego love, based on chemistry. It can turn to hate anytime.) and Love (based on Spirit, it is unlimited and unconditional), happiness and Happiness, trust and Trust, etc.

We talk about it, we sing about it, we fantasize about it, but none of us can say with certainty what love is. It appears to be some kind of spiritoid, lofty emotion.

Love definitely has its chemical counterparts. But there are thousands of loves. Some people love women, some sports, some chocolate, some parachuting, food, etc. Most of the time we perceive love as something we need.

This is the biggest screw-up, for we always need more. It is never enough.

Love is giving, not taking. Love is not what we say, love is what we do. When we give unconditionally nothing bad can happen. Love is the absence of any judgement.

LOVE is being one with. It is a realization you share consciousness with the other. See the other being through silence. Lovers are not aware of space separation or time. Lovers become ONE with the object of Love. TRUE LOVE is not an emotion. Love center is found in our hearts, and our soul is rooted in Love. Love does not judge. Ever! It is a tendency to unify instead to separate. Brain separates, heart unites. Can we feel what they feel, and what is happening inside them? Can we see ourselves in the other person? Can we love them as they are? If not, we are pretending. We need something.

True Love cannot exist without other.

But just knowing what love is, is not enough. Understanding is not enough. We need to take empty words and infuse them with feeling and true understanding. Feel what is happening to them now! Love is acceptance what is in the moment. When facing, bad and evil people, we need not love them, but we can remember SuperConsciousness within them and love that.

Love is patient, love is kind. It does not envy, it does not boast, it is not proud. It is not rude, it is not self-seeking. It is not easily angered. It keeps no record of wrongs. It always protects, always trusts, always hopes and always perseveres.

Love is made up of beautiful, precious moments!

Produce the moments of love as often as possible. Become a producer of love instead consumer. Fill in the future with them. Ask yourself what would be an act of love NOW? Just put yourself in the other person's position and feel it.

A Hindu saint who was visiting river Ganges to take bath found a group of family members on the banks, shouting in anger at each other. He turned to his disciples smiled and asked:

"Why do people shout in anger at each other?"

Disciples thought for a while, one of them said, "Because we lose our calm, we shout."

"But, why should you shout when the other person is just next to you? You can as well tell him what you have to say in a soft manner" asked the saint.

Disciples gave some other answers but none satisfied the other disciples.

Finally the saint explained:

"When two people are angry at each other, their hearts distance a lot. To cover that distance, they must shout to be able to hear each other. The angrier they are, the stronger they will have to shout to hear each other to cover that great distance.

What happens when two people fall in love? They don't shout at each other but talk softly because their hearts are very close. The distance between them is either nonexistent or very small."

The saint continued; "When they love each other even more, what happens? They do not speak, only whisper and they get even closer to each other in their love. Finally, they even need not whisper, they only look at each other, and that's all. That is how close two people are when they love each other."

He then looked at his disciples and said:

"So, when you argue do not let your hearts get distant, do not say words that distance each other more, or else there will come a day when the distance is so great you will not find the path to return."

Love is The Law of Life: All love is expansion, all selfishness is contraction. Love is therefore the primary law of life. Only he/she who loves truly lives. Therefore, love for Love's sake, just as you breathe to live.

Love is E- emotion, and it seeks two things, eternity and intensity. In the relation of the Lover and Beloved the seeking for eternity and for energy is instinctive and self-born. Love is a seeking for mutual possession, and it is here that the demand for mutual possession becomes absolute. Love is a seeking for oneness, and it is here that the idea of oneness, of two souls merging into each other and becoming one, manifests. Love, too, is a longing for beauty. Beauty does not lie in things, but in the emotions we give to them. This longing can never be fully satisfied because only in the Divine can it find its real and its final satisfaction. Therefore it is here the turning of human emotion Godward finds its full meaning and discovers all the truth, of which love is the human symbol.

Whatever we see of this Divine and fix our concentrated effort upon it, that we can become or grow into some kind of unity with it, or at the least in tune and harmony with it. The Upanishad put it pointedly in its highest terms "Whoever envisages it as the Existence becomes that existence and whoever envisages it as the Non-existence, becomes that non-existence; " so too it is with all else that we see of the Divine. It is something beyond; yet it is indeed already within us.

This joy of union is the ultimate achievement of all the varied experiences of spiritual relation between the individual soul and God where the One became many in this infinite universe.

Most intimate experience of divine love cannot come by the pursuit of the impersonal Infinite alone (as in science); for the Godhead we adore must become near and personal to us. It is possible for the Impersonal to reveal within itself all the riches of personality when we get into its heart, and one may discover in it things he had not dreamed of. The Existence has infinite surprises for us. The Divine is a Being and not an abstract existence or a status of pure timeless infinity; nevertheless a being outside time and space. All beings exist by this Being; all things are the faces of God; all thought, action, feeling and love proceed from "him" and return to him. Inwardly, the image of the Divine has to become visible to the eye within, dwelling in us as in his mansion, presiding over all our activities of mind and life as the friend, master and lover. A constant inner communion is the joy to be made, close, permanent and unfailing.

Now, take a look at your parents, you know them well, and ask yourself was I conceived through love or through sexual desire, the lowest energy center? Be honest about it. This is the 'stamp we wear on our foreheads', and we act accordingly.

Our head has five senses and our heart has none. Yet our heart is as powerful as our brain. It is powering the life in our body. Heart has a direct connection to Spiritual Heart, the one that gives life to everything living in this infinite universe. When our heart begins to beat in harmony with Universal Heart- the Life Itself, the gap with the existence is bridged and unconditional LOVE ensues.

Concentrating in meditation on the general heart area is very powerful practice. It is an important element in Christianity, Sufism, Hinduism, Taoism, Tantra, and other spiritual movements. The atom through which life pulses into our being is found in our heart. Existence of this energy portal is mentioned in Sita Upanishad, Maha Narayana Upanishad, Ashtanga Hridaya, and many other texts. It is experienced as the SuperConscious energy being aware of itself.

"God is born in heart and heart is born in God"- Meister Eckhart.

To the Christian Fathers of North African Desert heart was not just a physical organ, but a spiritual center of every human being. Heart for many is the ultimate symbol of the point of contact with that which we call God. Perception through our senses is indirect while our heart is the organ of the direct knowledge.

***

You cannot think, taste, smell, hear, feel, see, have an

emotion nor have any experience whatsoever, unless there are corresponding bio-chemical reactions in your body.

Imagine your body, if you will, as a giant bowl of soup containing thousands of chemicals. The human body is the greatest chemical factory on this planet. It can produce any chemical in the Universe, instantly. Imagine these chemicals (endorphins, neuropeptides and many others still undiscovered) combining, dissolving, and recombining every millisecond in a never-ending cascade right throughout your body. What do you think happens when we introduce man-made toxic chemicals into our internal chemistry?

We have over 600 trillion living beings on us and in us; each with its own energy intelligence chemistry and consciousness, affecting us in innumerable ways. Abdominal tract nervous system had been regarded as a digestive organ only 'till the discovery made by Michael Gershon that 90% of the body's serotonin, a daytime neurotransmitter, is located within the walls of the gastrointestinal tract.

The enteric nervous system is a subdivision of the autonomic nervous system that directly controls the gastrointestinal system. It is surrounded by a pool of more than 30 neurotransmitters like serotonin, dopamine, glutamate, norepinephrine and nitric oxide, and other chemical mediators like neuropeptides and enkephalins.

The normal gut flora is essential to maintain the gut-brain axis, thereby maintaining a good mood. The composition of normal gut flora varies from person to person. In addition, there are also variations based on the location of the gut microbes in the gut of different individuals. These variations create diversified patterns of intestinal nervous system in each individual as these microbes are essential for the production of serotonin.

Any disruption in the growth of normal microbes impairs cognitive and emotional balance whenever the gut is exposed to pathogenic microbes.

Gut also contains glia-like supportive cells and contains nearly 100 million neurons connected to the brain through vagus nerve.

Spirit Voyager should ensure his physical body is in good shape and well taken care of.

***

After 40 years of preparation, Mantak Chia was ready to present the ancient wisdom of the Dark Room Technology; starting February 10, 2002, with the Immortal Tao Practices of Kan & Li (Lesser, Greater and Greatest).

All spiritual traditions have used the Dark Room techniques throughout the ages, referring to it as the Perfect Inner Alchemy Chamber, including Christianity.

From Chi Kung perspective, and I quote:

"A dark room environment changes the body chemistry, which affects the Pineal, Pituitary and Thalamus/Hypothalamus glands."

In Europe, the dark room has often appeared in underground form as a network of tunnels; the Pyramids in Egypt, the catacombs in Rome or the caves used by the Essenes, near the Dead Sea in Israel. The Taoist tradition has used Cave Dark Room Technology throughout the ages for all higher level Inner Alchemy practices. Most famous are cave dwellers of India.

Every day the body needs tryptophan, an essential amino acid. This is converted into serotonin and melatonin (average 2-5mg./ day). When you are in the dark room, the melatonin can build up gradually. When this store reaches a sufficient amount (15-20mg.) the body then produces pinoline (a super conductor). It also realizes that it no longer needs any more melatonin.

At this point the tryptophan is then able to adopt a secondary function of producing 5MEO and DMT

(Dimethyltryptamine). When you reach the 'DMT state' you begin to function, preferably consciously, from the various psychic centers or chakras. The bodily processes of 'Healing Love' are then combined with those of the Dark Room. The human states of true compassion and sexual arousal create a new chemistry and a new vibration within the body. This 'special' vibration occurs at a frequency of 8Hz. 'As in the macrocosm, so it is in the microcosm'; hence if we make love, then all the cells and DNA actually make love as well. The DNA cross over, like two serpents intertwining in an erotic embrace (ureaus). You need the orgasmic vibration to arouse this crossover process which leads to the 'two giving birth to three'; the conception of new cells. The two vital states are compassion and arousal leading to orgasm. Both are inextricably linked to love. When this 'love-vibration' reaches the pineal gland a new hormone is produced, which in turn creates whole body conductivity. Only when you feel the waves of orgasmic vibration and unconditional love for the self and others can the process be activated and the essence of the darkroom magnified.

When the pinoline is triggered, you also activate your clairvoyant, clairsentient and clairaudient powers. You may see light and visions, hear music and gain phenomenal insight. Cosmic particles (?), which have the same cell structures as humans (and from which the Tao believes you evolved) are attracted to you magnetically. You are able to decode this universal information carried from outer space, which may be as old as nothingness itself. When you enter this primordial state or force you are reunited with the true self and divinity within. You literally 'conduct' the universal energy. You may see into the past and future, understand the true meaning of existence and begin to understand the order of things. You return to the womb, the cocoon of our material structure and nature's original Dark Room.

Mantak Chia Dark Room Enlightenment Program:
Day 1-3

"Complete isolation from external light causes the pineal gland to flood the brain with the neurotransmitter melatonin.

Three days of Internal Darkness and Sleep Therapy - During these 3 days one has the chance to catch up on all the lost sleep that has occurred over the last few years. Eyes get rested and give up trying to see.

This stage cannot be over emphasized, with regard to its importance in the overall process."

(However, light flashes and some phosphenes could be already appearing in experienced meditators and TR practitioners. We got familiar with them doing Paisley. Do yoga or other physical exercises daily to keep fit. Preferably diet should be vegan. Eat very slowly; you have all the time in the word, savor every morsel and every taste.)

Day 3-5

The pineal gland starts to increase the production of 'pinoline', whereby a greater fluidity of thought and healing of the body starts to occur. This period allows for transition, wherein numerous meditations will be carried out, which will incorporate projection of the energy body and astral travel along with (Iron Shirt) Chi Kung.

(You would agree nothing moves, nothing changes and nothing gets accomplished without energy. TR practitioners will commence energy exercises like Head & Lung Bounce, Energy Twerk, Spinal Breathing, Kumbhaka and Transcendental Rebirthing Method. Do the head and lung finger bounce for couple of minutes and then meditate. Do Twerking for 5minutes followed by 5 minute meditation. Do Spinal Breathing for 5 minutes followed by 10 minute meditation. Do Kumhaka for 10 minutes followed by 15 minute meditation. These suggestions are arbitrary. Improvise and meditate as long as you feel extra energy. You can do these techniques 2-3 times per day. Khumbaka energy is little denser and compacted. Just holding the breath for long period of time converts oxygen into carbon monoxide and acidifies the blood. Two-prong Khumbaka is designed in such a way so this does not happen.

It suffice to say that Kumbhaka method can be pretty hard to do, but we should remember that world record for holding the breath is 22 minutes and 22 seconds. Freedivers subject themselves to years of training to achieve such breath-defying feats. In the process, they actually modify their biology. Do the TR for 15 minutes with 15 minutes totally passive part. Dark room practices can be emotional and very visual but for the most part devoid of feelings. This is where our enhanced life-force is added. While fantastic, all this is based on body chemistry and physical. Higher goal is needed. Transcending physical body and accessing Dream Body (subconscious) without losing self-awareness is step one. Strong peripheral lights, like those of a car shining from the side could appear.)

Day 6-8

At this stage the pineal gland starts to produce the neurohormone 5-MeO-DMT. This psychoactive tryptamine is highly luminescent; it is also extremely phosphorescent due to the amount of phosphene that it transmits onto the visual cortex.

The neuro-transmitter 'akashon' is normally only active when we are in the womb and in the first months of our lives. It is now reactivated in the darkroom.

DMT switches at least 40% more of the cerebral cortex and awakens the nervous system to become self-aware. Hence, the possibility of meta-programming the nervous system's bio-computer, activating healing and message assortment of the nervous system.

DMT is the empathogenic neurotransmitter that expands the emotional body between 'infinity and zero'. It gives rise to telepathy in the emotional and intuitive bodies. It engages the awakening of the 'Flower of Life', the spine which begins to glow in a state of beingness and peace.

Many exercises will be practiced during this period; compacting Chi, consciousness and awareness into the nervous system, working with the Silent Self and anchoring the Immortal Body.

5-Meo-DMT discharges the darkness from the darkroom. A bright light will be activated.

This Great White Light, the manifestation of the astral body, enables the self to project externally.

At this point, some degree on 'N-Methyl-D-Aspartare Inhibition' (NMDA-I) usually occurs. This is a 'soft form' of the slowing of the glutamate input signals into the cells. This makes it easier for the nervous system to cause electrons to stop flowing within the cells, allowing for profound meditative trance states.

The 5-MeO-DMT prepares the nervous system, through its empathic state of being and self-awareness of the nervous system, for the DMT or dimethyltryptamine production of the pineal gland, in psychoactive milligram dosages.

(During meditations whole visual field can turn soft white, like fluffy clouds. Beautiful light gold colors and morphing images abound.)

Day 9-12

There is now enough 'Mono Amine Oxidase Inhibition' triggered by the pinoline, to allow the pineal gland's 'serotonin to melatonin cycle' to be intercepted by adrenaline and ephedrine activity and converted into a 'serotonin DMT pathway'.

When DMT levels reach more than 25mg, one's experience can become very visual. It is intensely energizing. At this stage of the Dark Room Retreat, the required amount of sleep tends to diminish dramatically. Although the day may last 24 hours, 3 hours of sleep can seem like 12.

During this period we will engage in further practices; psychic games and interactivity, Taoist Dream Yoga (advanced levels) and Imagination Expansion."

(Entire visual field can go bright white, which is amazing considering we are in a total darkness. Even weirder effect is appearance of The Clear Light, clarity of nothingness. Geometric, psychedelic morphing designs are mind boggling. Perception of one level above fifth-element and its ceaseless churning of images is beyond comprehension.)

You have sixteen hours, or more, to fill every day. Do not spend too much time doing nothing.

And so on to 49 days. As stated; this is for advanced practitioners or those crazy determined.

Now read this again but from energy point of view and not chemistry.

Here are couple of suggestions if you experience scary visions. Be in a double-arrow; this should be the mode you are in at all times, anyway. Do not look at images directly. If and when you do use your left eye to look into a left eye of the 'entity.' This gives you a sense of control. Tell it mentally you want to be a friend. If fear starts entering you quickly 'grab' the feeling (not an emotion but physical feeling in your body) with your double-arrow attention, let the feeling spread and dissipate, therefore harvesting its energy. Emotions are directly linked to the breath. Good way to calm ourselves is by regulating our breathing.

Images are perceived as external so they are not so hard to handle. It is a different story with voices. They are experienced as internal and coming from within your head. So ignore them. Think and do something different rather than putting your attention on a voice(s). You have that ability. Remember the times when somebody said something, but you did not have a clue what it was because your mind was elsewhere. Here all those concentration exercises I mentioned in my other works will come very handy. You can also use a Christian mantra to stop the voices by taking their space away. Softly chant "Jesus have a mercy on me." Not that he will; but this mantra is very effective. Gradually speed it up until spaces between the words are gone without losing the meaning of the mantra. Be in a double-arrow and speed it up some more until those words become a fast, continuous, harmonic, sounding whistle (See; Tuvan throat harmonics, Jonathan Goldman, Primordial Zikr, also my videos)

Nadabrahma humming works well too.

Sit in a relaxed position, either on a chair or a cross legged position on the floor, if you are comfortable with it, or lay down on bed. With mouth shut and lips together begin to hum, loud enough to create a vibration throughout the entire body. The humming should be loud enough so that the surrounding people could hear it. Hum and inhale at your own pace. If the body wants to move allow it. Visualize your body as a hollow, empty vessel. If you do this technique often enough after a while a point will come where you are just a listener. The humming will happen by itself. This is very helpful to "cleanse" the brain and enhance physical healing processes in the body. This can be a twenty minute meditation in itself.

Inner silence is a state of being in which there are no thoughts; it is a total suspension of the internal dialogue which is normally going on all day, every day. It is a state in which perception does not depend on the senses. Ability to be in inner silence gradually increases day by day. We should be aware of ourselves and let the thoughts go away and our mind will become quieter. This inner silence is reached by shutting off all the senses, shutting off all the thoughts, shutting off all the emotions. There are no dreams from inner silence; dreaming becomes optional. All the noise, inner and outer, is gone. "Be silent and know I am God." - says 'He'. Do a 'silent' meditation, hook Ooooo-Hoooo mantra to your breath. Let it go subtle until both disappear.

Responses to a Dark Room Retreat vary greatly. Young man before me was in for nine days and did not have a single vision. (Sometimes just giving yourself a permission to have them does the trick.) Few emotional memories and lot of thinking and that was it. Young couple before him wanted to do ten day dark retreat at the same time (to spiritually help each other?!). So they entered dark rooms on the opposite part of town. (Mazunte, Mx. is the only town that has two.) Young man run out of the dark room on the fifth day. He was very disturbed; said he had terrifying visions and voices in his head. He insisted on going to the other retreat center to rescue his wife from terrible danger. He even threatened to involve the police. When they finally allowed him to communicate with his wife, she told him to go away to the beach and enjoy himself and leave her alone, for she was having the best time of her life.

If you have on your night table a blue light digital clock, replace it with red LED; it does not affect circadian rhythm. Also get yourself a good quality sleep mask; the one that has thick foam around your eyes and allows for the eye movement and comfort. It will over time improve your melatonin and DMT production. You will sleep better and your dreams will be more vivid.

For several days after dark room experience eyes are supersensitive to television and digital advertising panels. Television is, for the most part, an idiot box. Walking through the airport of Mexico City I was assaulted by super-bright advertising images. Who the hell gives these corporate creeps the right to assault our minds in this way?! And then I thought of all nocturnal insects, moths and animals whose world is being destroyed by light pollution. City dwellers have become paranoid of darkness.

Look at the news we see on television or in the newspaper. Look at the media's enthusiasm for negative events. Look at the excitement that is generated, and the effort expended to try to find more interesting stories about a negative event that occurred in the world. So much intensity is focused there, but we don't have that kind of focus when something good happens. We tend to blame the media for that strong focus on the negative. Yes, it is true: They are actively pursuing negative news. On the other hand though, who is watching? We are; along with the rest of the world; and our media simply follows after the stories that people want to see.

There are different ways to deal with any negative situation, and any of those ways may be a good way as long as it is right for you at that very moment. Do not think one way is inherently proper, and another way is inherently wrong. It depends on the circumstances. The White Tantra view clearly says every negative situation can be transformed into the positive one. Yes, that is true. But the question is, are you able to do that? Is it possible to transform a negative situation into a positive path? Absolutely. Taking things further, from the point of view of spiritual teachings you don't even need to transform. When you consciously leave it as it is, it is self-transformed, it is self-liberated. You recognize that the conscious experience has the ability to liberate itself. So, rule number one, the simplest rule, for when you find yourself facing a negative situation is to do nothing. If you are going to learn one rule in those situations, then it would be don't do anything with your body, don't do anything with your speech, don't do anything with your mind. Catch the emotion with your awareness at the very beginning. Watch for the feeling in your body caused by its energy charge; stay in double-arrow and let the energy dissipate throughout the body. You have just harvested the energy of that particular emotion. As you get proficient, you will realize the emotions are just another of your tools. O yes, they are very powerful, spanning back eons upon eons, but are still subjects to the consciousness.

When you are trying to stabilize the experience of any practice, the progression moves from one's initial recognition; to familiarity; then to prolonging that familiarity; and then to extending that familiarity to outside the meditation session and into simple tasks, such as cooking, walking, writing or cleaning, etc. The development progresses sequentially. Expressed another way: It is just being conscious of that experience and then expanding on it. That's the only way.

One great thing about meditation is that when a big problem arises in your life; you can see it as an opportunity, not just as a problem. It is an opportunity to find out if your practice and what you have learned works. The only time you can really put it to the test is during those troubled situations. Having another beautiful practice of meditation is not necessarily of benefit in itself. The only time it really helps is when you are in trouble, and that will be when you find out whether your practice has developed or not.

Our minds are indeed constantly acting and acted upon by the minds of others through hidden currents of which we are not aware, and we have no knowledge or control of these agencies.

Actually man is not content solely with living in the present; he is moved to look before and after, to know as much as he can of the past and try to penetrate as far as he can, however obscurely, into the future.

Chemistry of Dark Room and other spiritual practices is very complex; here are some research results for whatever it is worth.

Soma Pinoline, the combination of the Pineal secreted DMT (Di-methyl-triptamine) and the MAO Inhibitor, Pinoline (Methoxy-tetra-hydro-beta-carboline) may be responsible for naturally occurring psychic experience. Furthermore, noradrenaline plays a significant role in the Pineal gland, when there is sufficient Pinoline saturation in the brain. It releases a serotonin site, enabling another serotonin site on the pineal gland to produce the potent visionary Dimethyltryptamine (DMT), neurotransmitter. Through meditative breathing, and whole body 8 Hz entrainment is the ultimate hormone precursor anti-aging pill. Not only does the pineal gland produce more Melatonin and Pinoline, which instigate 8 Hz ELF waves throughout the body, but these neurohormones signal the pituitary to release the life hormone Somatropin, which signals the adrenal glands to instigate cholesterol to convert to Pregnelenone then DHEA.

The extra Pinoline and other beta carboline levels that result, aid the body cells to replicate, and neutralize microorganisms, parasites, fungoids, and bacteria, and related harmful invaders. Melatonin and Pinoline are also strong antioxidants. Meditation is a rest break, an exercise session, an integration session, an energizer, and a body tuner, promoting antioxidant and antidepressant production. It is a healing state.

Dr. James Callaway detected this DMT molecule in the spinal fluid of people who were dying, or were having an "Out of body experience (OOBE)", or who were lucid dreaming. All of this relates to Tibetan dream yoga and various Bardo states.

It is Pinoline that enables the threshold levels of DMT to become active in the brain, but it requires an adrenaline burst. DMT with Pinoline increases brain activation, and with its cousin the 5-Methoxy-DMT, has been shown to activate the brain by as much as 40%, compared to our 10% maximum potential at present. This is a frightening prospect for the uninitiated, due to the absolutely overwhelming nature of DMT.

Dark retreat reopens the source code of embryogenesis - formation and development of an embryo.

The transformative core of Tibetan Buddhist practice is the Bardo Retreat, traditionally lasting 49 days or even longer. This experience, reserved for stabilized, advanced practitioners rends the mystic veil and opens the Third Eye wide in a retinal display of biophotons which only the Third Eye sees or even creates: the Light of Wisdom. The pineal gland becomes 'decalcified' as in youth and produces the endogenous hallucinogen, DMT, creating access to a whole other order of existence, somewhere between dreams and waking.

This 'Third Eye', in the center of the brain, is implicated in the production of natural DMT, dubbed the Spirit Molecule. The pineal synthesizes natural hallucinogens in response to certain psychophysical states, like Transcendental Rebirthing, meditation and Dark Room retreat.

This master gland is responsible for the internal perception of Light, the raising of Kundalini the serpent power, and for awakening inner sight or in-sight.

Many of us will only experience a glimmer of this deepest revelation in the most critical of circumstances. DMT production is stimulated, in the extraordinary conditions of birth, sexual ecstasy, childbirth, extreme physical stress, Life threatening accident, near-death, death, TR, as well as meditation.

Pineal DMT also plays a significant role in dream consciousness. This chemical messenger links body and spirit. Pineal activation awakens normally latent neural pathways.

"All spiritual disciplines describe quite psychedelic accounts of the transformative experiences, whose attainment motivate their practice. Blinding white light, encounters with demonic and angelic 'entities', ecstatic emotions, timelessness, heavenly sounds, feelings of having died and being reborn, contacting a powerful and loving presence underlying all of reality; these experiences cut across all denominations. They also are characteristic of a fully psychedelic DMT experience.

Meditative techniques using breath, sound, sight, the mind or heart may generate particular wave patterns whose fields induce resonance in the brain. Millennia of human trial and error have determined that certain "sacred" words, visual images, pranayama and mental exercises exert uniquely desired effects. These fields cause multiple systems to vibrate and pulse at certain frequencies. We can feel our minds and bodies resonate... Of course, the pineal gland also is buzzing at these same frequencies....The pineal begins to 'vibrate' at frequencies that weaken its multiple barriers to greater

DMT formation: the pineal cellular shield, enzyme levels, and quantities of anti-DMT. The end result is a psychedelic surge of the pineal spirit molecule, resulting in the subjective states of mystical consciousness." -Strassman, 2001.

Embryological rudiments of the pineal gland and the differentiated gonads of both male and female appear at 49 days, hence 49 day dark retreats for advanced practitioners.

Stress-related hormones cue the pineal activation to activate normally latent synthetic pathways, creating tryptamine and/or beta-carboline hallucinogens. When we face stress or potential death, or in meditative reveries, we "tune back" into the most well developed motif of such experiences - the birth experience. Perinatal themes and memories re-emerge.

Those with Cesarean deliveries report greater difficulty in attaining transcendent states of breakthrough and release during drug-induced states. They may not have a strong enough "template of experience" to fall back on, to let go without fear of total annihilation, because lesser amounts of pineal hallucinogens were produced during their births.

Through meditation, the pineal may be modulated to elicit a finely tuned standing wave through resonance effects.

The pineal is a superconducting resonator. Ananda claims it potentates DNA as a multidimensional transducer of holographic projection, through hadron toroids, and is crucial to staying youthful.

Melatonin is mostly made in the pineal gland, comprised of the same Tryptophane base materials as Pinoline. Melatonin induces mitosis.

The human Pineal gland not only produces the neurohormone melatonin, one of the body's most potent antioxidants, but the revolutionary pinoline, 6-methoxy-tetra-hydro-beta carboline, or 6-MeO-THBC. Pinoline is superior to melatonin in aiding DNA replication. Pinoline can make superconductive elements within the body. It encourages cell division by resonating with the very pulse of life - 8 cycles per second - the pulse DNA uses to replicate.

Caves were the original sensory deprivation chambers. The ancients associated caves with the womb of the earth, life and death, the afterworld, and the place of healing. Caves are the hotbed of incubation and transformation, of that which is concealed. Absolute darkness has an initiatory quality - the metaphor of moving from the darkness of ignorance into the illuminative light. But it is more than a metaphor. All wisdom traditions have used sensory deprivation and darkness (such as caves, tunnels, catacombs, or special chambers), as a shamanic mind-altering force.

Soma Pinoline and DMT are the source of visionary Light in transpersonal experiences. Its primary source, the pineal, has traditionally been referred to as the Third Eye. Curiously, this gland is light sensitive and actually has a lens, cornea, and retina. DMT production is particularly stimulated in the extraordinary conditions of birth, sexual ecstasy, childbirth, extreme physical stress, near-death, psychosis, and physical death, as well as meditation. Pineal DMT also plays a significant role in dream consciousness. As said elsewhere, our mind-body system can produce any chemical in the universe, including LSD and THC.

DMT is implicated in the wild imaginings of our nightly dreams, near-death phenomena, alien abduction experiences, and dream yoga. It is also a source of visionary phenomena in therapy, such as unusual psychophysical states attained in waking dreams, shamanic or psychotherapeutic journeys. DMT can be found everywhere in our body and in nature. DMT is omnipresent in the biosphere, found everywhere from a variety of botanicals to mammals: It has been documented in rat brains at birth. Not only is it found in seaweed, flowers, vines, acacia tree, toad skins, prairie-mimosa and Mimosa hostilis, Anadenanthera colubrina, lawn grass, etc., but also in our brains, lungs, heart and spinal fluid.

The pineal is the only unpaired gland in the brain,

this is why it is depicted as a single eye. The shape of the gland resembles a pine cone, hence its name.

Is this "ground zero" of the Mother Luminosity what the Lamas, gurus, Shamans, Swamis, and other sages, see when they look deeply within their meditations? Is what is true for subspace true for supraspace? It is a fact of physics that at the sub-quantal level the fabric of reality and our bodies flicker 'in and out of existence' each nanosecond at a phenomenal rate. Actually this is not quite true; everything flickers in and out of existence at such incredible speeds that we do not have a name for such high number. Creator creates always!

The Heart Sutra says the Void is all forms and all forms are void. The formless field gives rise to itself.

CHAPTER NINETEEN

DEATH -THE ULTIMATE DREAM

Science does not have the slightest clue what happens to a person after death, however, science is making some progress lately. Last year studies have shown that genes of a deceased person start working even more energetic and quick. This year science found out that brain activity continues even ten minutes after death. But on a more subtle level brain is active for another 3-4 days before life force finally disconnects. Again, not a single body cell, out of 70 trillion, has died yet; and remember, the whole system is holographic. What a person knows each cell knows.

Main problem with the human beings is that we don't entertain the possibility of death. We behave as if we are never going to die. Even more problematic is the sense of immortality that comes with the sense we can figure out this infinite universe with our Ego mind. Perceiving energy directly as it flows in the universe is an ability of conscious cognition. Spirit Traveler sees how energy flows and he flows with it. If the flow is obstructed the Spirit Voyager moves to something else. He/she does not oppose the Universal force, he/she sees that energy and feels its intent. For Spirit Traveler time is most important. Time is of the essence for we never know when it is going to end.

An important element to survival after death, to begin with, is to remember your dreams better.

Mind Traveler has an option at the time of death; he can retain his life force and gift universe his memories, the products of his life.

Infinity is a force, it is energy, and it is conscious of itself. Infinity, the fifth element, is a conscious force that at certain times deliberately intervenes in a life -force of Spirit Travelers. All our lives are spent in preparing for the impact of the fifth-element. Traveler must brace itself continuously and be prepared for the blow of tremendous magnitude.

For average human being, this means the termination of his awareness, and the end of his organism. For Astral Traveler, this is a unifying factor. Instead of disintegrating the organism, as is ordinarily the case, death unifies. All the senses are now shut down for good and enormous energy becomes available at that moment. What happens to the Psychonaut if he/she is able to access this hidden option of death? He turns his dream image into a very powerful, very specialized, very energetic, high speed Dream Body capable of stupendous maneuvers in perception and experience. The dreamscape, the infinity, becomes the realm of action. Human beings need not die to have this option available to them.

It might be a bit amusing for you to see "death" referred to as a dream.

'Death' can also be one of our best advisers, if only we would listen to it.

If you are too weak to prevent the fantasies and delusions of the moving mind during the day, and 60,000 mostly useless thoughts and many more useless emotions, you will most likely be bound by the same limitations in a dream, and most probably much worse limitations.

Human body, uses chemical reactions to produce both mechanical movements and electrical currents that flow through all our living cells.

Our Ego Mind is based on chemistry. When our time on this planet runs out and we exhale our last breath, the life-force that moves those chemicals departs, and chemistry stops functioning. Body turns cold and stiff and a person is pronounced dead. Our body also operates on chemistry. Every second there are over a quadrillion chemical reactions taking place. We cannot move, feel, think or have an emotion without a corresponding chemical reaction. All our organs, glands, and every cell, out of about 65 trillion we have, function through chemistry. These chemical reactions are powered by underlying energy, and directed by unfathomable inner intelligence.

Just like lucidity, awareness, consciousness, double-arrow cultivated in waking life is eventually carried into the dream state, so is the awareness lucidity and consciousness cultivated in a dream carries into the death. If a Dreamer fully masters conscious dream practices, by them he or she is prepared to enter the death and have a stability needed to attain liberation. So we need to be aware, conscious, self-conscious in a very first moments of any experience, be it waking, dream and even death.

You cannot start at the end, you need to start at the beginning; always examining your feelings and reactions to those feelings. Be aware, be conscious, be in a double-arrow every second of your life. See if you are thrown into emotional reactions by your attractions or aversions or can you remain self-aware in a presence of any situation. A successful lucid dreamer must become stable enough and avoid being swallowed by emotions and lost in a dream world. As the mind becomes stronger, dreams become longer and less fragmented. A dreamer can remember more easily and consciousness steadily rises.

There is a definite correlation with waking life for we can see that very increasingly we are able not to be carried away by habitual emotional reactions which draw us into the depths of despair and unhappiness.

The theory of Biocentrism implies that death does not exist. It is an illusion which arises in the minds of people. It exists because people identify themselves with their body. They believe the body will perish sooner or later, thinking their consciousness will disappear too. In fact, consciousness exists outside of constraints of time and space. It can be anywhere: in the human body and outside of it. That fits well with the basic postulates of quantum mechanics, according to which a certain particle can be present anywhere and an event can happen in several, sometimes countless, ways.

Death of the body is not something that only happens to somebody else, it will happen to you and me. Death is the one thing that has remained unadulterated. The human mind can corrupt everything else, but death has remained untouched. And death is the only certainty in your life. You never know what will happen and what will not happen. Life is constantly uncertain, but death is a 100 percent certainty. Have no doubt about it.

Being aware of your mortal nature is extremely important. If you remind yourself every day, at least once, that you will die, then you will naturally move toward knowing higher dimensions of perception. People think they are immortal that is why they have time to live foolish lives. But if you know today could be your last day, would there be time to get angry with anybody? Would there be time to do anything stupid with your life?

Many dying people want to resolve issues from their past, particularly with family members. They may want to write a letter or send email, or meet with the person in question. They may also have a desire to visit childhood places they frequented, or go through old family photographs. These experiences can be profoundly healing and often enable the person to let go and die at peace.

It is also not uncommon in the weeks or days before death for a dying person to speak of being 'visited' by dead relatives, friends and groups of children, religious figures or even favorite pets. They will say these apparitions have come to "collect" them or help them let go. Subconscious mind is creating images to pacify the mind. Visions and dreams hold profound meaning for dying people, helping them to come to terms with their dying process. The person may also talk about moving in and out of 'reality' and describe other-worldly realms. They may speak of embarking on a journey, or may suddenly stare at a point in the room or turn towards the window and experience a sense of amazement, joy or wonder. Even when semi-conscious and unable to communicate with those sitting with them, it may appear that they are reaching out to take hold of something and then feeling it between their fingers as if puzzled. They may also appear to be thinking deeply as if they are being 'shown' information they may not have considered before. Dying people, and those who witness these end-of-life experiences, usually describe them with loving, reassuring words such as calming, soothing, greeting, comforting, beautiful and readying.

Specify in your Will not to have your blood replaced by formaldehyde, this disgusting chemical is right from the bottom of hell. Even putting the body in cooler in a hospital or a morgue interferes with your normal dying process. Just like best place to be born is at home, so it is the best place to die; surrounded by your family.

When approaching death we should be in the double-arrow awareness, we should be self-conscious keenly observing the senses, before sensory experience begins to dissolve. Do not wait until you enter death. When one of your senses, like hearing for example, is gone but the other sense like sight remains, it is a signal to be completely conscious rather than be distracted by all other senses. Become super-conscious, super aware that death is coming. All the dream and sleep practices are on one level preparations for death. Even in a sudden death, such as a deadly car accident, there is always a moment to recognize that the death has come.

When our time runs out our senses begin to gradually close. Our life force is withdrawing from the outer material level. The consciousness is withdrawing from this outside world. This change of frequency can be experience as travelling in a counter-clockwise direction down the light tunnel. When arriving to the other side (same place we visit every night when FALLING asleep) you have entered the world of subconscious mind. This mind 'thinks' in virtual tridimensional live pictures 24 hours a day. Hopefully by now you have become friends with your subconscious mind and given it a gift of reason and empathy.

This subconscious world seems much brighter and more real than waking reality, and unless your conscious mind is trained and expanded, it will get swallowed up and forget about the waking world, and mistake the dream world for waking reality.

As all your senses, thoughts, emotions and feelings shut down, and enormous amount of energy is now not being used and is liberated. Now the power of envisioning, this creative power of subconscious mind, comes to be at our disposal also. If you have trained your intent properly, you can Will to 'ascend' toward a SuperConscious mind. You have come home; conscious, subconscious and super-conscious mind have become one. You are now free and you can INTEND what you want. Leave details to the Existence.

You can reincarnate and come again to this place of magic and beauty.

When we are dying, a large amount of Dimethyltryptamine (DMT, the God-molecule), one the most powerful psychedelic substances in the known world, is released from the pineal gland (Third Eye) into our brain, along with other chemicals. But this does not mean that the visions experienced during death are mere hallucinations as has typically been assumed by medical doctors. Subconscious Mind visualizes all the time, it creates tri-dimensional live movie pictures. Intend a direction. Up, up and away. When you arrive at the etheric energy, intend again and hold the intention.

Through the high practices of White Yoga Tantra, and others, Dream Yogi is aware, at the onset of death, of diminishing energy currents associated with physical elements; earth, water, fire, and air.

The death does not come when the last breath is exhaled and when the heart and brain stopped functioning. A dying person usually remains in the state of lucidity for three days. After three days the color of the skin starts visibly changing indicating dissolution and departure of consciousness. Only at this point it is safe to remove the body for disposal. Prior to that time the consciousness is still in the body. If skin is not turning yellowish-green, a person is not truly dead. The longest known case of coming back to life was recorded in Russia when a woman came back after 17 days. People of old, all over the world have known this. These modern "doctors" have lost this knowledge and sometime bury a person still 'alive'.

How would you like to wake up inside your grave? It happened many times.

All of our senses are facing outside, sensing Existence through electro-magnetic impulses, and are therefore indirect. Our heart faces inside and has a direct connection to the Life itself. Universe is there for us to travel. However, it does not make even a bit of difference if you are on Earth or in the next galaxy; your time will expire. Wise men prepare for Death.

CHAPTER TWENTY

KNOWLEDGE

The word "belief" is a difficult thing for me. I don't believe. I must have a reason for a certain hypothesis. Either I know a thing, and then I know it; I don't need to believe it. - C.G.Jung

No psychic value can disappear without being replaced by another of higher or equivalent intensity.

It has been written: "In all the world there are only two kinds of people; those who know, and those who do not know."

When pondering on knowledge person should remember that our subconscious does not differentiate between the past and the present, self and the others.

2+2=1; in a spirit world this can be true.

Knowledge has been defined as "A clear perception of a truth or fact; a skill from practice." Also; "to know; to perceive with certainty, to understand clearly, to have experience of."

On the other hand, 'belief' is an "Assent to anything proposed or declared, and its acceptance as fact by reason of the authority from whence it proceeds, apart from personal knowledge; faith; the whole body of tenets held by any faith; a creed; a conviction."

In regard to religion it will at once be evident that a great deal could be said on the subject of belief, it being, one might almost say, the principle on which most, if not all, Exoteric Religions are based. It will also be evident, that all these various religious beliefs, held by masses of people in all lands, must have arisen in the beginning out of the personal experience of a few who had somehow obtained a direct perception or knowledge of certain facts in regard to "The Absolute", "God", or at any rate some Being or Beings of a higher order than themselves, and that these revelations were then given out by them to others, colored to a certain extent by their own personality and limited by their own intellectual level.

"A true yogi learns" writes Swami Vivekananda, "that the mind itself has a higher state of existence, beyond reason, a SuperConscious state, and that when the minds gets to that higher state, then this knowledge beyond reasoning comes. Just as subconscious work is beneath consciousness, so there is another work which is above consciousness, and which, also is not accompanied with the feeling of egoism. There is no feeling of 'I', and yet the mind works, desireless, free from restlessness, objectless, bodiless. Then the Truth shines in its full glory, and we know ourselves; for what we truly are, free, immortal, omnipotent, loosed from the finite, identical with Universal Soul."

Christian Mystic, St John of the Cross; "In this Union of Love the Deity co-penetrates the soul, but in such a hidden way that the soul finds no terms, no means, no comparison whereby to render the sublimity of the wisdom and the delicacy of the spiritual feeling with which she is filled we receive this mystical knowledge of God clothed in none of the sensible representations, which our mind makes use of in other circumstances. Accordingly in this knowledge, since the senses and the imagination are not employed, we get neither form nor impression, nor can we give any account or furnish any likeness, although the mysterious and sweet-tasting wisdom comes home so clearly to the inmost parts of our soul."

"Man know thyself and thou shalt know thy God." "Seek ye first the Kingdom of Heaven (which is within you) and all these things shall be added unto you."

Speaking of the Absolute the Atmabodha says: "That should be known as Brahman, which, beyond the gaining thereof there remains nothing to gain, beyond the bliss thereof there remains no possibility of bliss; beyond the sight thereof there remains nothing to see; beyond becoming which there remains nothing to become; beyond knowing which, there remains nothing to know."

And again in the Kenopanishad we read: "That which is not spoken in speech but that whereby all speech is spoken. That which does not think in the mind, but that whereby the mind proceeds to think. That which does not perceive with the eye, but that whereby the eye receives its sight. That which does not hear with the ear, but that whereby the ear hears. That which does not breathe the breath of life, but that whereby life itself is kept up. Know thou that that is the Absolute, not this that people worship."

"Where is the man who doubts the fact of his own existence? If such a one be found, he should be told that he himself, who thus doubts, is the Self he denies."- Svatmanirupana.

Consider the fact that little real knowledge is better than a great deal of belief.

It is useless to tell you to "become knowledgeable" if you don't know how to accomplish this for yourselves.

"Way" or "Path" which lies within rather than without. The time has come when man, having vainly sought among the externals of life and failed to realize the ideal, turns again and retraces his steps towards the Source whence he came. Only when he does this consciously does he find the true entrance to the Path. Then will begin for him that great struggle, which brings with it an ever increasing joy.

The first thing then is a definite effort in the right direction.

Then will the Voice of the Silence tell us that having reaped we must sow. Then shall we also learn to sow rightly, but not till then. It is impossible to help others till you have obtained some certainty of your own.

This must be the certainty of Knowledge and not of Belief, and even if the attainment of Knowledge is not the final goal (for it still implies duality, Knower and a thing known), and someday, perhaps, this too must be transcended.

The capital city of Croatia is Zagreb: fact; chickens lay eggs; fact; $2 + 2 = 4$: fact. This mix of observation and logic serves to produce 'facts' that are indisputable, even for an idealist. But all these are only relative facts; they are only so if something else is so. This is relative knowledge and not some Absolute Knowledge. So let's take a closer look at this 'indisputable fact' that $2 + 2 = 4$. Any 'objects' in my dreams are just imaginary and just by intent they can become many or zero. Adding them up is nonsense. Let us for a second assume that this outer existence is similar to dream world and that universe is of a mental nature, which it is. Than $2+2$ is not necessarily 4. Let's take it one more level up where infinitely many = One.

Knowledge comes from experiential information. Belief comes from feeling.

You do not know where my house is nor where I live. But you can believe and always be wrong. However, if you make an effort and come to my home, you will know where it is and where I live. Now belief instantly drops. It is no longer possible to have it. You can believe all you want you can swim, but if you do not know how, you will drown if you enter deep water. Same principle holds for playing a piano; or for anything else.

Belief can be derived from knowledge but knowledge can never be derived from belief. But it can arise from a belief, if belief is accompanied by desire to convert the belief into knowledge, like in the case of Wright brothers, Tesla, and countless others.

"The fool doth think he is wise, but the wise man knows himself to be a fool." - William Shakespeare

We believe things with our minds. Beliefs are ideas. They are concepts. They give us a picture of reality that others can agree with or disagree with. Beliefs are thoughts that can be put into words and these words can be communicated to others. Beliefs, however, are not absolute truths. They are opinions about reality, not reality itself. In the realm of belief we can have our own opinions, others can have their opinions, and we can agree or disagree, remembering that the truth of our beliefs is relative.

Having faith in something is different from this. Faith, in a spiritual sense, does not have to do with relative truths but with absolute truths - truths that exist for all time. Faith relates us to an underlying reality we share in, one we assume exists whether we believe in it or not. Unlike beliefs which are of the mind, faith is not just of the mind but of the heart as well.

Faith comes into play when we tell ourselves that our concepts are true; when we hold them to be true, even though we have no proof they are true. Then we have crossed the line. Faith is not concerned with proof. This is because faith is of the heart as well as the mind. Faith occurs not just because we think something is true, but because we want it to be true and our minds tell us it may be true. Faith combines our heart's wish and our mind's belief into an inner affirmation that the possible is real. Faith is the affirmation of this reality.

When we have faith, we believe in the invisible, in the unperceivable.

Knowing is based on our experience of something. In knowing something, we do not think or speculate about it. We perceive it so deeply within ourselves as true we don't have to discuss it, and no matter what anyone else says about it, it does not alter our reality. In this sense, we can say that experience just is. (Like swimming or playing a piano.)

To experience something is to know it. To experience something deeply is to know it with a degree of certainty that gives it more power and influence over our lives than other things. Here is a common example of our knowing something: When the sun shines on our skin we feel warmth. We don't need anyone else to tell us what we feel. We know we feel something we call 'warmth'. In relation to the sun, we have it easy with our knowing since others share our experience and can understand it. But we can experience things that are just as real as the sun shining on our skin that others cannot see and know them to be true with equally strong conviction. Our problem in doing so is that when others cannot validate our experience for us, we frequently invalidate it ourselves. (Tetrachromats, Dream sun, SuperConscious, fifth-element)

Inner experience is complicated by the fact that it is also difficult for us to put such experiences into words because we don't have the language to do so. And so we try to do the best we can, knowing all the while that words are inadequate in communicating our experience to others. We know the experience of that which we call God or Light of Consciousness can be felt in our bodies, and it is unlike thinking about something or having faith in it.

In the realm of spiritual experience, there are many people who are afraid to know what they know. They may have had intuitions about things that are quite deep. They may have had experiences of God's presence that have come to them like a whisper or a gentle breeze that hardly lets you know it's there. Yet, because an experience doesn't last, they are inclined to say it wasn't there in the first place.

Here is fear speaking; the thought of being seen as foolish or crazy. Within the spiritual realm, we can know something for a moment and it can change our life forever. Many people have had such an experience and have been afraid to claim it for themselves because of the lack of proof it actually occurred. As a result, they let go of something that could have changed the rest of their life because they were afraid to claim it as real. The imprint of spiritual reality does not exist in time, it exists in depth, and if we claim our knowing, a moment is more than enough to convey to us the impression of eternity. This is how powerful spiritual reality can be.

Pre-established understanding tends to be lifeless. Lack of awareness and knowledge constraints the freedom to think in truly creative ways far more effectively than any dictatorial regime. The two safeguards for freedom of thought is an active, open inquiry that stimulates the mind and encourages creative intelligence. We should question all beliefs and doctrines. Inquiry the best suited to activating a more subtle intelligence is one that goes beyond words and concepts, judgments and distinctions, and the sense that the Ego gains knowledge. Investigation can certainly make use of such basic concepts as higher, lower, process, path, progression, transformation, etc. but if the words take on the reality of their own the pursuit of knowledge degenerates into word games. Ideas, no matter how interesting, do not lead to change at the deepest level.

Space is not only an active component of our own being. Space is not only the empty container for objects, or the distance that separates one thing from another, it is the background, a substance for everything that appears within it.

Time is not only the measure for what happens, but the active intensity within experience, which manifests equally in anxiety, fascination, or sharp awareness. Knowledge is not simply the accumulation of facts and methodologies, but a creative engaging of the potential. Deep appreciation and enjoyment of experiential inquiry can open space, energized time and make knowledge available, restoring harmony to the way we live our lives. Complete commitment to inquiry can be maintained only by the activation of a subtle, probing intelligence. Human knowledge has attained great heights, establishing a body of known facts far beyond the capacity of any one person to master. Yet our own active knowing remains undeveloped.

Our lives are shaped by what we know. Knowledge determines what to hold true, what you stand for, and how we act once we have learned to accept the knowledge that comes from outside. We may find it difficult to question and think carefully on our own when we first try to do so. Our inner resources seem limited and we may grow discouraged. When Spirit Traveler persist in seeking new knowledge, new strength develops. And with it comes new confidence in our ability to know what goes beyond the range of the familiar. Going beyond what everyone knows to be true gives us access to the world where knowledge can work its wonder; this natural development of knowledge is based on inquiry. Putting established through the test, letting knowledge lead to unexplored realms, inquiry opens to an understanding and intelligence that allows us to choose for ourselves how to think and act. If he cannot advanced our own knowledge to match the achievements of the technology, we may one day be incidental participants in the world that has escaped from our control. But based on the forms of knowledge in operation today, one fact remains predictable, the course of future development will continue to operate largely out of our control.

If we hope to affect the future, rather than be the subject to it, we must start now to gain a more comprehensive knowledge of Knowledge itself.

When we act on the basis of our desires and the emotions are we really choosing our own path? Where do desires come from, and what momentum do they reflect? If dreams and fantasies shape our actions and our lives, can we truly say we ourselves are responsible for the constructs we rely on to define our potential?

If we look to tradition, the advice of the friends or experts, the guidance of a supernatural power, or perhaps simply to the accumulated memories of prior acts of knowing; the outcome is always the same; the substitution of a belief for knowledge, or the communication for knowledge.

Transfer of beliefs will succeed only to the extent we have the capacity to understand what is being communicated. Beliefs insert themselves between our own experience and our knowledge of that experience. Even if a belief contains knowledge, we have no way of knowing whether that knowledge is complete. We could only determine this on the basis of another belief. As long as we import knowledge from outside our own knowing we will lack the capacity to determine the depth and the scope of what we know. In relying on believes, we are accepting an imperfect substitute for knowledge. When beliefs replace knowledge, vision is foreclosed, leading to stagnation.

Beliefs may be accurate in their content and useful in their operation, but in being passed from one person to another, they bypass our most fundamental concerns. We touch the true significance of beliefs only by discovering for ourselves the knowledge they embody.

We are usually not willing to face what we know of our own physical circumstances and the threats to our person. Each day people are disabled, fall sick, lose their sight or hearing, contract fatal diseases. They are robbed of their possessions, their sense of inner worth. Many are killed or starve to death. Some sink into depression and grow mentally unbalanced; any of these calamities might strike us without prior warning. Our bodies grow feeble and succumb to the passing of time, our strength fades and the vision alters. Even now, just a in few hours, illness or a passing problem sap our energy and leave us without the real resources to act. Yet we maintain to ourselves that we are prepared when we encounter real adversity.

Again and again the choices we make, collectively and individually, breed difficulties and dangers, yet we continue to believe that by old ways of acting we choose wisely. We brake our wows and resolutions, tire of our pleasures, and watch our dreams of transformation go unfulfilled.

When Spirit Voyagers break through the accepted limits, so we find ourselves standing outside the circle of the known, we will have to face the frustration of trying to communicate with those who have not made the same move. If the sense of isolation becomes too great, it may be tempting to reset our new understanding to conform with the old. In that case every new knowledge will quickly be lost from sight. So do your best to surround yourself with the people who had similar experiences, or intend to acquire them.

***

As long as we lack a deeper knowledge, time will unfold in a way that leaves us powerless in the in the face of its onrushing momentum, assuring conflict and establishing barriers to understanding; knowledge will fail to provide insight that would lead us to transform our lives. Whatever the changing circumstances of our lives may bring we will remain bound by inherited patterns of knowing. Even if we live in accord with the highest moral code, profound spiritual practice, or dedicate our energy to mental and physical discipline that challenges our resources and commitment to the fullest, these limits will persist.

If deeper knowledge becomes available, the potential for the transformation appears within our present situation, not as a future possibility, but as a present actuality of some significance. If you learn to see more, New Vision will arise. And engaging the Spirit Traveler's mind actively allows this region to expand so that the imagination learns to imagine the unimaginable. Knowledge is more likely to make itself known when we do not judge in advance what is worthwhile and what is not.

Among the indications that a new vision is knowledge it puts into operation tolerance, and less judgement, of ourselves and others.

Openness to different knowledge brings with it the energy and skill to accomplish more expanded knowing. It may present time and even space in a wholly different way.

Knowledge at a deeper level may respond to a time and space that extends beyond the specific position; or individual mind may be connected with everybody and each body with every other body.

Let's take a careful look at our senses in particular the sense of a vision for all other senses functions similarly. Simple model of visual perception describe; light is reflecting off an object and entering the eye, then excites a cascading sequence of processes that are in some way converted into a datum of knowledge. But is the knowledge gained in this way accurate. What guarantees that the object has remained unchanged in the interval between then and now or that the image formed here is a true likeness of an object there. Let us look at this from the point of view of the perceiver. Having directed attention to the object the perceiver sets out on the journey from here to there, and from now to then; but when he arrives at its destination, he finds that there has become here and then it has become now.

The original object of inquiry will always be situated in a time and space that remains wholly inaccessible. The difficulty is twofold. Knowledge is possible only in the future when the perceiver makes contact with the perceived; yet what can be known is only the object as it was in the past. If the bridge between the moments is a phenomenon different from the moments, what is it? From within moment to moment contradictory knowledge, it makes sense only to describe it is a gap between. If this is truly empty, how can it serve as a bridge? If it is not empty, is it occupied in some way? And is this occupant possibly some different kind of perceiver?

The problem also arises with a reference to the initial moment of knowing, which stands in an intermediate relation to previous moment of not knowing. How can a moment of not-knowing connect itself to a moment of knowing? For the link to be established, there must be some common ground between the first moment and the second. But how can an unknown have anything what it does not yet know?

Linear time is not only an unbroken flow, rather it is sharply divided into the three domains of the past, present, and the future. The present moment stands at the exact center, to one side is the past, fixed and immutable, the other is the future not yet known but the partly predictable in principle. The threefold division of time is fundamental to direct experience. The being of what exists only in the past is completely different from the being what exists only in the future.

In terms of this division it seems accurate to say only what exists in the present is real. What happened in the past may once have been real but it no longer is; what will happen in the future may later be real but it is not yet. Something remarkable is at the work in the view that the present alone is real, for the location of the present in time is established only by the presence within it of me. So the existence of all that is seems to hinge on a fact of my being here. Thus the existence of all that is seems to hinge on the wholly subjective fact of my being there. We also need to account for the fact that the presents itself is constantly shifting; each present moment is different from every other; except that there can only be one present moment at a time. Since what is real is only what exists in the present moment, does this mean that my being is what created each moment? And if this is so what has become of the original cause and effect, which determine what is real, when we look at the face of linear time.

Change is the only constant; affecting the world of objects and the world of the self with equal power. Without change experience and the interaction could not arise and the Ego could not establish itself as the owner of the experience. Active across the individual moments of time, although the past is no more, it reaches out to create the future from its being. Future is not yet come, it unfolds to create the past.

The meaning and design of a problem does not lie in its solution, but in our working at it ceaselessly; for every solution creates three new problems. And rightly so, for what would we do if all the problems suddenly disappeared.

On a personal level even when the desired results are obtained, no satisfaction can be found. At best it is temporary.

Confronted with an unusual experience that might be viewed as an invitation to inquire further the Ego may simply respond by preoccupation, deciding that he has no time for such concerns, or no interest in them. Instead it turns back to the well-known stories that proliferate from the founding story, stories of success and failure sorrow and joy, gain and loss, praise and blame. Other concerns are rejected as childish and useless, better left to the professional thinkers.

Judged by a single nontraditional standard, all traditions are found wanting, making attachments to one over another by simple accident of birth. Without methods they have diminished to a level of dogma and useless rituals. While traditional teachings may be honored as a guide to morality or ethical conduct, they lose their role as sources for direct knowledge of reality. To replace tradition, philosophy has sometimes put forward pure reason as an alternative to temporal knowledge. But history suggests that the reason can support countless conflicting positions, even those most destructive to the human beings. How then can reason ever yield trustworthy knowledge? The advance of the formal logic has only confirmed the reason's limitations and its ultimate incompleteness.

Is absolute only in a comparison to what is not absolute? It might be that the absolute, though inaccessible to logic, can be directly experienced, assuming a human faculty for recognizing the absolute. No matter how direct knowledge claims to be, it is mediated by structures of knowing; including language, concepts, images, reasoning and ability of our senses. Whatever we can know by such means will not be absolute. Just as we are positioned by language and by culture; we are also bound by our understanding of space and time. Where does the space come from and how does it originate? Is even our idea of space correct? Can anything exist outside of space? Was there a beginning to time? If so, what was there before the beginning? If time had an origin outside of time, is it different temporally? Is different temporality in operation somewhere else? How might knowledge operate in such an elsewhere?

Mind Traveler knows deeper knowledge is not likely to make itself comprehensively known until the old understanding of space and time begins to lose their hold.

We may suspect that there are gateways to new knowledge, but those gateways will not open within linear time, nor will it be accessible in a space, which is just the 'emptiness' between.

Is each earlier moment already encompassed with the potential for all succeeding moments of time? Did the first moment contain in some unexpressed form everything that has ever happened and will ever happen? So what can be said about the first moment of time? Did anything precede it? How could the first moment come into being without having a past of its own? If you have a beginning, did this originating act come into being in another, different, kind of time? So many questions for the Spirit Voyagers to entertain. SuperConscious gives perfect answers. Make sure you ask relevant questions from it?

All personal development, psychological, spiritual or holy books of the world, including mine, will do you no good unless you acquire experiential knowledge.

All the knowledge in the world is not any good if you cannot remember it. There would be no value in learning if you forgot and then have to relearn the same thing all over again.

The memory expresses organization, forgetfulness expresses disorganization of the self.

"Memories are the cabinet of imagination the treasury of reason, the registry of conscience, and the Council chamber of thought." - Basil the Great

Unconscious mind functions on yet even deeper level of inherited memories, which Carl Jung called 'collective unconscious' and contains the entire evolutionary history of man from the very beginning of the mankind itself.

The subconscious mind is literally responsible for over 99.9% of your everyday thoughts, feelings, motivations, desires, prejudices, anxieties, tensions, illnesses, personality problems, social state, and daily behavior.

"Memory performs the impossible for man; it holds together past and present and gives continuity and dignity to the human life. This is the companion, this is the tutor, the poet, the library, with which you travel."- Mark van Doren

One fundamental Law of Memory is; the conscious mind cannot remember anything.

Most people strain the conscious mind to recall things, when in fact only the subconscious mind can remember. Our conscious mind can and does initiate the recall but it cannot remember what happened just a split second ago. It must always go to the unending ocean of memories contained in the subconscious mind for recall.

Memory has remained an elusive mystery because it is impossible to isolate the faculty of memory in anatomical tissue, memory is not, and never has been localized in flesh. Memory has no limits; the subconscious mind has unlimited capacity to store memories.

"There is no such a thing as ultimate forgetting, traces once impressed upon the memory are indestructible." – Thomas DeQuincey

Our subconscious mind is the ceaseless "manufacturer" of memories. Our mind can never stop recording even during the deep sleep. Our subconscious mind always automatically records and remembers every experience permanently, regardless if it is perceived consciously or unconsciously.

Every perception is preserved in the minutest detail and it continues to exist and is always in the present. Every experience is permanently stored in your subconscious mind; everything you have ever been exposed to is **alive now** in your memory, and that includes prenatal, and even primordial memories. Your memory span is infinite, your memory is always instantly available, always present, always now, always here, always total, always perfect.

And not only that, your mind is accurately keeping a record of every sensory sensation present at all times, as well as your feelings and thoughts, and in the sequence of their occurrence. Further proof of the infallibility of your memories is when under hypnosis and the suggestion your mind plays back instantly vivid details of childhood events that you no longer remember. Upon a command you can recall any thought or feeling you have ever experienced in your lifetime including prenatal memories. This simply means that your subconscious mind has hundred percent memory right now of everything that ever happened.

Memories are authentic extrasensory perception, you do not have to be born with it nor can you ever develop it; this extrasensory perception is ever present and is a natural function of your mind that can only be released.

It is very important that when an idea comes to you immediately write it down wherever you are, regardless of how insignificant or ridiculous it may at first appear to be. What at first appears to be a foolish idea may eventually prove to be extremely viable. Remember, nothing evaporates into the ether quicker than a genuine idea that has made itself known to you by the process of intuition.

Every human being possesses memories spanning the entire evolutionary history of a man. The memory of the entire human race is available to those individuals who consciously seek to free themselves from all limiting concepts. Such a Spirit Voyager, if liberated from the false assumptions taken for granted by our culture, would have an instant knowledge and skills bordering on supernatural.

Proper understanding of the function of our own mind is all that is necessary.

"Pure memories are spiritual manifestation. With memory we are in the domain of the Spirit. Any attempt to derive pure memory from an operation of the brain should reveal a radical illusion. Itself an image, the body cannot store up images, since it forms a part of the images. This is why it's useless enterprise to seek to localize past or even present perception in the brain; they are not in it; it is the brain that is in them" – Henry Bergerson.

Some researchers go as far as claiming we use less than 1/10 of 1% of our innate potential to think, feel, act, and be conscious.

The major problem of life is the ignorance of who and what we really are.

Believe nothing; know everything.

Do things!

CHAPTER TWENTY-ONE

TRUE INTENT

In the beginning that NEVER was, there was Intent. Oh, yes, the book says: "In the beginning there was a word". But for it to be a word, someone had to hear it and understand it, and that someone was not created yet. So it was a sound. Again someone or something had to hear it for it to be a sound. Well, it must have been a vibration then. Vibration of what, nothing yet existed. So, it was an Intent of the Spirit, pure infinite Consciousness, the Clear Light, the "material" everything is made of. God intended and everything became. Let me clarify this. That which we call God did not create the universe and since then he just sits on his ass and pronounces judgements. Creator CREATES every millisecond. That is "his" job.

God is not He, She, nor even an It. What we call God is outside of matter, space and time.

Even cosmologists agree that during the first few moments of the universe, time and space may have acted in unimaginable ways. This is what they believe, but that beginning never existed. Existence was here always.

There is something deep inside, only a glimmer perhaps, but something that emanates a feeling of warmth, love and goodness within you. It is an unforgettable moment, because it feels so good. You may not remember the specifics of the moment, but you remember the felt sensation. You remember that, for that moment, you felt good about yourself. For that moment, you loved yourself. And when you form an intention for yourself, it is ultimately an intent to feel that experience again, to feel it on a more consistent basis. You may not verbalize your intent in that way, but that is ultimately what you want.

The Law of Effortlessness is based on the fact that

nature's intelligence functions with effortless ease and abandoned carefreeness. This is the principle of the least action, of no resistance. This is, therefore, the principle of harmony and love. When we learn this lesson from nature, we easily fulfill our desires. Meditation must be effortless. When travelling along a parasympathetic nervous system effort is counterproductive. But something is taking place during meditation and that something can only be described as non-doing.

The Law of Intention is based on the fact energy and information exist everywhere in nature. A flower, a tree, or a human body, when broken down to its essential components, are energy and information. The whole universe, in its essential nature, is the movement of energy and information. That infinite energy field is subject to our Intent.

The Law of Detachment says to acquire anything in the physical universe, you have to relinquish your attachment to it. This doesn't mean you give up the intention to create your desire. You give up your attachment to the result.

The Law of Purpose in Life: This law says we have taken manifestation in physical form to fulfill a purpose. Your own purpose; the Existence does not have one for you or anyone else.

The Law of Humility. Humility may be one of the most misunderstood and under-appreciated aspects of human experience. It doesn't mean putting yourself below others, letting people "walk all over you," or acting like you're inferior or unworthy in any way. It means being neutral; letting go of the need to place yourself above or below others.

The Law of Optimism states we have to be of proactive state of mind, whose predisposition is toward acting in such a way as to cause good things to happen. It is action that determines future. Pessimism is detrimental; so is being overly optimistic. Be a realist.

Whenever we have thoughts our energy moves in the

direction of that thought. Thoughts are like leaders causing the body to move along a certain path. In the movement from one thought to the next, a force of attraction emanates from a specific thought, creating a momentum that pulls thought forward. Some thoughts loom large and other small, exerting a different gravitational pull accordingly. Silent awareness is the Spirit, the consciousness, it is an all-encompassing force that manifests itself differently in different things. This is pure energy communicating with us. As said; the Fifth Element, the one everything is made of, is an infinite force that has no interest whatsoever in us, but responds to a powerful Intent. The more powerful intent the more response we get. But do not mix Intent for a thinking process.

***

Eventually there is an opening of new powers in all the senses, an extension of range, a stretching out of the physical consciousness to an undreamed capacity. The supramental transformation extends to the so called physical consciousness far beyond the limits of the body and enables it to receive the physical contact of things at a distance. And the physical organs become capable of serving as channels for the psychic and other senses so we can see with the physical waking eye what is ordinarily revealed only in the supernatural states and to the mystical vision, hearing or other sense knowledge.

The SuperConscious mind in its descent into the physical being awakens consciousness; veiled or obscure in most of us, which supports and forms the energy sheath. When this is awakened, we no longer live in the physical body alone, but also in an energy body which penetrates and envelops the physical, and is sensitive to impacts of another kind. We become aware of the forces around us, and coming in on us from the universe, or from particular person, or group, or from things, or else from energy planes and worlds which are behind the material universe.

For there is a continuous scale of the planes of consciousness, beginning with the mental and other realms attached to and dependent on the material plane, to the worlds of the gods and the highest supramental, and spiritual planes of existence. And these realms are in fact always acting upon our subconscious selves, unknown to our waking mind, and with considerable impact on our life and nature. The physical mind is only a little part of us and there is a much more significant range of our being in which the presence, influence and powers of the other levels are acting upon us and help to shape our external being and its activities.

The awakening of the paranormal consciousness enables Spirit Traveler to become aware of these powers, presences and influences in and around us. In the impure, or yet oblivious and largely undeveloped mind this unveiled contact has its dangers. If rightly used and directed, it enables us to no longer be their subject, but their master, and to come into conscious and self-controlled possession of the inner secrets of the nature of our being. This SuperConsciousness reveals this interaction between the inner and the outer planes, partly by an awareness of their impacts, communications to our inner thoughts and conscious being, partly through many kinds of symbolic, transcriptive or representative images presented to the different mystical senses. But there is also the possibility of a more direct, concretely sensible, almost 'material' communication with the powers, forces and beings of other worlds and planes.

Make an intent when you reach the "edge" of Creation and Uncreation once your time expires, and you close your eyes forever. Come back to experience this magical beauty again, and again.

CHAPTER TWENTY-TWO

CRYSTAL BODY

After all, scientists have short while ago created time-crystals; new type of matter which nobody could even conceive of until recently.

At the time of death as the physical body becomes inactive the vital energy used for its functioning is liberated into the Universe; unless Dream Body is made 'solid' and functional.

The Dream Body has the vital force or prana as its chief constituent. It is revealed by the self-luminous Atman–sense of Self. When the subtle body rises, the Atman also can goes with it.

Upon exiting the dream world, through the inner direction, we are 'facing' consciousness. No body, no objects, just pure consciousness. But consciousness CAN create the body on any level of existence. By now you will have developed the power of spiritual Intent. Spirit Traveler intends the "liquid" Crystal Body, rudiment of which he/she already has; the body that nothing can latch on, the body that is perfectly transparent, yet by some magic perfectly capable of reflecting infinite number of colors making up White Light. The body that cannot contain a single low thought- an emotion- or an image. Once the work of creating a Crystal Body is completed, the Eight Door opens and Holy Traveler enters supra-celestial realm. When the consciousness of the being returns wholly into itself, it is aware only of itself, of its own being, its own consciousness, its own love of existence, its own ultimate force of being.

The supra-mentalising of the physical sense brings with it a result similar in this field to that which we experience in the transmutation of the thought and consciousness. As soon as the sight, for example, becomes altered under the influence of the supramental seeing, the eye gets a new and transfigured vision of things and of the world around us, like in Tetrachromats and Pentachromats. Sight acquires an extraordinary totality and an immediate and embracing precision in which the whole and every detail stand out at once in the complete harmony and vividness of the significance meant by Existence.

There is at the same time a subtle change which makes the sight see in a sort of fourth dimension, the character of which is a certain internality, the seeing not only of the surfaces and the outward form, but of that which in-forms it and subtly extends around and within it. The material object becomes to this sight something different from what we now see; not a separate object on the background or in the environment of the rest of Nature, but an indivisible part of the unity of all we see. All light becomes to the spiritual eye the light of the Creator shining its infinite colors upon the Creation.

All the other senses undergo a similar transformation.

All that the ear listens to, reveals the totality of its sound-body and sound, its rhythmic energy, the soul of the sound and its expression of the one universal Spirit. The sense going into the depths of the sound and the finding there of that which informs it and extends it into unity with the harmony of all sound, including the harmony of all silence, so that the ear is always listening to the Infinite in its expression and the voice of its silence. All sounds become to the spiritual ear the voice of the God, himself born into sound.

Universe sings.

The End

BIBLIOGRAPHY:
SELECTED SOURCES

Are You Dreaming? - Daniel Love

Autobiography - Gopi Krishna

Biocentrism - Robert Lanza

Creatures from Inner Space - Stan Gooch

Darkness Technology - Mantak Chia

Dreams of Awakening - Charlie Morley

Dream Yoga - Namkhai Norbu

Dreaming Yourself Awake - Alan Wallace

Dreaming: The Paradox of Consciousness During Sleep - Celia Green

Exploring the World of Lucid Dreaming - Stephen LaBerge

Kundalini, Psychosis or Transcendence - Lee Sanella

Lucid Dreaming - Stephen LaBerge

Lucid Dreaming for Beginners - Mark Mcelroy

Lucid Dreaming, Plain and Simple - Robert Waggoner & Caroline McCready

Lucid Dreaming - Robert Waggoner

Owning Your Own Shadow - Robert A. Johnson

Painless Effortless and Natural Birthing Method - Ivan Kos

Play of Consciousness - Swami Muktananda

Psychology and the Alchemy - Carl Gustav Jung

Psychology of the Unconscious - Carl Gustav Jung

Realms of Human Unconscious - Stanislav Grof

Sleep Paralysis - Ryan Hurd

SuperConscious Meditation - Ivan Kos

The Archetypes and the Collective Unconscious - Carl Gustav Jung

The Art of Dreaming - Carlos Castaneda

The Life Divine - Sri Aurobindo

The Theory and Practice of Meditation - Rudolph Ballentine

The Tibetan Yogas of Dream and Sleep - Tenzin Wangyal Rinpoche

The Lucid Dreamer - Malcolm Goldwin

33 Pillars of Life - Ivan Kos

Tibetan Book of the Dead - Evan Wents

Transcendental Rebirthing - Ivan Kos

Your Home and Body Toxic Alert - Joanne & Ivan Kos

Tao Garden Dark Room Retreat 2013 Part1 - YouTube

Directory of Other Darkness Retreats

ABOUT THE AUTHOR

IVAN KOS

IVAN KOS is a successful businessman in Edmonton, Alberta, Canada. He made esoteric disciplines his hobby and is familiar with over 65 personal development methods.

Ivan is a Certified Firewalking Instructor; he pioneered 'Painless, Effortless and Natural Birthing Method,' and modified Rebirthing into an extensive personal development 'Transcendental Rebirthing' system.

He is the author, workshop and seminar facilitator with international experience, and has taught in Peru, Croatia, USA and Canada. Ivan also speaks, writes and presents seminars on various subjects, including Lucid Dreaming, Transcendental Rebirthing, Scalar Pointholding, Meditation, Firewalking, Kundalini and other subjects related to extraordinary personal development.

www.ingramcontent.com/pod-product-compliance
Lightning Source LLC
Chambersburg PA
CBHW061942070426
42450CB00007BA/878